S104 Exploring science
Science: Level 1

The Open University

Earth and Space

Prepared by Stephen Blake, Stephen Serjeant and Sandy Smith

This publication forms part of an Open University course S104 *Exploring science*. The complete list of texts which make up this course can be found on the back cover. Details of this and other Open University courses can be obtained from the Student Registration and Enquiry Service, The Open University, PO Box 197, Milton Keynes MK7 6BJ, United Kingdom: tel. +44 (0)845 300 60 90, email general-enquiries@open.ac.uk

Alternatively, you may visit the Open University website at http://www.open.ac.uk where you can learn more about the wide range of courses and packs offered at all levels by The Open University.

To purchase a selection of Open University course materials visit http://www.ouw.co.uk, or contact Open University Worldwide, Michael Young Building, Walton Hall, Milton Keynes MK7 6AA, United Kingdom for a brochure. tel. +44 (0)1908 858793; fax +44 (0)1908 858787; email ouw-customer-services@open.ac.uk

The Open University
Walton Hall, Milton Keynes
MK7 6AA

First published 2007

Edited and designed by The Open University.

Typeset by SR Nova Pvt Ltd, Bangalore, India.

Printed and bound in the United Kingdom by University Press, Cambridge.

ISBN 978 0 7492 2667 1

1.1

Contents

Chapter 1
Introduction

The Earth seems vast on a human scale but, compared with the entire Universe, it is extremely small. Yet the whole Universe is the realm of science, from the huge distances faced by astronomers studying remote celestial bodies to the tiny sizes of the atoms that make up the human body. Being of intermediate size, humans are well placed to look up to the skies and to look down into the structure and make-up of matter. For example, Book 1 showed how the Earth's surface temperature depends on interactions between the very large (the Sun) and the very small (the molecules of greenhouse gases in the atmosphere). To understand these interactions it was necessary to have some knowledge about the different parts of the Earth's climate system – the Sun, the atmosphere and the various reservoirs of water and carbon (including all living things) that influence the chemical composition of the atmosphere. Similarly, to understand the Earth and indeed the Universe, you need to gain knowledge of their component parts and then see how they interact to produce the fascinating and sometimes puzzling array of phenomena that make up the natural world.

So, the first part of this book (up to the end of Chapter 10) concerns the planet we live on (Figure 1.1): what it is made of, how its outer surface is shaped, and what goes on within it. You'll find answers to questions such as 'What is at the centre of the Earth?' and 'Why don't earthquakes happen everywhere?'. The Earth's component parts of atmosphere, ocean and the solid, rocky part of the planet, are introduced in Chapter 2. Earthquakes, volcanoes and the formation of rocks are dealt with in Chapters 3 to 5 and our picture of the Earth is completed in Chapter 6 with a look at the hidden interior of our planet. To make sense of the observations of the Earth's active solid surface, the theory of plate tectonics is introduced and explored in Chapters 7 to 9. This wonderfully simple theory, in which the Earth's surface is analogous to a jigsaw of about twelve slowly jostling plates, emerged in the 20th century as the best way of explaining how the Earth works. You'll also learn, in Chapter 10, how our planet's solid surface is continually being formed and re-formed by a linked system of interactions between its interior, surface, oceans, atmosphere and biosphere.

The second part of the book (Chapters 11 to 15) starts by comparing the Earth with its planetary neighbours within the Solar System (Chapters 11 and 12), before embarking on an exploration of the great distances of space, taking you to the edge of the observable Universe in Chapter 13. Chapter 14 will show how the motion of the planets, and indeed almost anything you care to think of, can be understood, explained and successfully predicted by a simple set of rules known as Newton's laws of motion (named after their discoverer, the 17th century British scientist Isaac Newton). Here you'll find answers to questions such as 'Why doesn't the Moon fall out of the sky?'. Chapter 15 is a short chapter that draws the whole book together.

Your study of this book will introduce you to some key scientific ideas concerning the Earth and the Universe. These are the realms of geology (the study of the Earth) and astronomy (the study of the cosmos). While

Figure 1.1 The Earth from space, photographed from about 3.6×10^4 km above the Earth's surface by astronauts on the *Apollo 17* lunar landing mission in 1972.

you study this book, particularly through doing the activities, you'll also be developing a range of skills used in doing science. These include making your own observations and interpretations from maps and rock specimens, and using information held electronically. You'll also find that diagrams, maps, graphs and tables are used extensively in this book to convey and summarise information about the Earth, the Universe and the way they work, so you will develop skills both in reading information from these sources and in producing them for yourself. Another aspect of doing science that you'll continue to develop is the ability to handle quantitative information and find the answers to questions involving calculations – something that, like all skills, comes with practice.

1.1 Planning your study of Book 2

You should now look at the course Study Calendar to check the period over which you should study this book, and to start planning your personal timetable for your study (Activity 1.1). The chapters in this book are of unequal length and, as you probably found with Book 1, the length of a chapter is not always a guide as to how long you'll take to study it. The time taken to answer assessment questions can also disrupt initial estimates of study times. Including relevant assessment questions, Book 2 can be broken down into four fairly even segments:

Chapters 1 to 5

Chapters 6 to 8

Chapters 9 to 11

Chapters 12 to 15.

Activity 1.1   Planning your study of Book 2

We expect this activity will take you approximately 30 minutes.

How happy are you with the work pattern you developed while you worked through Book 1 (Activity 4.3)?

Did you fare best when working in regular sessions of a couple of hours, or in fewer but much longer sessions? Is there anything about your study regime that you'd like to change, or experiment with doing differently?

To help your planning of Book 2 notice that some of the activities in this book require you to go online (Activities 1.1, 3.2, 3.3 and 4.1), use the Practical Kit (Activity 5.1), or use multimedia material (the linked set of Activities 6.1, 6.2 and 6.3). Activity 5.1 forms a major part of Chapter 5, and Activities 6.1 to 6.3 are woven around the book text of Chapter 6 so, particularly if you do a lot of your studying away from home, you'll need to think ahead so that you'll have all the necessary materials to hand when you are ready to study those chapters. In general, think about the most effective way to include practical and computer-based activities into your study plan. Now go to Activity 1.1 on the course website to access the timetable template and fill it in for your personal study timetable. As well as having your personal timetable easily to hand, you may wish to keep a copy in your study folder so that you can refer back to it when planning your work on later books.

Does your study plan for Book 2 differ from your plan for Book 1? Note down your thoughts now on how well you feel you are organising your study and managing your time. If you have any queries or concerns, you can discuss these with your tutor.

There are no comments on this activity.

Chapter 2
The Earth: an introduction

As a first step in studying the Earth, it is useful to recognise that the Earth comprises a number of different parts. For example, the **biosphere** is that part of the Earth inhabited by life, and you will learn more about life on Earth in Book 5. You are also familiar with the oceans, lakes, rivers and ice caps that make up the **hydrosphere** – the part of the Earth composed of water. The Earth's atmosphere and solid, rocky surface complete the picture. In Book 1, you found that the atmosphere consists of a number of layers. In the lowermost layer, temperature decreases with height; this layer is called the troposphere and is about 10 km thick. It is this layer that contains weather systems, driven by unequal heating across the Earth's surface and the transfer of energy associated with evaporation, condensation and precipitation of water. This chapter concentrates on the oceans (the main part of the hydrosphere), and the shape of the Earth's surface, from mountain ranges to the deep ocean floor.

2.1   The Earth's oceans

As land-dwellers, it can be easy to forget that less of the Earth is covered by land than is covered by ocean. The ocean makes up about 70% of the Earth's surface, is several kilometres deep, and at the present time there are about 1.4×10^{21} kg of water in the ocean, cycling through the hydrosphere and constantly on the move within great ocean currents. These currents have a role in sustaining the water cycle and in controlling the Earth's climate, and they have influenced the historical development of civilisations through their effects on fishing grounds and sea-trade routes. A simple place to start investigating the origins of these currents is with a look at the temperature of ocean water.

2.1.1   Temperature in the oceans

Imagine that someone decides to measure the temperature at several depths beneath the sea surface as follows. First, they arrange to be aboard a ship anchored at sea. Next, they lower a long piece of rope with a heavy weight and a thermometer attached to the end over the side of the ship. The intention is then to wait a few minutes, pull up the rope and read from the thermometer the water temperature for the depth corresponding to the length of the rope. By repeating this procedure for different depths, a series of readings will be obtained showing how temperature varies with depth.

■ The design of any scientific experiment should ensure that the results are reliable and not likely to give a misleading impression. Do you think this method would give reliable results?

☐ No. There are several problems. For example, many thermometers are delicate and could easily break when being hauled around. If the thermometer passed through warmer or colder water while it was being pulled to the surface then the temperature reading would be different from that at depth. In short, this is a badly designed experiment.

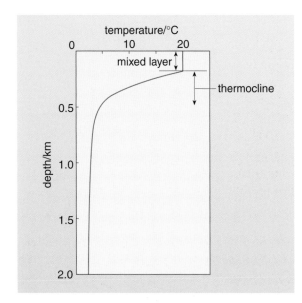

Figure 2.1   Graph showing how temperature typically varies with depth in the uppermost 2 km of the ocean in mid-latitudes. The terms mixed layer and thermocline are explained in the text.

The method that has just been described was used when the scientific exploration of the oceans was starting in the early 1800s. Not surprisingly, the results led to confusion and some very heated debate about the reliability of the measurements, which prevented any agreement being reached on what the measurements actually meant. The practical problems were gradually acknowledged and new instruments were designed to overcome them. The present practice for obtaining reliable results is to lower an electronic temperature sensor that sends the temperature measurements to a computer on board the ship. The results are best presented on a graph such as Figure 2.1 in which the vertical axis represents depth increasing downwards. This has the advantage of letting us visualise how the temperature changes downwards into deeper waters.

Question 2.1

Describe how the seawater temperature varies with depth in Figure 2.1. Consider:

(a) the temperatures at the surface and at the deepest levels measured

(b) the way in which temperature changes with depth – does it change at the same, unchanging rate, or, if the rate is not constant, over what depth range does it change most rapidly?

So, the measured temperature structure of the ocean shows that there are two layers in which temperature changes only slightly with increasing depth, separated by a layer in which temperature decreases by several degrees over a few hundred metres (the exact thickness of this layer varies from place to place). The water in the warm uppermost layer is stirred by the action of wind and waves, so this layer of water is called the mixed layer. This is where phytoplankton live and, as Book 1, Section 7.3.4 shows, this makes it an important reservoir in the global carbon cycle. Below it lies the zone of steep temperature change, called the thermocline (combining the Greek words *therme*, 'heat', and *klinein*, 'to lean'). The temperature of the deep ocean below about 1 km hardly varies with depth, and is no more than a few degrees Celsius.

■ Why is the water in the mixed layer warmer than deep ocean water?

□ Energy from the Sun is absorbed by the surface water which becomes heated. This energy is distributed throughout the uppermost few hundred metres by mixing, but the mixing does not penetrate to the deep ocean, so deep ocean water remains colder.

Because of the Sun's influence you might expect to find a seasonal variation in surface water temperature. This is indeed the case, especially in high latitudes – a swim in the sea in late summer is not as chilling an experience as it is in late winter. It is also the case that lower amounts of solar energy reach polar rather than equatorial parts of the Earth (remember Activity 8.1 and Section 8.2.2 in Book 1) with the result that surface water near the Equator is about 20 to 25 °C warmer than Arctic and Antarctic surface water.

2.1.2   Ocean currents

In the troposphere, winds transport heat and moisture around the atmosphere. In the oceans, the equivalent of winds are ocean currents. By tracking the paths of buoys and other floating markers, ocean scientists have identified currents in the upper part of the ocean, involving the mixed layer. These surface currents are shown in Figure 2.2a. In the North Atlantic Ocean the surface currents move in a roughly clockwise circulation pattern. The prevailing winds in this region also travel in the same direction, so is there a connection between the motion of the surface current and that of the overlying atmosphere? It turns out that there is; surface currents are driven by prevailing winds, with the seawater being 'dragged along' and set in motion by the moving air.

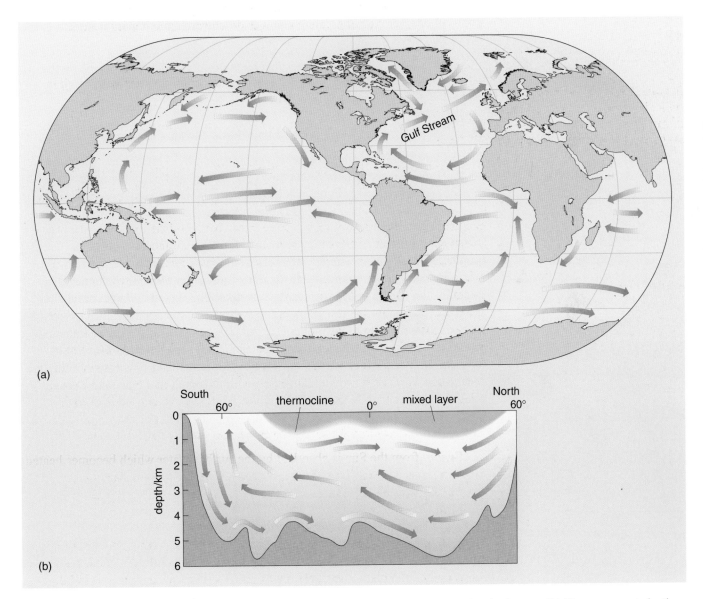

Figure 2.2   (a) Map of surface ocean currents, e.g. the Gulf Stream in the Atlantic Ocean. (b) Deep currents in the Atlantic Ocean illustrated on a south–north cross-section.

There are also currents in the deep ocean, beneath the thermocline, and these transport cold polar water towards the Equator by flowing beneath warmer surface water. Because this involves the vertical as well as horizontal flow of water, the deep currents are best illustrated on a cross-section (i.e. a vertical slice viewed from the side; Figure 2.2b) rather than on a map. These currents are driven by the differences in the density of the seawater that result from differences in temperature and/or salt content (salinity) – relatively dense water flows downwards and beneath less-dense water. For example, at very high latitudes, surface cooling makes seawater cold, and therefore denser, so it sinks and flows towards the Equator, while a shallower warm current flows in the opposite direction. In the case of the North Atlantic, the northward flow of warm surface water allows northern Europe to have a milder climate than it would otherwise have. Although the variations in density are tiny, being measured in tenths of one per cent, they are enough to drive the slow circulation system in the ocean that has a major influence on climate.

Changes in the density of seawater that keep ocean circulation patterns on the move can come about by heating (which lowers the density) or cooling, or by making the sea more saline (which increases the density) or less saline.

■   What processes can you think of that would change the salinity of seawater?

☐   Adding freshwater to seawater reduces its salinity. This occurs when rain falls into the sea, where rivers flow into the sea, and when ice melts into the sea. On the other hand, when freshwater is removed by evaporation this increases the salinity of the seawater because the salt is left behind.

The input of rain and rivers may seem fairly constant, but in a world in which climate changes take place, any changes to the rates of flow in the water cycle can potentially have important effects in the ocean. Warming of polar regions could lead to melting of the ice caps, causing cold, fresh meltwater to flow into the sea, reducing its salinity. Although it is cold, this low-salinity seawater can be less dense than normal seawater and will float on the surface, thereby reducing or even stopping the tendency for the polar surface water to sink. This could have the dramatic effect of slowing or even stopping the strong ocean circulation that brings warm water to high latitudes, with the result that Northern Europe could become colder. Notice that the word 'could' has been used a lot in this paragraph. The possibility that climate-driven changes in the pattern or scale of ocean circulation could cause further changes in climate is one of serious concern but, like the studies of global warming you read about in Book 1, it will require careful measurement, interpretation and modelling to assess the degree to which any such changes are actually happening. This is an active area of scientific research.

2.2   The Earth's surface

The Earth's atmosphere and oceans are constantly on the move, driven by energy from the Sun. However, the solid Earth (in other words, the rocky surface and everything below it, down to the centre of the Earth) is also restless. Not only are there obvious signs of this activity such as earthquakes and volcanoes, but the surface of the Earth also moves, although most of us never notice this. The Earth's surface is composed of a dozen or so separate interlocking blocks (known as plates) which are constantly moving around the globe – albeit very slowly – driven by energy from the Earth's hot interior. For much of the following eight chapters you will be investigating the solid Earth and exploring the evidence for the movement and interaction of the plates – plate tectonics – one of the great scientific discoveries of the 20th century.

Our starting point is the large-scale shape of the Earth's surface, shown in Figure 2.3. This shows the shape of the Earth's solid surface as if the oceans had been drained. Probably the most familiar features are the coastal outlines of the land masses and the major mountainous regions such as the Alps in Europe and the Himalayas in Asia. The map of the world in Figure 2.4 or an atlas may be helpful for identifying places that are mentioned in the rest of this chapter.

2.2.1   Mountain belts

In Figure 2.3, places that lie more than 2000 m above sea level are shown in shades of reddish-brown. Many of these mountainous regions extend for thousands of kilometres; they are known as **mountain belts**. Notable mountain belts are found along the western side of North America (the Rocky Mountains), the western side of South America (the Andes), and there is a chain of mountain belts running east from central Europe (the European Alps), through the Middle East to Nepal and Tibet (the Himalayas, which includes the

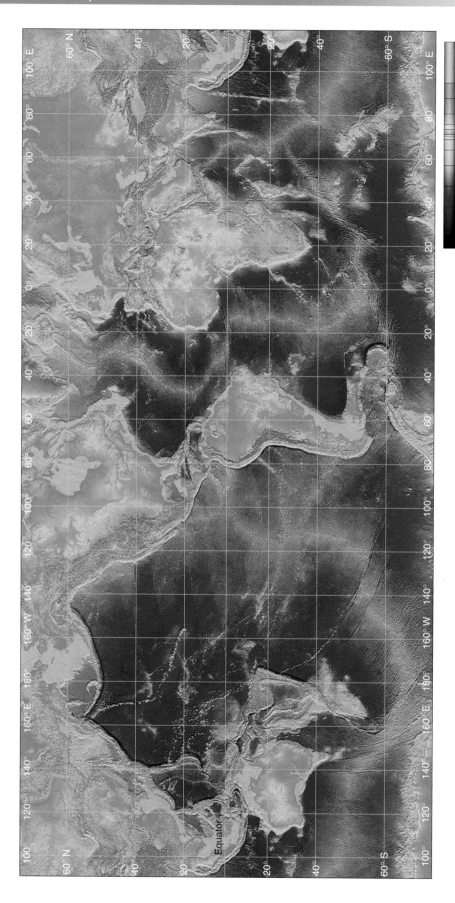

Figure 2.3 A colour-coded map of the Earth's surface between latitudes of about 70° N and 70° S, showing height above sea level (in green, yellow and red with increasing altitude) and distance below sea level (i.e. ocean depth in increasingly dark blue with increasing depth). The shape of the surface appears as if illuminated from the left. This applies both over the land areas and on the ocean floor. For example, the ocean floor slopes down to the west off the western coast of Africa, showing up as a pale, illuminated band. The eastern side, however, appears dark and in shadow even though the depths are the same as on the west side. The course website has a link to an electronic version of this map.

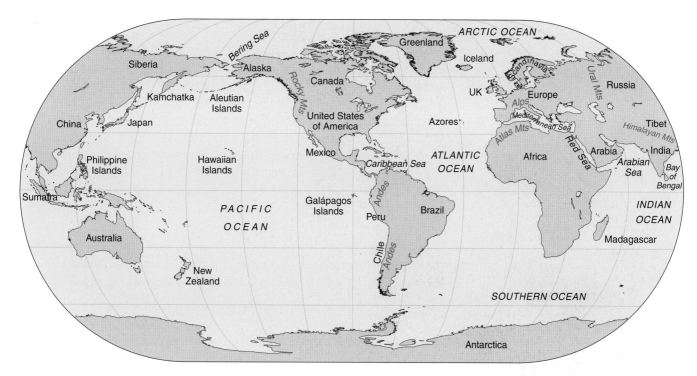

Figure 2.4   A map of the world identifying countries, mountain ranges and seas mentioned in the text.

Earth's highest point, Mount Everest, at 8848 m above sea level). In northwest Africa, along the coast, lies another mountain belt – the Atlas Mountains. Other mountain belts occur along the east coast of the USA (the Appalachians), across Norway and Sweden, and running north–south in central Russia (the Urals) (Figure 2.4).

Mountain belts are more than scenic attractions because they influence the climate by interrupting the flow of air across the surface of the Earth, forcing air to rise to high altitudes, causing it to cool. As a result, water vapour in this air condenses into clouds and then falls as precipitation. Precipitation then supplies rivers, which return the water to the ocean. For example, the Himalaya–Tibet region, which contains all but one of the world's peaks higher than 7000 m, supplies about 10% of the river water flowing into the oceans. Rivers with their headwaters in these mountains provide freshwater for more than one-fifth of the world's population.

2.2.2　The ocean floor

It is a triumph of science and technology that the depths of the oceans, and the shape of the ocean floor, are known for virtually all of the oceans, as you can see from Figure 2.3. Notice that around the areas of land, the ocean floor does not always plummet to great depth. Around many coastal areas, the ocean floor lies no more than 200 m below the ocean's surface (shaded pale blue in Figure 2.3). This is the **continental shelf**, and it is in the rocks beneath the continental shelf where the world's offshore oil and gas reserves are found. Deeper water lies beyond the continental shelf, shown in Figure 2.3 by the dark-blue colours of much of the ocean basins.

Question 2.2

Consider a voyage across the Atlantic Ocean from the southern British Isles to North America. In three or four sentences, describe in qualitative terms (i.e. numerical values of depth are not required) how the ocean depth changes as you travel westwards.

An alternative to describing the shape of the ocean floor in words is to draw a picture, in the form of a cross-section. For example, Figure 2.5 shows a cross-section between the eastern Pacific Ocean and western Africa. It illustrates the relief along a roughly west–east line that crosses South America and the South Atlantic Ocean. The continental shelf on the west coast of Africa is labelled on the extreme right-hand side of this diagram. Immediately to the west of the continental shelf lies a much steeper part of the ocean floor, called the **continental slope**. This in turn lessens in slope as the deep ocean floor is approached; this region is called the **continental rise**. In Figure 2.5 it appears as if these features are quite steep, but this is because of the exaggeration of the vertical scale, and the actual slopes are very gentle. The continental shelf, slope and rise have average slopes of just 0.1°, 4° and 0.5° respectively. To put these figures into context, a slope of 4° amounts to a change in height of 7 m over a horizontal distance of 100 m, whereas a slope of 0.1° amounts to an essentially imperceptible change of just 17 cm over the same 100 m distance.

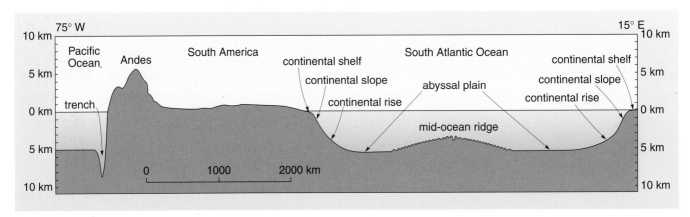

Figure 2.5　Labelled cross-section between 20° S 75° W and 8° S 15° E. Note the difference in vertical and horizontal scales. On the horizontal scale, a distance of 2 cm represents 1000 km, whereas 2 cm represents only 10 km on the vertical scale. The vertical scale has been stretched out, or exaggerated, by a factor of 100. The reason for doing this is that it allows the topography, or shape of the surface, to be visible on a small diagram.

Beyond the continental rise, and several hundred kilometres from the coastline, lies a flat expanse some 4 to 6 km below sea level, shown by the deeper blue tones in Figure 2.3. These areas are called the **abyssal plain**; 'abyssal' because they are deep, and 'plain' because they are so flat and extensive. But the abyssal plain does not extend uninterrupted across the Atlantic to the continental rise of South America. As you found when answering Question 2.2, the ocean floor becomes considerably shallower in the mid-Atlantic, forming a broad elevated region known as the Mid-Atlantic Ridge. In Figure 2.3, you can see that it snakes its way along the mid-Atlantic from south to north, meeting Iceland on the way.

Question 2.3

(a) What is the width of the Mid-Atlantic Ridge in the South Atlantic Ocean shown in Figure 2.5? (You can assume that the cross-section cuts the ridge at right-angles to its length and therefore shows its true width rather than an oblique section.)

(b) What is the water depth above the crest of the ridge crest, and above the adjacent abyssal plain?

(c) What is the height of the ridge above the adjacent abyssal plain?

It is not only the Atlantic Ocean that contains a large, symmetric ridge. As Figure 2.3 shows, a system of **mid-ocean ridges** extends around the Earth. These ridges extend for about 65 000 km and form the Earth's most spectacular mountain ranges, yet their full extent was not known until the 1960s. The locations of the mid-ocean ridges, along with their names, are shown in Figure 2.6.

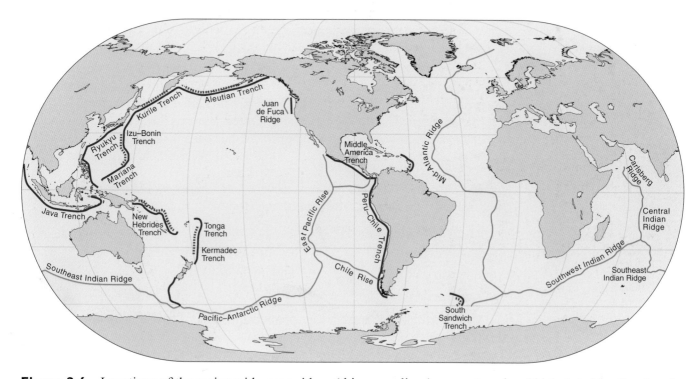

Figure 2.6   Locations of the major mid-ocean ridges (thin green lines), ocean trenches (thick dark-blue lines) and island arcs (red dotted lines). Trenches and arcs are explained in the text.

Question 2.4

In Figure 2.3, follow the Mid-Atlantic Ridge southwards until it meets two other ridges. From there, follow the mid-ocean ridge system eastwards around the maps in Figures 2.3 and 2.6, noting the names of the most prominent ridges. Are there any mid-ocean ridges to be seen in Figures 2.3 or 2.6 that are not connected to the system you have followed?

In following the mid-ocean ridge system in Figure 2.3 while answering Question 2.4, you probably noticed that the crest of the ridges is not continuous, but is frequently offset to one side or the other. On the Mid-Atlantic Ridge, these displacements are quite closely spaced but on the East Pacific Rise, for instance, they are more widely spaced. The significance of these offsets is considered in Chapter 8. For the time being, it is sufficient to note that they are a feature of the global mid-ocean ridge system.

Now return to Figure 2.3 and consider the ocean floor at the edges of ocean basins by answering the following question.

■ In what ways is the ocean floor along the Pacific coast of South America different from that along the Atlantic coast of South America?

☐ Off the Pacific coast of South America, the continental shelf, slope and rise appear to be absent or at least very much narrower than on the Atlantic coast. The abyssal plain is separated from the land by a narrow band. Its western side is dark, being in shadow, whereas the eastern side is illuminated and bright, so it represents a trench of very deep water. There is no trench along the east coast of South America.

The deep trench off the Pacific coast of South America can also be seen on the left-hand side of Figure 2.5. It is known as the Peru–Chile Trench, and in places it extends to 9 km below the sea surface. The **ocean trenches** are extremely long narrow troughs in the ocean floor, extending down from the abyssal plains to the greatest depths of the oceans. The major trenches are named in Figure 2.6. The Mariana Trench, in the western Pacific Ocean, contains the deepest known point in the oceans (the Challenger Deep) where the ocean floor is 11 034 m below sea level.

■ How does the depth below sea level of the Challenger Deep compare with the height above sea level of Mount Everest?

☐ Mount Everest is 8848 m above sea level; at 11 034 m below sea level, the Challenger Deep is over 2 km deeper than Everest is high!

2.2.3   Island chains and island arcs

Many small islands and conical submarine mountains (seamounts) lie within the ocean basins. Some are isolated individuals, but others stretch out along lines thousands of kilometres long. In Figure 2.3, chains of islands and seamounts can be noticed rising from the Pacific Ocean's abyssal plain. Some of these chains extend roughly east–west at about 20–30° S, while another prominent chain defines a large open 'L'-shape in the northwest Pacific. Other chains of islands lie alongside some of the ocean trenches and are known as **island arcs** because of their long curved shape. Examples of island arcs occur in the Caribbean, in the northern Pacific (the Aleutian Islands between Alaska and Siberia) and in the western Pacific, for instance north of New Zealand (Figure 2.6). All of these island arcs contain many active volcanoes, and you will learn more about these in Chapter 4.

2.3 Why isn't the Earth's surface flat?

Clearly, the Earth's surface is not flat, and there is a total height difference of almost 20 km between the highest point on the continents (Mt Everest, 8848 m above sea level) and the lowest point in the oceans (Challenger Deep, 11 034 m below sea level). But is most of the Earth's surface near sea level, with only small areas towards the highest and deepest levels? To answer this question requires information about how much of the Earth's surface area actually lies above, below or between given levels. Figure 2.7 shows this information as a **histogram**, with the length of each bar giving the percentage of the Earth's surface area (read from the vertical axis, although in this case the values are also written above each bar) within each 1 km interval (read from the horizontal axis). For example, it shows that 4.5% of the Earth's surface area is at an altitude of between 1 and 2 km above sea level. Rather than referring to Figure 2.7 as 'a histogram of the heights and depths of the Earth's solid surface', which is a bit long-winded, it is more convenient to use a shorthand term. So, combining the two Greek words *hypsos*, 'height', and *metron*, 'measure', Figure 2.7 is called a **hypsometric plot**.

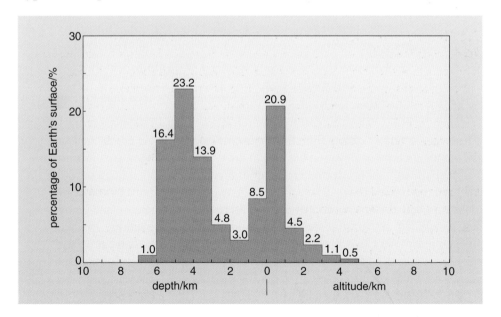

Figure 2.7 A histogram showing the percentage of the Earth's surface area lying within specified intervals of height and depth, relative to sea level. This type of histogram is known as a hypsometric plot. The percentages of the Earth's surface above 5 km altitude and below 7 km depth are too small to show at the scale of this diagram.

■ Does the shape of the hypsometric plot indicate that most of the Earth's surface is near sea level?

□ No. Although 8.5% + 20.9% = 29.4% of the surface lies less than 1 km above or below sea level, an even larger proportion of the surface lies 3 to 6 km below sea level.

The hypsometric plot has two peaks, one centred on 0 to 1 km above sea level and the other centred on 4 to 5 km below sea level.

■ How do these observations compare with the picture of the Earth's surface presented in Figure 2.5?

□ They compare well – the most common heights or depths apparent on Figure 2.5 are, on the one hand, the vast expanse of the abyssal plains between 4 and 6 km depth, and, on the other hand, the areas of land and the continental shelves that lie near sea level (between 1 km below and 1 km above sea level).

The Earth's surface has two common levels (the two peaks on the hypsometric plot) and a first reaction is to think that these correspond to 'below sea level' and 'above sea level'. To a good approximation this is the case, but a fair proportion of the high areas actually lies below sea level – the 8.5% of the Earth that is covered by up to 1 km of seawater.

Despite the familiar division of the Earth into areas lying above and below sea level, the two peaks on the hypsometric plot suggest an alternative division at between 1 and 2 km below sea level, within the continental rise. This means that the continental shelf, such as that beneath the North Sea and to the west of the British Isles, is really part of the continents rather than the ocean floor. During the last glacial period (between approximately 75 000 and 10 000 years ago, Book 1 Section 3.4.2), when sea level was up to 130 m lower than today, large areas of the continental shelves were actually dry land. Sea level and the position of shorelines that define the outline shapes of the land thus turn out to be accidental consequences of the amount of water in the oceans.

The deep ocean floor differs from the continents (including the continental shelf and slope) not only in elevation but also in the type of rocks they are made from. The deep ocean floor is covered in a layer of mud, but beneath it lies a dark-coloured rock called basalt. The continents, however, contain many other types of rock as well as some basalt. Some, such as sandstone, limestone and granite, may be familiar to you from their use as building stones. The uniting aspect of these continental rocks is that, on average, they are less dense than basalt, the characteristic rock of the deep ocean basins. The rocks on the continental land masses have an average density of about 2.8×10^3 kg m^{-3}, whereas basalt has a density of about 3.0×10^3 kg m^{-3}. To an Earth scientist, the difference between the ocean basins and the continents is not that one is submerged by seawater, but that they are made of different types of rock having different densities. In other words, the Earth has two geological domains, the continents and the ocean floor, and the boundary between them lies beneath the continental rise, not at sea level. It just so happens that seawater covers the boundary between oceanic and continental rocks. At the present time, about 25% of the continental area is actually covered by the sea.

The division into relatively lower density continental rocks and higher density ocean-floor rock accounts for the essentially twofold division in the level of the solid Earth's surface. Yet both the sea floor and the continents have striking topographic features: the mid-ocean ridges, ocean trenches and mountain belts. This might seem surprising, as weathering and erosion (Book 1, Section 7.5) might be expected to level off high peaks and fill in trenches. So, to rephrase the question posed in the title of this section of Chapter 2, why hasn't the continual action of erosion during the many millions of years of Earth's history produced a flat or at least subdued topography? The explanation that answers this question must involve some process (or several processes) that maintains the mid-ocean ridges, ocean trenches and continental mountain belts against the destructive action of erosion. In the following chapters, you will find out what these processes are and how they operate.

2.4 Summary of Chapter 2

This chapter has given an overview of two important aspects of the Earth – the oceans and the surface form of the solid Earth. Like the atmosphere, the ocean has a layered structure with a relatively thin upper mixed layer above colder water. Ocean surface currents are driven by the prevailing wind, whereas deep currents are driven by differences in the density of seawater caused by variations in the temperature and the salinity (saltiness) of seawater. Changes to temperature and salinity brought about by climate change could potentially change the strength or pattern of major ocean currents. Similarly, changes in ocean circulation patterns could potentially influence the Earth's climate because ocean currents move heat around the Earth's surface.

The Earth's solid surface comprises extensive areas of rather flat terrain, principally the abyssal plains of the ocean basins and much of the continental areas. The major features of the Earth's solid surface are the mid-ocean ridges, ocean trenches, mountain belts and island arcs. Mid-ocean ridges form a system of submarine mountains rising from the abyssal plain and encircling the globe. Deep ocean trenches extend to great depths below the abyssal plains. These trenches are often parallel to the edges of continents and volcanic island arcs. Mountain belts occur as linear regions on the edges of continents or in their interiors.

A hypsometric plot illustrates that over half of the Earth's surface lies between 3 and 6 km below sea level, whereas nearly a third of it lies between 1 km below sea level and 1 km above sea level. These represent oceanic and continental areas respectively; the oceanic areas are made from basalt, whereas continental areas are made from a wide range of rock types whose mean density is lower than that of basalt. The boundary between these areas does not coincide with sea level, but lies beneath the continental rise.

In studying this chapter you have made use of graphs, maps, cross-sections and histograms to make observations and find information.

Chapter 3
The active Earth: earthquakes

The next three chapters deal with processes that shape the surface of the Earth. This chapter, and the next one, look at two of the most dramatic: earthquakes and volcanoes.

3.1   What happens during an earthquake?

During an earthquake, the ground shakes for a few minutes as waves of energy move through the Earth. The ground surface can split apart or move up and down. You probably have some idea from news reports or perhaps even personal experience, of just how powerful earthquakes can be. In a matter of minutes earthquakes have devastated cities and killed huge numbers of people.

One of the most destructive earthquakes in recent times occurred about 95 km northeast of Islamabad, Pakistan on 8 October 2005. Extensive damage occurred throughout northern Pakistan. The region hardest hit was Pakistan-administered Kashmir, with much of the capital, Muzaffarabad, destroyed (Figure 3.1). Landslides blocked roads and there was extensive damage to the electricity, water and telephone infrastructure and all the city's hospitals. At least 54 000 people were killed in Pakistan and 75 000 people were injured. Over 30 000 buildings collapsed. An estimated 4 million people were left homeless.

Figure 3.1   Residents walk through the rubble of destroyed houses in Muzaffarabad, 11 October 2005.

As well as being highly destructive in their own right, the ground movement during earthquakes can also trigger two other very destructive natural events – landslides and tsunamis.

3.1.1   Earthquake-triggered landslides

A landslide is a movement of earth materials down a slope, the materials ranging from huge boulders to soil. Landslides can involve the movement of just a small amount of material or enough to bury whole towns in their path. They can have a number of causes, of which earthquakes are just one. The shock of an earthquake may be sufficient to start the slide.

One of the most destructive earthquake-induced landslides occurred on 31 May 1970, following a large earthquake beneath the Pacific Ocean about 25 km from the coast of Peru. The tremors produced by the earthquake loosened rocks and ice on Mount Huascaran, one of South America's highest mountains, 130 km away from the earthquake. This initiated a gigantic landslide, which increased in speed and size as it moved down the mountain, reaching a speed of over 200 km h^{-1} (kilometres per hour). It swept along the valley at the foot of the mountain, filling it with rock, mud and ice, and partially destroying the town of Ranrahirca, 12 km from the mountain. Part of the landslide branched off to one side, swept over a ridge and roared through the village of Yungay. The village was obliterated; only a few of its inhabitants managed to escape by running to higher ground as the landslide approached. Survivors described the landslide as like a gigantic ocean wave with a deafening roar and rumble. The earthquake also triggered many other smaller landslides in the region, destroying thousands of buildings and causing even more deaths. The final toll was 67 000 dead and 800 000 homeless, making this one of the worst earthquake-induced disasters.

3.1.2   Earthquake-triggered tsunamis

The second natural event that can be triggered by an earthquake is the **tsunami** (pronounced 'tsoo-nam-ee'). Tsunamis are ocean waves caused by the displacement of the ocean floor by an earthquake beneath the ocean. The water is moved as if it were being pushed by a giant paddle, producing powerful, fast-moving waves that spread out from the region of the earthquake across the ocean. Tsunamis are hardly detectable in the deep open ocean as their wave height is low – less than a metre. However, when they reach shallow water at coastlines their wave height increases dramatically due to the slowing of the wave causing water to 'pile up', such that waves over 30 m high can break against the shoreline, with disastrous effects.

Scientists use the term tsunami, which is a Japanese word meaning bay or harbour wave, and is particularly apt as it is only along the shore that they become noticeable or destructive. Japan has suffered greatly from their destructive effects. The term tidal wave is sometimes used in news reports of tsunamis but this is inaccurate as they are not related to tides. One of the most damaging tsunamis in recent times was the 2004 Indian Ocean tsunami, caused by a massive earthquake that occurred on 26 December 2004 beneath the eastern margin of the Indian Ocean, just off the northern tip of Sumatra, Indonesia. It was the largest earthquake for 44 years, since one in Chile in 1960. The Indian Ocean earthquake caused a rupture in the ocean floor around 2000 km long, extending from Sumatra to Burma. It generated a tsunami travelling at speeds of up to 600 km h^{-1} across the ocean and struck the surrounding coastlines with devastating effect. In the deep ocean its low wave height was nearly undetectable, but upon approaching the coast of Sumatra it built up to a height of over 30 m. Further away in Thailand, India and Sri Lanka the wave height was lower, but it still reached up to 10 m.

The tsunami struck with little warning. Over 200 000 people died, with just over half of the casualties in Sumatra. Many more were made homeless. This tsunami was the most destructive in recorded history. Although the destruction was confined to the Indian Ocean, the wave travelled around the world, being detected as far away as the UK.

3.2   Why do earthquakes occur?

What causes the apparently solid and rigid Earth to move and so produce an earthquake? Earthquakes mainly occur when the different parts of the Earth's surface move relative to each other (Figure 3.2a), causing distortion in the rock (Figure 3.2b). The distortion builds up very slowly, over tens or even hundreds of years. When rocks are distorted very slowly they behave as if they were springs, or pieces of elastic, being able to store energy when they are stretched or compressed. (You will investigate the concept of a spring storing energy in Book 3.) Prior to an earthquake, the rock is like a spring-loaded system waiting to go off. Eventually the distortion is enough to cause the rock to break and move, releasing energy in the form of an earthquake. The break is called a **fault**. It starts as a small fracture (Figure 3.2c), but grows rapidly (Figure 3.2d). In general, the larger the area of the fault, the greater the size of the earthquake.

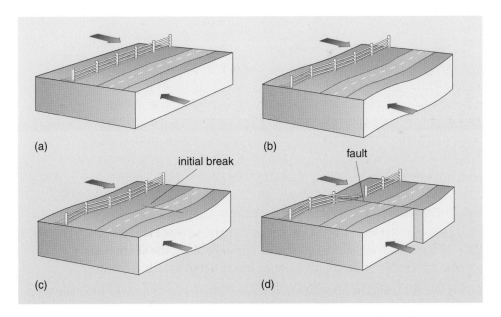

Figure 3.2   The circumstances of an earthquake. These are block diagrams, illustrating both the surface of the Earth and the Earth in cross-section. Movement directions are shown by the arrows. (a) Part of the Earth where areas of rock are trying to move in opposite directions. (b) Before a fault develops, the rocks stretch and bend. (c) When the distortion is enough to cause the rocks to break, the break starts at one point. (d) The break spreads rapidly, creating the fault, so accommodating the distortion and releasing energy. Note that faults are not always vertical, and movement often results in the rocks on either side of the fault being displaced up or down.

The fault length (the length of the break along which rocks are displaced) can vary from metres for a small earthquake to thousands of kilometres for a very large earthquake.

Question 3.1

Figure 3.3 is an aerial view of part of the San Andreas Fault in California.

(a) What is the evidence for a fault in this photograph?

(b) What are the relative directions of motion of the blocks on either side of the fault?

Figure 3.3 An aerial view of part of the San Andreas Fault in the Carrizo Plain National Monument, California, looking northeast. The fault is in the middle of the picture and runs from left to right. The flat area in the foreground with a stream running towards the viewer and road running from left to right across it lies on one side of the fault. The hilly ground cut by many river valleys lies on the other side of the fault.

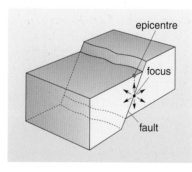

Figure 3.4 The focus and epicentre of an earthquake.

What is the real place of origin of an earthquake? As the break propagates, it releases energy along the fault, so in a sense the earthquake originates from the entire fault – which may be 1000 km long. However, it is useful to refer to the initial break as the place of origin of an earthquake. This is called the **focus** (plural foci) of the earthquake. This is usually well below the Earth's surface. The point on the Earth's surface directly above the focus is called the **epicentre** (Figure 3.4).

A large earthquake is frequently followed by a series of smaller earthquakes on the same fault, called **aftershocks**. These can continue for months after the main earthquake. They are caused by the readjustment in the positions of the rocks following the main earthquake, releasing smaller, localised accumulations of energy on the fault. Sometimes the main earthquake is preceded by one or more smaller **foreshocks**, although they cannot be identified as foreshocks until after the main earthquake has occurred.

Following an earthquake in California in 1989, a sequence of aftershocks revealed the size and orientation of the fault. The epicentre was about 100 km southeast of San Francisco. Referred to as the Loma Prieta earthquake after the mountain just to the east of the epicentre, movement occurred on a fault about 40 km in length. It was large enough to cause destruction not only in the nearby city of Santa Cruz but also in San Francisco and its surroundings, where buildings, bridges and raised roads collapsed.

Figure 3.5a is a map showing the location of the epicentres for the Loma Prieta earthquake and its aftershocks. The earthquake and aftershocks occurred along part of a well-known fault in California – the San Andreas Fault (shown in Figure 3.3). Figure 3.5b is a vertical cross-section of this area *along* the fault, from point B to point B′ on Figure 3.5a. This shows the positions and depths of the earthquake and aftershocks, i.e. their foci.

■ Over what length of the fault did the aftershocks occur?

☐ About 70 km.

■ What was the depth of the main earthquake, and what was the maximum aftershock depth?

☐ The main earthquake had a depth of about 17 km and the maximum depth of the aftershocks was about 21 km.

Figure 3.5c is a cross-section showing the foci *across* the fault beneath the line joining point C to point C′ on Figure 3.5a.

■ Is the fault vertical?

☐ No. The earthquake foci become deeper towards the southwest, indicating that the fault slopes down to the southwest (at about 25° to the vertical).

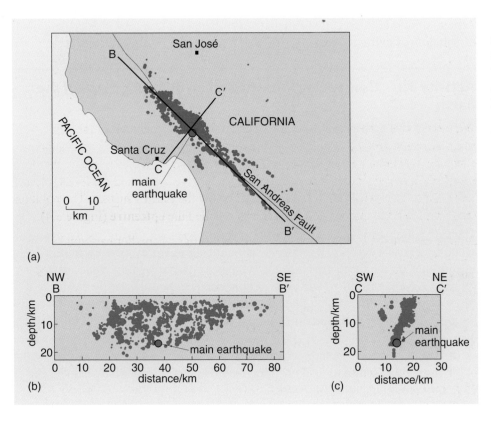

(a)

(b)

(c)

Figure 3.5 (a) Map of epicentres, and (b) and (c) cross-sections, showing the foci for the main earthquake and aftershocks of the Loma Prieta earthquake, California, 1989. BB′ and CC′ on (a) are the locations of cross-sections in (b) and (c) respectively, which show foci along and across the fault. Larger earthquakes are shown by larger dots.

The San Andreas Fault is the largest and possibly the most active of many faults in California. As well as the Loma Prieta earthquake, movement along this fault has caused other large earthquakes, including a major San Francisco earthquake in 1906. This resulted in the almost total destruction of the city by fire, following the rupture of gas mains; rupturing of the water mains made it impossible to put out the fires. The land to the west of the fault moved as much as 6 m north relative to the other side during this earthquake.

3.3   Where do earthquakes occur?

How deep in the Earth do earthquakes occur? Most earthquake foci are within a few tens of kilometres of the surface. Earthquakes less than 70 km deep are classified as shallow-focus. Earthquakes with foci 70–300 km deep are classified as intermediate-focus and those below 300 km are deep-focus (Figure 3.6). No earthquakes are known to have occurred below about 700 km. At greater depths, the rocks are very hot and under high pressure so they deform by flowing rather than breaking and faulting. Shallow-focus earthquakes occur more often than deeper ones. Unfortunately, the shallower an earthquake, the more damage it can produce at the surface; intermediate- and deep-focus earthquakes are rarely destructive. About 75% of the total energy released from earthquakes is from shallow-focus ones. The first earthquake that you looked at in this chapter, in Pakistan in 2005, had its focus at a depth of 26 km, and so this was a shallow-focus earthquake. The depth to the focus is called the **focal depth**.

Do earthquakes occur everywhere, or only in some parts of the Earth? So far, this chapter has discussed earthquakes in Pakistan, California, the Indian Ocean and the Pacific Ocean near Peru. You may also recall hearing of earthquakes in Italy, Armenia, Iran, Mexico City, China and even Britain. Figure 3.6 shows the global distribution of earthquakes.

Activity 3.1   Comparing information on different maps of the Earth

We expect this activity will take you approximately 45 minutes.

This activity will give you practice in translating information from diagrams to written form.

(a) Use Figure 3.6 to describe the main geographical patterns of earthquake distribution.

The use of the word 'describe' in an activity or a question means 'give a detailed account'. For this activity, it involves summarising in words the pattern of earthquakes on the Earth's surface. As with any piece of writing, your answer should have a logical flow, and your writing needs to be sufficiently clear that it could convey the information from the map to someone who cannot see it. Study Figure 3.6 carefully and structure your answer in a way that relates to the actual distribution of the earthquakes. Will you describe the pattern from west to east across the map, or continent by continent, or on land then at sea, or will you start by giving a short summary followed by more detailed information? Try to keep your answer within about 100 words.

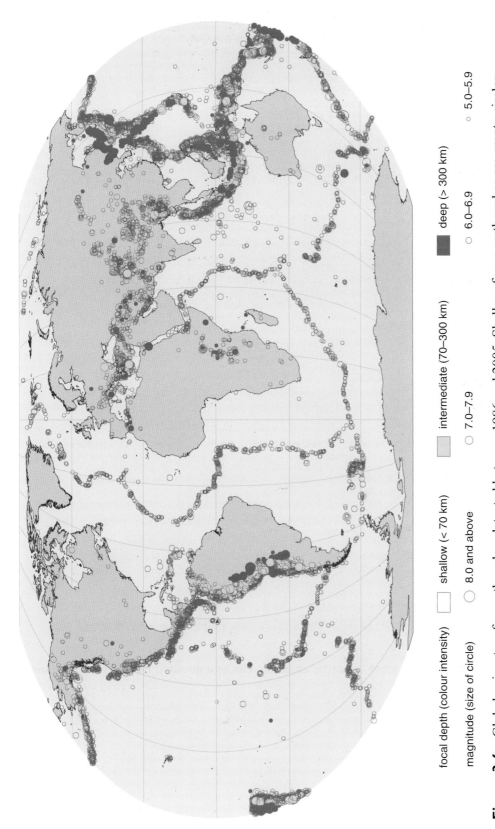

Figure 3.6   Global epicentres for earthquakes detected between 1986 and 2005. Shallow-focus earthquakes are empty circles, intermediate-focus earthquakes are light red circles and deep-focus earthquakes are deep red circles. Only earthquakes of magnitude 5 and above are included (earthquake magnitude is discussed in Section 3.4; > means 'greater than'; < means 'less than'). Data are from the British Geological Survey World Seismicity Database. This figure is also on the course website.

focal depth (colour intensity)   ☐ shallow (< 70 km)   ▨ intermediate (70–300 km)   ■ deep (> 300 km)

magnitude (size of circle)   ○ 8.0 and above   ○ 7.0–7.9   ○ 6.0–6.9   ○ 5.0–5.9

(b) Use Figures 2.3, 2.6 and 3.6 to identify which surface features on the Earth appear to have (i) shallow, and (ii) deep earthquakes associated with them. (You may wish to refer to the version of Figure 3.6 on the course website to help you distinguish where shallow and deep earthquakes occur.)

You are asked to use world maps that look quite different because they have different scales and they use different map bases. So you might start by looking for clearly recognisable features like continents that you can identify in each map, and by comparing the scales, indicated by the spacing of the lines of latitude and longitude. Once you have worked out how the two maps relate to each other, it becomes more straightforward to identify the position on one map that corresponds to a particular feature on the other map, and specifically to see how shallow- and deep-focus earthquakes relate to surface features.

After you have completed (a) and (b), look at the comments on this activity at the end of this book.

Earthquakes are largely confined to specific areas of the Earth, called **seismic zones** (derived from *seismos*, the Greek word for 'shaking'; **seismology** is the study of earthquakes). Most of the rest of the Earth is relatively free of earthquakes, or at least free of large earthquakes (Figure 3.6). However, even the UK has some earthquakes, although they are usually fairly small. The largest one recorded (in 1931) had about a thousand times less energy than the 1906 San Francisco earthquake. This 1931 earthquake occurred under the North Sea but was felt over most of the UK. Two earthquakes just a little smaller occurred in the Dover Straits in 1382 and 1580, causing significant damage in London. In 1863, Charles Dickens experienced shaking caused by an earthquake and was moved to write to *The Times* describing its effects (Figure 3.7). All UK earthquakes occur at shallow depths; the greatest recorded depth is only 42 km.

You have seen in Activity 3.1 that most earthquakes are associated with certain features of the Earth's solid surface – mid-ocean ridges, ocean trenches and some mountain belts. You have also seen that deeper earthquakes are characteristic of ocean trenches, whereas shallower earthquakes are more typical of mid-ocean ridges. This relationship between the surface features of the Earth, and the movement of the Earth that causes earthquakes, is one of the observations of the active Earth that can be explained by the theory of plate tectonics (Chapter 8). For now, however, earthquakes will continue to be the specific object of study.

> *THE EARTHQUAKE.*
>
> TO THE EDITOR OF THE TIMES.
>
> Sir, — As you may think any accurate observation of the shock of earthquake which was felt in various parts of England last Tuesday morning worth publishing I send you mine.
>
> I was awakened by a violent swaying of my bedstead from side to side, accompanied by a singular heaving motion. It was exactly as if some great beast had been crouching asleep under the bedstead and were now shaking itself and trying to rise. The time by my watch was 20 minutes past 3, and I suppose the shock to have lasted nearly a minute. The bedstead, a large iron one, standing nearly north and south, appeared to me to be the only piece of furniture in the room that was heavily shaken. Neither the doors nor the windows rattled, though they rattle enough in windy weather, this house standing alone, on high ground, in the neighbourhood of two great rivers. There was no noise. The air was very still, and much warmer than it had been in the earlier part of the night. Although the previous afternoon had been wet, the glass had not fallen. I had mentioned my surprise at its standing near the letter "i" in "Fair," and having a tendency to rise. It is recorded in the second volume of the *Philosophical Transactions* that the glass stood high at Oxford when an earthquake was felt there in September, 1683. Your faithful servant,
>
> CHARLES DICKENS.
>
> Gad's-hill-place, Higham by Rochester, Kent, Oct. 7.

Figure 3.7 Charles Dickens' letter about the 1863 Hereford earthquake.

3.4 The size of earthquakes

Why are some earthquakes more destructive than others? There are three main reasons: location (an earthquake with a focus under an ocean at a large distance from land, for example, is not usually destructive, unless it generates a tsunami); depth (shallower earthquakes can be more devastating); but, most importantly, the *size* of the earthquake.

3.4.1 Earthquake intensity

A straightforward way to measure the size of an earthquake is to look at the damage it causes. This is a crude measure of the strength of the ground shaking caused by an earthquake, and is called the **earthquake intensity**. To estimate the intensity of an earthquake at a single place, descriptions of what happened to people and structures during the earthquake are collected, and the description compared with a scale of earthquake effects, such as 'objects fall off shelves' or 'most chimney pots fall off'. The descriptions are given numbers on a 12-point intensity scale, with intensity 1 being not felt, intensity 8 including 'most chimney pots fall off' and intensity 12 being total devastation. This intensity scale is a qualitative scale because it is not based on specific measurements, even though it is numerical. The intensity of the 8 October 2005 earthquake in Muzaffarabad, Pakistan (Figure 3.1) was 9.

It is important to realise that intensity refers to the damage caused *at a particular place* by an earthquake. An earthquake has different intensities in different places, so it is wrong to refer simply to *the* intensity of an earthquake. It is necessary to state its intensity in, say, Los Angeles, or 'the maximum intensity'. The intensity at the epicentre of the 1989 Loma Prieta earthquake was intensity 8, but the maximum intensity (and damage) was in parts of San Francisco and Oakland, about 100 km to the northwest of the epicentre, where intensity 9 was recorded. This was mainly due to the presence of a loose sand layer at the ground surface in the San Francisco Bay area which did not support built structures as well as the solid rock nearer to the epicentre.

Intensity scales have two major disadvantages: they are no use for describing earthquakes under the oceans or in uninhabited areas. Even in inhabited areas, the effects of an earthquake can depend on the local building standards. To overcome these problems in measuring the size of earthquakes, a different way of measuring their size is normally used.

3.4.2   Earthquake magnitude

The **earthquake magnitude** is a quantitative measure of the amount of seismic energy released. The first and most well-known scale of earthquake magnitude is called the **Richter scale**. Many scientists contributed to the evolution of the earthquake magnitude concept, but it was Charles Richter, at the California Institute of Technology, who set up a scale on the basis of many years of observations and applied it to well-known earthquakes. He explained the scale in a now classic scientific paper published in 1935. Professor Richter modestly never attached his own name to the scale. He even refused to call it the Richter scale in his own subsequent papers, long after the press and public had made the 'Richter scale' synonymous with 'earthquake magnitude scale'.

Professor Richter often had trouble explaining to people that the Richter scale is a mathematical scale involving measurements and calculations on paper. 'They seem to think it is some sort of instrument or apparatus. Every year they come by, wanting to look at my scale', he once said in an interview. Richter borrowed the term 'magnitude' from astronomy, in which he had an amateur interest. In astronomy the brightness of stars is measured on a magnitude scale.

Unlike earthquake intensity, any earthquake has only *one* Richter magnitude. The Richter scale is also quantitative, being based on numerical measurement. The Richter scale has no upper limit, but in reality the Earth itself provides an upper limit due to the strength of rocks. The largest earthquakes ever recorded had Richter magnitudes of 8.9.

The Richter magnitude is calculated by first measuring the size of the largest ground motion recorded by a **seismometer**, which is a sensitive instrument that detects the ground movements produced by earthquakes. It consists of a heavy object that is suspended from a spring (Figure 3.8). The frame of the seismometer is attached firmly to solid bedrock. When an earthquake vibration (called a **seismic wave**) shakes the ground, the suspended heavy object stays relatively still, whereas the frame moves with the shaking ground. The relative motion between the object and the moving frame is traced by a pen, fixed to the heavy object, onto a chart that moves with the ground, and is also recorded electronically. The paper record of ground motion with time is called a **seismogram** (Figure 3.9).

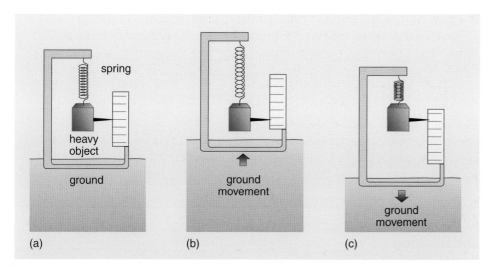

Figure 3.8   How a seismometer works. (a) A heavy object is suspended by
a spring from a frame (attached to the ground). (b) When the ground moves
upwards, the object stays relatively still and the attached pen moves down on the
chart, which moves with the ground. (c) As the ground moves downwards the
pen moves up on the chart. This seismometer measures vertical ground motion: a
slightly different supporting system can be used to measure horizontal motion.

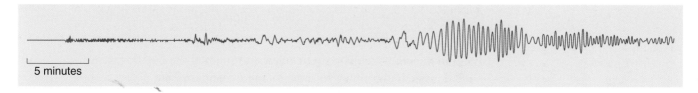

5 minutes

Figure 3.9   A seismogram of the 8 October 2005 Pakistan earthquake, recorded at Sutherland, South Africa. Time
elapsed increases from left to right.

Before the seismic waves arrive at the seismometer, the ground is still,
and the seismogram trace shows little or no motion (the far left-hand side of
Figure 3.9). The earthquake produces a number of different seismic waves, which
are recorded at different times on the seismogram, and produce different amounts
of ground motion. The effect of this earthquake on the seismometer lasted over
an hour. To measure the earthquake magnitude, the size of the ground motion is
then modified to account for the distance from the earthquake, since the closer the
seismometer is to the earthquake, the larger the ground motion will be.

The sizes of earthquakes vary enormously, so the size of the ground motion
produced can differ by a factor of thousands or even millions from earthquake
to earthquake. In order to deal with such enormous variation, the Richter scale
is based on powers of ten, which means that an increase of one unit on the scale
implies a tenfold increase in the amount of ground motion. For example, a
magnitude 2 earthquake produces 10 times more maximum ground motion than
a magnitude 1 earthquake. A magnitude 3 earthquake produces 10 times more
again, which is $10 \times 10 = 100$ times greater maximum ground motion than a
magnitude 1 earthquake.

■ How many times greater is the maximum ground motion of a magnitude 6 earthquake compared with that of a magnitude 3 earthquake?

□ Magnitude 6 is 3 points more on the Richter scale than magnitude 3, so a magnitude 6 earthquake has $10 \times 10 \times 10 = 1000$ (or 10^3) times greater maximum ground motion than a magnitude 3 earthquake.

Similarly, the difference between earthquakes of magnitude 3 and 7 (4 points on the Richter scale) will be 10^4 in terms of maximum ground motion. What appears at first to be a small change in Richter magnitude of an earthquake (say from 3 to 7, i.e. 4 points) really represents a very large change in earthquake size.

Activity 3.2   Investigating links between earthquake magnitude and location

We expect this activity will take you approximately 20 minutes.

You saw in Activity 3.1 that the ocean trenches, mid-ocean ridges and certain mountain belts have earthquakes associated with them, and that some of these features have both deep-focus and shallow-focus earthquakes. In this activity, you will investigate whether there is also a relationship between the size of an earthquake and its location relative to the major surface features.

(a) Study Figure 3.6 (we recommend you use the electronic version on the course website), and for each of the surface features (i), (ii) and (iii) listed below, decide what is the highest earthquake magnitude usually associated with the feature:

   (i)   mountains and ocean trenches surrounding the Pacific Ocean
   (ii) mountain belts in Europe; mountain belts in Asia
   (iii) mid-ocean ridges.

(b) Now fill in Table 3.1 (which is also available in electronic form on the course website if you wish to do this electronically), using your answers from part (a) of this activity and the answer to Activity 3.1. The completed table will provide a summary of the relationships between earthquake depth, size and location.

Table 3.1 The depths and sizes of earthquakes at different locations.

	Mountains and ocean trenches surrounding the Pacific Ocean	Mountain belts		Mid-ocean ridges
		Europe	Asia	
Depth (shallow-focus, intermediate-focus, or deep-focus)				
Largest magnitude (up to magnitude 7.9, or magnitude 8.0 and above)				

In Chapter 7 you will find out how these observations about the distribution of seismic zones on the Earth can be explained by plate tectonics.

Now look at the comments on this activity at the end of this book.

Not all earthquakes are associated with major Earth features, and the next activity looks at some of these earthquakes.

Activity 3.3 Earthquakes in the UK

We expect this activity will take you approximately 20 minutes.

A number of historical earthquakes in the UK have already been mentioned or described. This activity updates your knowledge of UK earthquakes to the present day. To do this requires a source of data that is continually updated. The best source for this is the internet. For the UK, a good website is maintained by the British Geological Survey (BGS). Go to the course website for instructions of where to find and how to use the BGS earthquakes pages to do this activity.

(a) Look at the locations of earthquakes in the UK. Are they randomly distributed or clustered in certain areas? Do the higher magnitude earthquakes occur in particular locations?

(b) Now look at the most recent earthquakes in the UK. How many have occurred in the last 30 days?

Now look at the comments on this activity at the end of this book.

3.4.3 Seismic energy

It is also possible to relate earthquake magnitude to the seismic energy released by an earthquake, as well as the amount of ground motion. An increase of one unit on the Richter scale represents an increase of about 40 times in the amount of seismic energy released.

Question 3.2

How many times greater is (a) the maximum ground motion, and (b) the energy released between an earthquake that measures 6.1 on the Richter scale and one that measures 8.1?

Earthquakes with magnitudes of 8 and greater occur rarely, but when they do occur they can lead to almost total devastation over a large area (Table 3.2).

Table 3.2 Numbers and effects of earthquakes of different Richter magnitude.

Richter magnitude	Average number per year	Radius of region of strong ground shaking/km	Effects of shallow earthquake
>8.0	<1	80–160	almost total destruction
7.0–7.9	15	50–120	serious/great damage
6.0–6.9	140	20–80	considerable damage
5.0–5.9	900	5–30	slight damage
4.0–4.9	8000	0–15	felt by many

Smaller earthquakes occur more frequently, but their combined energy release is small compared with that from one great earthquake; it would take almost 3 million earthquakes of magnitude 4 to release as much seismic energy as a single magnitude 8 earthquake. Earthquakes with the highest Richter magnitudes are not necessarily the most devastating, nor do they necessarily cause the greatest loss of life. The damage also depends on the depth; as mentioned previously, shallow earthquakes are generally more destructive than deeper ones. It also depends on other factors such as surface rock types and soil conditions as well as local building standards and population density.

Finally in this section, it is instructive to compare the energy produced by earthquakes with other energy sources. The amount of energy released by the Hiroshima atomic bomb was about 10^{12} J, whereas the largest earthquake ever recorded (magnitude 8.9) released about 10^{18} J of seismic energy. This is a million times more energy (i.e. a factor of 10^6) than the Hiroshima bomb. The amount of energy used every day in the UK is around 10^{16} J, which is more than 100 times greater than the seismic energy released by the largest UK earthquake. Figure 3.10 shows these comparisons in the form of a graph. However, the seismic energy (responsible for ground motion and the resulting damage) is only a few per cent of the total earthquake energy. The rest is involved in breaking, crushing and heating rocks around the fault, and moving the adjoining blocks of the Earth.

Figure 3.10   The seismic energy released by earthquakes of different Richter magnitude, compared with the Hiroshima atomic bomb and the UK daily energy use. Energy is given in joules. Each step on the vertical scale represents a tenfold increase in energy.

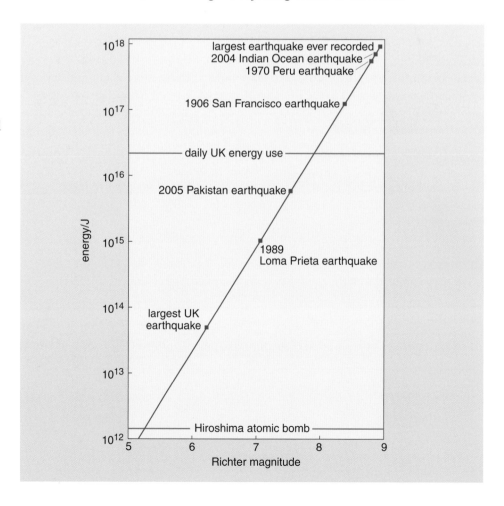

3.5   Summary of Chapter 3

Earthquakes shake the ground surface, can cause buildings to collapse and disrupt transport and services. They can trigger landslides and tsunamis.

Earthquakes occur as a result of Earth movements, involving parts of the Earth moving relative to each other, creating a fault. Smaller earthquakes, called foreshocks, may precede the main earthquake, and aftershocks may occur after the main earthquake. Earthquakes are mainly confined to specific areas of the Earth known as seismic zones, which coincide mainly with ocean trenches, mid-ocean ridges and mountain ranges.

The point of origin of an earthquake is called the focus. The epicentre is the point on the Earth's surface directly above the focus. Most earthquake foci are within a few tens of kilometres of the Earth's surface. Earthquakes less than 70 km deep are classified as shallow-focus. Intermediate-focus earthquakes are 70–300 km deep, and deep-focus earthquakes are more than 300 km deep. Shallow-focus earthquakes occur in all of the Earth's seismic zones, but intermediate- and deep-focus earthquakes are almost exclusively associated with seismic zones near ocean trenches.

The destructiveness of an earthquake depends on its size, depth (shallow ones are more destructive) and location. Earthquake size can be stated in terms of the damage caused (the intensity) or the amount of ground motion and the energy released by the earthquake (related to the Richter magnitude). A powers of ten scale (Richter magnitude) can be useful for measuring a quantity that can vary in size by factors of up to a million or more.

In studying this chapter you have compared information given in diagrams and maps and practised summarising your interpretation of that information.

Chapter 4
The active Earth: volcanic activity

In some parts of the world, the landscape is dominated by the elegant shapes of volcanoes, such as Fuji in Japan (Figure 4.1). Fuji is one of about 1500 volcanoes that have erupted at least once in the last 10 000 years (Fuji last erupted in 1737), and these are conventionally designated as active volcanoes. As with earthquakes, volcanic eruptions can destroy life and property but they can also reveal information about processes that shape the Earth's surface and which operate within the inaccessible depths of the Earth. The scientific study of earthquakes and volcanoes is therefore important for two reasons: to help understand these natural hazards and to learn about the Earth processes that produce them. In this chapter, and in keeping with the general scientific approach of making observations and then trying to explain them in a consistent way, you will look at some volcanic eruptions, the processes that cause them, and how different eruptions can be classified.

Figure 4.1   The print 'A sudden gust of wind at Ejiri' is one of the series 'Thirty-six Views of Mount Fuji' produced around 1830–1 by K. Hokusai and expresses the beauty of Fuji and its place in the world.

4.1 Volcanoes and their eruptions

In the popular imagination, a volcano is thought of as a steep majestic cone which every now and then suddenly explodes catastrophically, but this picture is not always accurate, as the examples in this section will show. To begin with, you'll recall that Book 1, Section 8.2, dealt with the effect that large volcanic eruptions can have on the GMST and that the eruption of Pinatubo (in the Philippines) in 1991 was a case in point. What actually happened during this eruption, and how typical was it of volcanic eruptions?

Mount Pinatubo is a high volcanic mountain on the island of Luzon, in the Philippines, that had last erupted about 500 years ago. Then, in March 1991, small earthquakes started to be detected, with foci beneath the volcano, signalling that the sleeping volcano might be becoming restless. Starting on 2 April, steam and other hot gases escaping from underground caused occasional explosions that sent pulverised rock to heights of a few kilometres. As time went on, the seismic activity continued and gas emissions and explosions increased, all the while being carefully observed and measured by a growing international team of scientists. On 7 June, molten rock (**magma**) reached the surface and over the following days generated a series of explosions as gas bubbled and frothed out of the magma, sending plumes of torn magma fragments and hot gas up to 25 km into the air (Figure 4.2a). The magma fragments, in the form of pumice full of very many small gas bubbles (Figure 4.2b) fell to the ground, blanketing a huge area in rock fragments. As

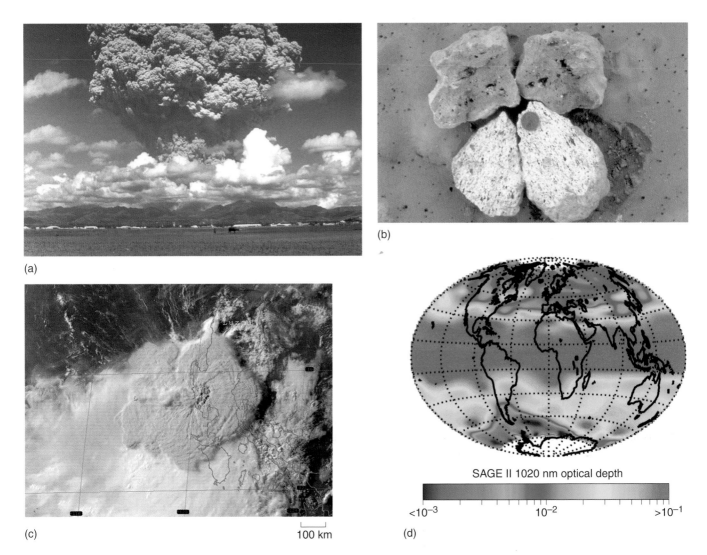

(a)

(b)

(c)

100 km

(d)

SAGE II 1020 nm optical depth

$<10^{-3}$ 10^{-2} $>10^{-1}$

Figure 4.2   The June 1991 eruptions of Mount Pinatubo. (a) View of the eruption on 12 June. (b) Fragments of pumice several centimetres across from the 15 June 1991 eruption. (c) Satellite image showing a roughly circular cloud of ash and gas at an altitude of about 35 km centred above the volcano on 15 June. (d) Satellite data showing that sulfuric acid aerosol particles formed in the atmosphere from erupted gases had covered 42% of the Earth's surface by mid-August 1991. The colour scale reflects the amount of aerosols in the atmosphere; red (right end of scale bar) is highest amount, blue (left end of scale bar) is lowest amount. SAGE II is the name of the satellite.

the volcano became evermore restless, the scientists felt that an even more destructive eruption was possibly imminent and made the difficult decision to evacuate nearby cities and a US Air Force base. On 15 June, the volcano burst into its most intense activity. Continuously rising magma exploded out of the volcano's summit, sending pumice and hot gas aloft in a lighter-than-air, buoyant mixture that rose to a height of 35 km (well into the stratosphere) and darkened the sky. This kept going for nine hours. Pumice rained down to cover an area of about 2000 km^2 to a depth of more than 10 cm in a snow-like blanket of pumice. Overall, pumice fell across tens of thousands of square kilometres of land and sea. At the same time, denser mixtures of rock and gas fell from the edges of the rising cloud and spilled over the edge of the crater. The dense mixture rushed down valleys on the sides of the volcano, burying all in its path and filling some valleys with volcanic ash to depths of up to 200 m. Torrential rain associated with a typhoon that was coincidently passing by 75 km away, turned a lot of the fallen pumice layers to a watery, muddy mixture with the consistency of wet concrete. Floods of this dense mud sped away from the volcano, bringing more destruction. In the stratosphere, ash and gas spread out in a layer several kilometres thick and up to 1000 km across which was easily spotted by satellites (Figure 4.2c). Satellites also tracked the dispersal of the 20 Mt (20 megatonne, or 2×10^{10} kg) cloud of sulfur dioxide (SO_2) gas and the layer of sulfuric acid aerosol particles that shrouded the Earth (Figure 4.2d), causing the GMST to decrease by about 0.5 °C in 1991–1992.

Within the space of nine hours, Pinatubo had discharged some 12.5 billion tonnes of magma and produced a 2.5 km diameter crater at the volcano's summit. The enormity of this is difficult to envisage, but in terms of the volume of magma being erupted every second it is equivalent to about 1.5×10^5 m^3 s^{-1}, roughly 100 times the rate at which water flows over Niagara Falls.

Luckily, such events are rare – on average about 1 to 3 eruptions of that size occur somewhere on Earth during a human lifetime. But some of the phenomena that occurred are not so rare. In general, the lumps of broken rocks and magma emitted by an explosive volcanic eruption are known as **pyroclasts**, so explosive eruptions are often described as **pyroclastic eruptions**. (The word pyroclast comes from the two Greek words *pyros*, 'fire', and *klastos*, 'shattered', so it means 'broken by fire'. However, volcanic eruptions and magmas are not caused by burning; it is just that magma is extremely hot, anything from about 700 to 1200 °C. Coincidently, another fire-related term used in describing pyroclastic rocks is ash (or volcanic ash), but this refers to small solid fragments of rock (strictly speaking, less than 2 mm in diameter) rather than the fluffy ash produced when wood or coal is burnt.)

The driving force behind pyroclastic eruptions is the hot gas that bursts out of the erupting molten magma, tearing it apart into frothy blobs (Figure 4.2b) which solidify in mid-air. Although gas is a small proportion (by mass) of the material produced in an eruption, it can be an impressive source of natural air pollution. For example, the SO_2 injected into the atmosphere by Pinatubo in June 1991 in less than a day is about one-seventh of the annual global SO_2 output from all industrial sources.

Explosive eruptions produce a mixture of hot gas and pyroclasts, but the behaviour of the erupted mixture depends on whether its density is less than or greater than that of the atmosphere. Figure 4.3a shows the case where the mixture is less dense than the atmosphere, so it rises high into the atmosphere, eventually spreading out in an umbrella-shaped cloud. As happened at Pinatubo, pyroclasts fall out of the umbrella cloud, blanketing the ground in a layer of pumice, ash and other volcanic rock debris (a pyroclastic fall deposit) which may be many metres thick near the volcano and cover many thousands of square kilometres. The extremely widespread distribution of the pyroclastic material reflects the fact that the umbrella cloud spreads out to great distances from the volcano and is also carried downwind. In the case where the erupted mixture is denser than the atmosphere (Figure 4.3b), the mixture fountains out of the volcano and flows down the side of the volcano as a **pyroclastic flow**, leaving a deposit of pumice and ash on the ground it travels across. Pyroclastic flows move very quickly, and their speeds range from less than 10 m s^{-1} to more than 100 m s^{-1}.

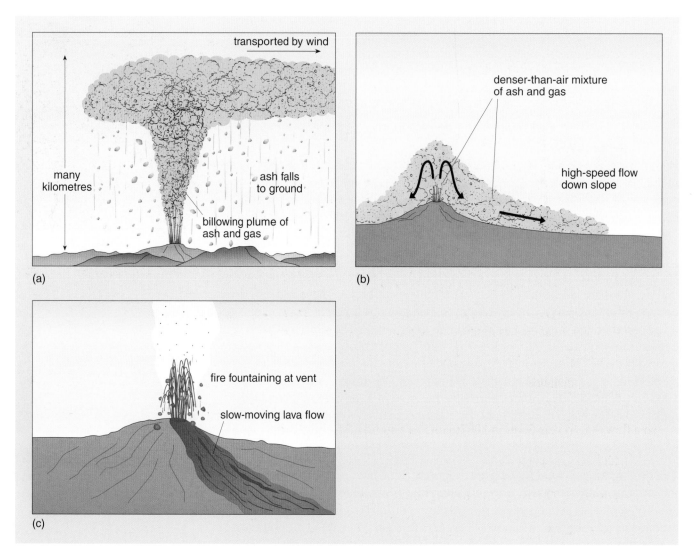

Figure 4.3 Three styles of pyroclastic eruptions: (a) a buoyant plume of gas and pyroclasts that rises high into the atmosphere where it spreads out and is dispersed, allowing the pyroclasts of pumice and ash to rain down onto the ground over a wide area; (b) a dense mixture of gas and pyroclasts cascades to the ground and rushes over the ground as a pyroclastic flow; (c) a fire fountain that produces a lava flow.

Explosive eruptions are often reported by the news media, especially if they happen close to where people are living, but you may have seen reports of less dangerous volcanic eruptions. Good examples of these occur on the island of Hawaii in the central Pacific Ocean. Hawaii is built from five separate but overlapping volcanoes with slopes that are rarely more than 6° – much less steep than, say, Fuji (Figure 4.1). The active volcanoes on Hawaii typically spring to life when a row of craters opens up on the side of the mountain, along a line extending away from the summit. Fountains of red-hot magma lumps and gas erupt from the craters and rise a hundred metres or more into the air (Figure 4.3c and 4.4a). Most of the pyroclasts fall back to the ground in a molten state and coalesce when they land to form rivers of **lava** that flow down the volcano's sides (Figure 4.4b). These can travel for tens of kilometres before coming to a halt once they have cooled and become solid rock.

(a)

(b)

Figure 4.4   Examples of volcanic activity at Kilauea volcano, Hawaii: (a) a fire fountain rising 100 m into the air; (b) lava flow (towards the camera) in a 4 m wide channel.

■ Lava flows on Hawaii typically take 5 to 100 hours to advance 5 km. At what speed (in km h^{-1} and m s^{-1}) do they advance (to 1 significant figure)?

□ The average speed is the distance travelled divided by the time taken:

$$\text{speed} = \frac{\text{distance}}{\text{time}}$$

so a flow that travels 5 km in 100 hours has a speed of:

$$\frac{5\ \text{km}}{100\ \text{h}} = 0.05\ \text{km h}^{-1}.$$

Because 1 km = 1000 m, and 1 hour = 60 minutes = 60 × 60 s = 3600 s,

this is equivalent to $\dfrac{5 \times 1000\ \text{m}}{100 \times 3600\ \text{s}} = \dfrac{5000\ \text{m}}{360\,000\ \text{s}} = 0.01\ \text{m s}^{-1}$ to 1 significant figure.

Similarly, 5 km in 5 hours is $\dfrac{5\ \text{km}}{5\ \text{h}} = 1\ \text{km h}^{-1}$.

This is equivalent to $\dfrac{5 \times 1000\ \text{m}}{5 \times 3600\ \text{s}} = \dfrac{5000\ \text{m}}{18\,000\ \text{s}} = 0.3\ \text{m s}^{-1}$ to 1 significant figure.

To put these speeds into context, this is much slower than average walking pace so although these eruptions are dangerous, and can destroy land and property, they are much less violent than the June 1991 eruption of Pinatubo. Typically, eruptions on Hawaii produce between 10^5 to 10^9 m^3 of lava at average rates of 10 to 200 m^3 s^{-1}.

A third example of volcanic activity is the eruption of Mount Saint Helens in Washington State, northwest USA. In May 1980, Mount St Helens erupted explosively, forming pyroclastic fall deposits and pyroclastic flows that devastated the surrounding area. In the years since, and at least until the time of writing (2007), this volcano intermittently pushed out very viscous magma that slowly formed a dome-shaped mound of lava (Figure 4.5). The eruption rate was less than 1 m^3 s^{-1}. This is an example of an eruption in which magma flows directly onto the surface, rather than exploding out in a stream of gas and pyroclasts, and is known as an **effusive eruption**.

Figure 4.5   The lava dome in the crater of Mount St Helens, USA, photographed on 20 November 2004. Height is approximately 200 m above the crater floor.

The three eruptions (Pinatubo, Kilauea and Mount St Helens) that have been described in this section certainly show great variety in explosivity, the amount of magma erupted, and the rate of eruption. The explanation for this depends on at least two factors – the viscosity (resistance to flow) of the magma and the amount of gas within the magma. Well beneath the Earth's surface, the pressure is so high, due to the weight of overlying rock, that gas is dissolved in magma, like gas is dissolved in a bottle of fizzy drink. When the magma moves closer to the surface, the pressure becomes less and eventually the pressure becomes so low that the gas can no longer remain dissolved and it starts to form bubbles, expanding the magma (like opening a bottle of fizzy drink). The more gas, the greater the amount of expansion. And if the liquid has a high viscosity, then it resists the rapid expansion of gas, allowing pressure to build up until the magma eventually explodes into fragments and an expanding stream of hot gas. Magmas with low gas content produce effusive eruptions, whereas magmas with high gas content and high viscosity tend to produce the most dangerous pyroclastic eruptions (e.g. Pinatubo).

4.2 Sizes of volcanic eruptions

You saw in Section 3.4.2 that the size of earthquakes can be measured by the Richter magnitude scale – a powers of ten scale that measures the amount of ground motion generated by the earthquake and is related to the amount of energy released. Is there a similar way of measuring, or quantifying, the size of volcanic eruptions? As with earthquakes, different types of measures can be thought of – for example, the destructiveness of an eruption, the rate at which magma is erupted, or the amount of magma erupted.

■ Which of these three measures do you think would be the best way to gauge the size of a volcanic eruption?

☐ As with earthquake intensity, a measure based on destructiveness will depend on how close the eruption is to a city or other populated centre, not just on the scale of the eruption itself. To measure the rate of eruption would require information about how long the eruption lasted, and this won't be available if the volcano wasn't closely observed; for example, if it was in a remote area, or if the eruption took place a long time ago, before records were kept. Thus it is best to consider the amount of material erupted needs to be known, as this can be worked out at any time after the eruption has stopped.

The most commonly used measure is the **eruption magnitude**, which is based on the mass of magma erupted. This is calculated after the eruption by measuring the thickness and area of the volcanic deposits produced, whether lava flows or pyroclastic deposits, to estimate their volume. This volume is then converted into a mass by multiplying by the density of the deposit (because mass = density × volume). Volcanic eruptions on Hawaii can produce as little as 10^8 kg (100 million kilograms) of magma, whereas the Pinatubo eruption produced about 10^{13} kg. Much larger eruptions are known to have occurred in the past because their deposits are preserved. The largest known eruption produced almost 10^{16} kg of magma. The difference in the sizes of these eruptions varies by a factor of 10^8 so, as with earthquakes, a powers of ten scale is appropriate. An eruption that yielded 10^8 kg of magma is defined as having magnitude 1, and an eruption of 10^{16} kg is defined as having magnitude 9.

Whereas news reports of earthquakes typically say that 'the 'quake registered such-and-such a value on the Richter scale', reports of volcanic eruptions don't give any measure of size because this can only be found after the eruption has stopped and it is safe to enter the area to make the necessary measurements, by which time the eruption will no longer attract the attention of news reporters. The important points are that (i) the eruption magnitude provides a quantitative measure of eruption size, and (ii) a powers of ten scale is necessary in order to deal with the enormous range in magma volumes erupted.

4.3   Where do volcanoes occur?

Figure 4.6 shows the locations of the world's active volcanoes.

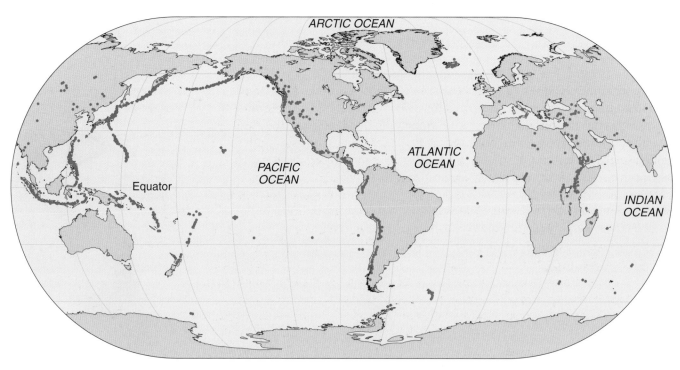

Figure 4.6   Map showing the locations of active volcanoes (indicated by red dots). These are defined as volcanoes that have erupted at least once in the past 10 000 years.

■ Referring to Figure 4.6 and maps of the Earth's surface features (such as Figure 2.6), what is the relationship between the distribution of volcanoes and major topographic features?

□ A great many of the volcanoes are arranged in long narrow rows along island arcs (Section 2.2.3) and along the edges of some continents. In both cases, these rows of volcanoes lie beside ocean trenches. Other volcanoes are associated with mid-ocean ridges, as in the case of Iceland and the Galápagos Islands. But not all volcanoes belong to arcs or lie on a mid-ocean ridge; some are built on the abyssal plains (e.g. Hawaii) and on the continents (e.g. East Africa).

The rows of volcanoes alongside trenches are called **volcanic arcs**. Examples include the Aleutians (an island arc in the North Pacific) and the volcanoes of the Andes in South America. These and many of the volcanoes that have had notoriously explosive eruptions in historical time – Krakatau (1883), Tambora (1815), Mount St Helens (1980), Pinatubo (1991) – lie around the edge of the Pacific Ocean. Together with the volcanoes that make up volcanic arcs in New Zealand, the Philippines, Japan, Kamchatka, and western America, this array of explosive volcanoes has been dubbed the Pacific Ring of Fire. Coincidentally, large numbers of people live in most of these regions, and many of the world's major cities lie near volcanoes that have produced explosive eruptions in the past. In Europe, the most threatening volcano is Vesuvius, which is close to Naples (population 1.2 million). It was a pyroclastic flow from Vesuvius that destroyed the town of Pompeii in AD 79.

On the other hand, volcanoes that lie within ocean basins and that are not associated with ocean trenches tend to have fewer catastrophically explosive eruptions, often producing only lava flows. Some examples are the volcanoes on Hawaii and the Galapagos Islands in the Pacific, and those on Iceland in the Atlantic Ocean.

4.4   Magma chambers and the subsurface

Clearly, volcanic eruptions happen above the ground, but every volcano must have a hidden underground part where the hot magma is stored and transported before it reaches the surface. At an active volcano, clues about the subsurface 'plumbing system' can be obtained from careful measurements of how the ground swells before eruptions, indicating that magma is collecting below the surface in a reservoir or **magma chamber**. Other clues can come from the locations of individual craters. For example, in many eruptions on Hawaii craters open up along a fissure that stretches for many kilometres. The long row of craters indicates that a long subterranean channel has opened, allowing magma to flow from a magma chamber to the surface (Figure 4.7a). The magma is said to *intrude* the rocks around the magma chamber. A long row of craters at the surface suggests a long intrusion at depth, and the solidified remnants of these can often be found at extinct volcanoes, after erosion of its upper parts have exposed the solidified rocks beneath. A long narrow intrusion such as this is known as a **dyke**. A spectacular example is in the desert of New Mexico, USA, where a dyke made of resistant volcanic rock some 3 m thick sticks out of the desert floor, forming a jagged wall about 9 km long (Figure 4.7b).

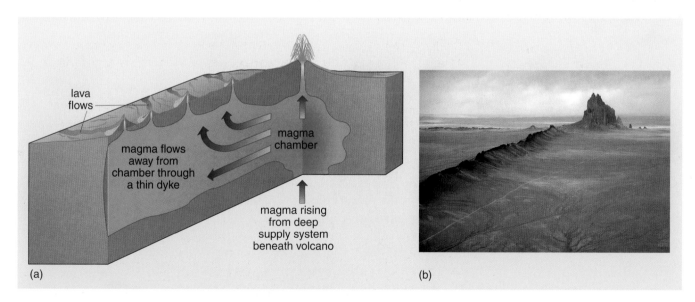

(a)

(b)

Figure 4.7   (a) An interpretation of the subsurface structure of a volcano. It shows a magma storage chamber and a dyke that has intruded the surrounding rock, allowing magma to flow sideways from the chamber and erupt. (b) Photograph of a dyke at Shiprock, New Mexico, USA. The jagged mountain in the distance is the eroded remnant of the feeder pipe to a volcano that was active some 30 million years ago. Magma that flowed vertically through the feeder probably erupted on the surface (0.75 to 1 km of overlying rock has been stripped away by erosion), whereas magma that flowed sideways intruded to form a dyke.

4.5   Volcanoes and earthquakes

Volcanoes and earthquakes are dramatic examples of activity within the solid Earth, but are these two phenomena related in any way?

■ Compare a map of the world showing the locations of volcanoes (Figure 4.6) with a map of earthquake distribution (Figure 3.6). Are volcanoes and earthquakes found in the same places?

☐ Usually, but not always. For example volcanoes occur in the seismic zones around the Pacific Ocean basin and on parts of the mid-ocean ridge system, yet in the Himalayas and large areas of the Middle East, for instance, there are many earthquakes but no volcanoes.

What can be made of these observations? Think first about areas where there are both volcanoes and earthquakes. One reason why earthquakes can happen in volcanic regions is that when magma moves into a magma chamber or intrudes beneath a volcano, rocks must be broken apart, causing earthquakes. It is often the case that the number of shallow earthquakes at a volcano increases before an eruption, while magma is intruding its way to the surface. Monitoring how the number and size of these earthquakes changes over time can be a good way of anticipating that an eruption may be about to happen, as was the case at Pinatubo. However, successfully predicting exactly when the volcano will erupt is still only very rarely possible.

On the other hand, the observation that earthquakes can happen where there are no volcanoes means that volcanoes cannot be the cause of every earthquake. Indeed, in Chapter 3 you saw how movement of rocks on either side of major faults produces most earthquakes. These earthquakes happen whether or not volcanoes are present.

4.6   How many volcanoes have erupted in the past week?

Only if a volcanic eruption has caused loss of life, or threatened communities, is it likely to be reported in the usual international news media. Nonetheless, there are a few volcanoes around the world that are almost constantly active; one of these is the Italian volcano Stromboli and the craters at its summit have been ejecting bursts of red-hot pyroclasts several times an hour for well over a thousand years. Most volcanoes aren't so persistent, and their eruptions are recorded by the Global Volcanism Program run by the Smithsonian Institution in Washington DC in collaboration with the United States Geological Survey. The Global Volcanism Program's website serves the scientific community, news media and the general public by providing an archive of observations of volcanic activity. Not only does it include information reported by people who observed the eruption, but it also includes information about ash clouds and hot ground that have been detected by instruments on Earth-orbiting satellites. Before the eras of rapid communication and satellites, many of the world's volcanic eruptions went unreported, but this is now far less likely, even for volcanoes in uninhabited regions.

Activity 4.1   Summarising recent volcanic activity

We expect this activity will take you approximately 30 minutes.

Go to Activity 4.1 on the course website. Follow the links to the Global Volcanism Program website and click on the Weekly Reports link to find the most recent summary of eruptions in a week-long period.

Task 1

The website explains that the quality of the information it holds can be of variable quality, or incomplete for various reasons. Write two sentences explaining why the information in the Weekly Report can be incomplete.

Task 2

Summarise the week's reported activity by noting the dates of the week in question, then for each volcano list its name and geographical location and the type of activity reported, noting which of the following are mentioned:

- emissions of hot gas or steam (sometimes referred to as fumaroles)
- lava flows (including lava domes)
- ash plumes and/or ash fall (is the height of any ash plumes reported?)
- pyroclastic flows (including varieties known as block and ash flows)
- mud flows (sometimes referred to as lahars, an Indonesian word for rapid flows of watery mud and debris that can be generated on the steep sides of volcanoes when water mixes with volcanic ash)
- earthquakes

You may find terms that are unfamiliar to you, although many of these will link to the course glossary. However, try to avoid getting side-tracked into exploring the meaning of every new term. You may find it helpful to record the information in a table, using the bulleted points above as column headings.

Task 3

How many volcanoes were active? What was the most common type of activity?

Now compare your findings with those given in the comments on this activity at the end of this book. How do the two weeks compare? How many of the volcanoes are mentioned in both weeks?

4.7   Summary of Chapter 4

Volcanoes erupt mixtures of molten magma, hot gas and, in some cases, pulverised fragments of rock which were part of the volcano.

Volcanic eruptions can be classified according to the behaviour of the erupting mixture of magma, gas and rock. When the magma releases gas and breaks violently into fragments (pyroclasts) which solidify in mid-air, the eruption is said to be explosive (or pyroclastic). Explosive eruptions can be divided into two types depending on whether the erupted mixture is lighter than air, and rises in a tall eruption plume high into the atmosphere, or is denser than air and flows at high speed across the ground as a pyroclastic flow. When the magma erupts without exploding, a lava flow or lava dome is formed and the eruption is said to be effusive.

Volcanic eruptions vary in the rate at which magma is erupted and in the mass (or volume) of magma erupted. The explosivity of an eruption increases with the amount of gas in the magma and the viscosity of the magma. The size of eruptions can be classified using a powers of ten scale, based on the mass of magma erupted.

Explosive volcanic eruptions are typically associated with volcanoes in island arcs and volcanic chains at the edges of certain continents, especially around the Pacific Ring of Fire. These volcanic arcs lie parallel with ocean trenches.

Earthquakes occur beneath volcanoes when rocks get forced apart by magma moving into magma chambers beneath volcanoes or when magma is creating pathways to the surface. Other earthquakes near volcanoes are caused by movement of rocks along faults.

In studying this chapter you have continued to use maps and web-based archives of scientific data to learn about the Earth.

Chapter 5
The active Earth: how rocks are formed

So far not much has been said about the rocks that make up the surface of the Earth. Although rocks are frequently seen in cliffs and road cuttings, solid rocks also lie below the vegetation and soil in every landscape. Some of these rocks are useful as building stones, others are sources of the metals needed to make many of the trappings of civilisation that are taken for granted, such as coins, railway tracks or electrical components. Although rocks often appear to be permanent features of the landscape, you have already found, in Book 1, Chapter 7, that rocks are formed and destroyed during the gradual operation of the water and carbon cycles. And, of course, active volcanoes are producing new rocks right now.

Different types of rock form in different ways, and the processes involved leave their marks on the rocks they produce. The purpose of this chapter is to use the set of rock samples provided in the Practical Kit to explore the links between processes occurring on the Earth and the rocks that they produce. First, it is necessary to elaborate on the meanings of two key terms – rocks and minerals.

5.1   Rocks and minerals

The terms rock and mineral, and the distinction between the two, need to be clearly understood. A **mineral** is a solid material, formed by natural processes and with a chemical composition that falls within certain narrow limits. Its constituent atoms are arranged in a regular three-dimensional array or pattern and because of this, minerals form crystals with a characteristic shape.

Five common minerals are shown in Figure 5.1 to provide you with some specific examples. They range in shape from cubes (pyrite) and thin sheets

Figure 5.1   Crystals of some common minerals. From left to right: (back row) mica, calcite, quartz; (front row) feldspar and two cubes of pyrite.

(mica) to more complex shapes. This is because each is built from atoms of different chemical elements, and different combinations of atoms fit together into differently shaped structures. You can also see that they have different colours and that their appearance varies from glassy to metallic to matt. These differences also come about because minerals have different chemical compositions and atomic structures. Although for the purposes of this book there is no need to know the details of these minerals' chemical compositions, it can be noted that quartz, mica and feldspar are common examples of the many kinds of minerals that contain silicon and oxygen – the two most common elements at the Earth's surface. Quartz contains only silicon and oxygen. Pyrite contains iron and sulfur. Calcite contains calcium, carbon and oxygen – it is calcium carbonate, the main constituent of limestone that, as you saw in Book 1, Chapter 7, is part of the largest reservoir of carbon on Earth.

There are several thousand different kinds of minerals but only a few are very common; for example, most of the sand grains on a beach or in a desert are grains of quartz. Others, such as gemstones and the minerals that are used to supply metals, are rather rare.

Figure 5.2   A piece of granite, shown at approximately actual size.

A **rock** is a solid assemblage of mineral grains that can range from a few micrometres to a few centimetres in size. The mineral grains rarely show their characteristic shapes because they are broken or are interlocked with each other. A rock may consist of only one type of mineral but more usually it consists of several different minerals. For example, in the piece of granite shown in Figure 5.2 some of the grains are white, others are grey and glassy, and others are black with a shiny appearance. It is therefore an assemblage of several minerals: the black shiny mineral, mica; the grey glassy mineral, quartz; and the white mineral, feldspar; all of which are shown individually in Figure 5.1.

Now that the important terms mineral and rock have been defined, you will investigate the dynamic processes that produce the different types of rock found at the Earth's surface.

Activity 5.1   An introduction to rocks and their origins

We expect this activity will take you approximately 2 hours, although it is not necessary to do it all in one go.

Rocks are formed by many different geological processes on the Earth, and in this activity you will examine a number of rock specimens and discover that they contain clues to the processes that formed them. This will involve first making observations and then interpreting them in terms of the processes by which rocks are formed. The activity is split into a number of tasks, which serve to guide you through the work. The overall aims of this activity are:

1   To examine rock specimens from the Practical Kit, and to link observations of the specimens to the processes that formed them.

2   To develop practical science skills associated with making observations and recording information.

Safety warning

Read the whole of this section before starting the activity and make sure that you have read the section on 'Practical activities' in the *Course Guide*.

When carrying out practical activities, you should always take care to observe the simple safety precautions highlighted in the course book. Very often, as in the case of this activity, these precautions will seem quite obvious and just a matter of using common sense. However, that does not mean that you should ignore the safety instructions. The Open University has a duty to give advice on health and safety to students carrying out any activities that are described in the course. Similarly, *you* have a duty to follow the instructions and to carry out the practical activity having regard for your own safety and that of other people around you. Whenever you do practical activities you should think about the hazards involved, and how any risks can be minimised.

Important safety precautions

Take note of the following safety precautions, which apply to all practical activities:

- Keep children and animals away while you are working.
- Clear your working area of clutter. Put all food away. Ensure there is nothing to trip on underfoot.
- Always wash your hands thoroughly after a practical activity.
- Any household items used should be thoroughly cleaned before returning them to domestic use.

In addition, you should note the following precautions specific to this activity:

- Take care when handling the rock specimens not to touch your eyes. Some rock dust can be an irritant. If you get dust in your eye, wash it out with copious amounts of water for at least 5 minutes. If irritation persists seek medical help.
- When using vinegar (Task 5) note that this can be an irritant. If you get vinegar in your eye, wash it out with copious amounts of water for at least 5 minutes. If irritation persists seek medical help.

Equipment required

KIT ITEMS:

Rocks and mineral specimens 1–6

Hand lens

NON-KIT ITEMS:

Sticky labels or sticky tape for labelling the specimens

Ruler marked in millimetres

Vinegar (optional, for Task 5)

Empty jam jar or similar (optional, for Task 5)

Task 1   Getting started

Along with this book you were sent a Practical Kit packed in a box with a clear plastic lid. For this activity you will need the hand lens and the six rock and mineral specimens.

The rock and mineral specimens in the Kit are not individually labelled, but each can be distinguished using Figure 5.3 – rather like identifying the contents of a box of chocolates. The Kit has been packed with each compartment containing a particular specimen, recognisable by shape and/or colour and described in the caption to Figure 5.3. You should label the specimens for yourself so that you will be able to identify them when you have taken them out of the box. A small sticky label or piece of sticky tape can be used to label each specimen with its number according to Figure 5.3.

Figure 5.3   Key to the rock and mineral specimens in the Practical Kit. Specimen 1 is colourless, transparent and glassy. Specimen 2 is pale-coloured and granular, and is inside a plastic bag. Specimen 3 is a dark-coloured, rounded and polished pebble, with some lighter patches. Specimen 4 is grey with jagged edges, and has a shiny surface made up of flakes of glittering material. Specimen 5 is very dark grey or black, with some white flecks. Specimen 6 has white, grey and black patches.

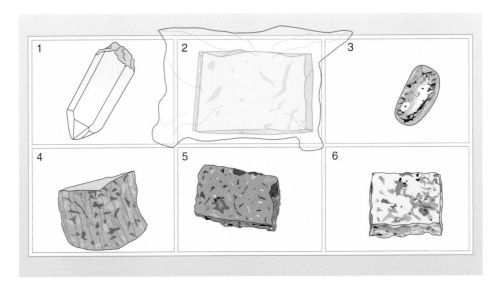

Every rock specimen is unique, so if you compare your example of Specimen 2, say, with that of another student it is likely that you'll be able to see subtle differences in perhaps grain size or colour, even though all the samples of Specimen 2 are of the same rock, collected from the same rock outcrop.

Specimens 2, 4, 5 and 6 have been prepared by sawing up larger samples, so they have at least one flat sawn surface, as well as rough, naturally broken, surfaces. In some cases the sawn surfaces may have curved markings on them – this is just an effect of the sawing process and is not a characteristic feature of the rocks themselves, so please ignore any of these curved marks. Also, Specimens 4 and 5 can have brown or orange surface stains, caused by chemical alteration of the rock after it formed, and these should be ignored too. The features on sawn surfaces can often be enhanced by wetting the surface with some water.

Before starting to examine the specimens, take a little time to familiarise yourself with using the hand lens. The correct way to examine objects with a hand lens is shown in Figure 5.4.

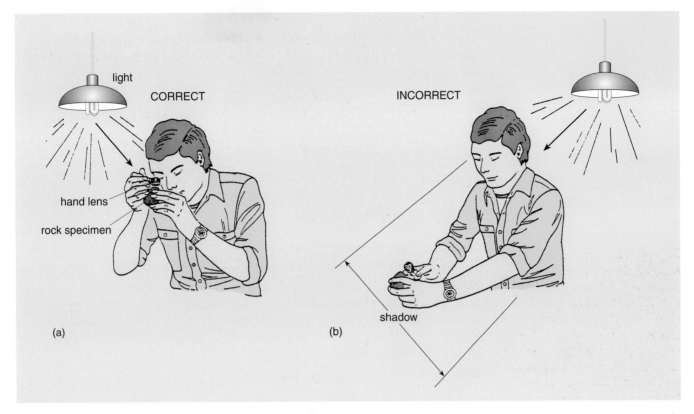

Figure 5.4   (a) Correct use of the hand lens. (b) Incorrect use of the hand lens.

Some additional useful hints are:

- Hold the hand lens 2–3 cm from your eye and bring the specimen up towards the lens until it is in focus.
- Make sure the surface of the specimen is well lit from the side.
- Keep the hand lens and the specimen surface parallel to each other and hold both steady.
- With rough surfaces, you may have to move the specimen up and down to bring different parts into focus.

You might like to practise using the hand lens by looking at the end of one of your fingers, or the millimetre divisions on a ruler. How many ridges on your fingertip are there to a millimetre?

There are no comments on this task.

Task 2   A preliminary classification of the specimens

The six specimens labelled 1 to 6 from the Practical Kit are all different, but some share common features. Take a few minutes to look carefully at the six specimens (you do not need to use a hand lens at this stage) and decide how you might divide the specimens into groups based on similarities and differences.

If you thought there could be several possible ways of dividing the six specimens then you'd be right. You could divide them according to whether they are light or dark in colour, or whether they have shiny or rough surfaces;

these are just two of the possible ways of dividing or classifying the specimens based on their appearance. However, perhaps the most obvious division is between Specimen 1 and all of the others. Unlike the others, Specimen 1 has a regular shape and is transparent or faintly cloudy in appearance, and its surfaces are flat with a glassy sheen or lustre. The others are opaque, have irregular shapes, uneven surfaces (unless cut or polished) and contain patches with different colours. These differences single out Specimen 1 as a crystal of a mineral, whereas the others are aggregates of different mineral grains, and are therefore classified as rocks.

Specimen 1 is a crystal of the mineral quartz. Whereas some of the rock specimens have flat, cut sides, the quartz specimen is uncut and unpolished – this specimen occurs naturally like this. Quartz is a mineral composed of silicon and oxygen atoms arranged in a regular way, and it is this internal structure that gives the crystal its regular shape. Quartz is one of the most common minerals on the Earth. (You will learn more about minerals in Books 4 and 6.)

You are now left with five rock specimens. Geologists call these 'hand specimens' because they are the right size to be examined in the hand, in contrast to examining a large outcrop of rock in a cliff or crag. In order to find out more about the different origins of these rocks, you need to examine them more closely. You will start with Specimen 2.

There are no comments on this task.

Task 3 Describing Specimen 2

Take Specimen 2 out of its protective bag and examine closely the flat sawn surfaces and the natural broken surfaces. Feel its surface with your fingers; look at the rock close up and through your hand lens.

- What colour is the specimen?
- Are its broken surfaces rough or smooth?
- How large are the individual grains that make up the rock? (Use your hand lens and a ruler to estimate the typical size of the grains.)
- Using the hand lens, look more closely at individual grains and their neighbours. Do the grains interlock with each other, or do they look more like individual fragments that have become stuck together?

Your observations should have enabled you to decide that the specimen is made of small grains or fragments of a pale material, typically 1–4 mm in size, and that these grains are stuck together to form a rock with a rough surface. If you are not sure, look again at the specimen through your hand lens. Notice that many of the grains have rounded or broken corners, indicating that they are fragments broken from larger pieces of material. The form of the grains that a rock is made of, and how they are arranged together, is called the rock's **texture**. This rock has a **fragmental texture**, meaning that it is composed of broken fragments of various materials.

Table 5.1 is provided for you to record your observations and other information about the rock specimens, and at this point you should fill in details of the texture, colour and grain size for Specimen 2. (A larger template is available on the course website.)

Table 5.1 Observations and interpretations of rock specimens.

Specimen number	Texture	Colour(s)	Typical grain size(s)	Rock type (metamorphic, sedimentary or igneous)	Process of formation	Rock name	Additional comments
2							
3							
4							
5							
6							

Interpreting Specimen 2

The texture of a rock contains evidence about the processes that formed the rock. Most of the larger fragments in this rock are fragments of quartz – the same material as Specimen 1. You may be able to see this by examining some of the grains closely; the glassy, broken surfaces are similar to the glassy, broken surfaces of Specimen 1. So how can this information be used to interpret the origin of this rock specimen?

■ In what type of place might you find many small grains of quartz?

☐ On a sandy beach or river bed.

■ So, where might the quartz grains that make up Specimen 2 have come together?

☐ On an ancient beach or river bed.

The rock formed by the accumulation of sand grains; hence it is called sandstone. The sand grains were deposited and then buried under more layers of sand. Over a very long period water would have percolated through the deeply buried and compacted sand, slowly depositing very small particles called cement which stuck the sand grains together. By this process, the loose sand has been hardened, or lithified, into solid rock. The larger grains are only loosely held together (cemented) by the much finer grains, and they are fairly easily dislodged.

The quartz grains in this rock have somewhat rounded shapes, suggesting a long history of buffeting, abrasion and breakage. Buffeting would have taken place by collisions with other rocks and mineral grains during each grain's journey down a river or along a shore to its final resting place. Accumulations of rock and mineral fragments that are transported and deposited in this way, by water, wind or ice, are called **sediments**. The sandstone formed by lithification (Book 1, Section 7.4.3) of sedimentary grains, so it is a **sedimentary rock**.

You may be able to see layers of different grain size in your sandstone specimen. These are original sedimentary layers, formed when layers of different-sized grains accumulated on top of each other.

Now complete the 'Specimen 2' row of Table 5.1.

There are no comments on this task.

Task 4 Describing Specimen 3

Specimen 3 is particularly attractive to look at because its features have been emphasised by polishing. Examine it closely and decide on its colour and grain size, as you did for Specimen 2. Enter these in the 'Specimen 3' row of Table 5.1.

You may have found this rather difficult, because the specimen contains different types of material. Some of the rock is made of dark grey, almost black, fine-grained material (in fact, the grains are too fine to distinguish individually, even with a hand lens). This is known as the rock's **matrix**. Set within the matrix are some intriguing pale grey, brown or pinkish objects, mostly a few millimetres across. What shapes do these pale objects have? Does this rock have a fragmental texture (i.e. is it composed of broken fragments)?

You probably concluded that the rock contains a lot of pale-coloured, broken fragments (do not be confused by the smooth surface of the sample, which is the result of polishing). Some of the pale-coloured objects are circular and sometimes have a circular or star-shaped 'hole' at their centre. Others are elongate, and are sometimes divided into faint, evenly spaced segments. Still others have broken edges. And the smaller objects look as if they are broken fragments of larger pieces. So this is another fragmental rock, and it is therefore another example of a sedimentary rock.

Interpreting Specimen 3

So what are the pale-coloured objects in this rock? You might be able to get a feel for their three-dimensional shape by turning the specimen to see edge-on and side-on views of the same object. This will confirm that some of the larger fragments are actually cylinders. On a flat surface you sometimes see their circular cross-section and sometimes you see a longitudinal view.

These regular-shaped fragments are the fossil remnants of organisms known as crinoids (Figure 5.5) that live on the floors of clear, shallow seas. Crinoids (which vary greatly in size) are animals related to sea urchins and starfish, although at first sight they look rather plant-like. The fossil fragments in Specimen 3 are parts of broken stems and other parts of the animal.

The texture and composition of this rock enable you to interpret it as a sedimentary rock, formed when crinoid fragments were deposited on the muddy bottom of a clear, shallow sea. The individual mud particles are too small to be

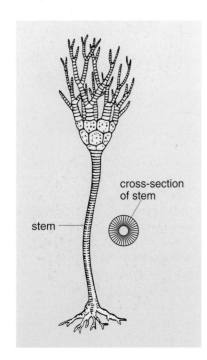

Figure 5.5 Reconstruction of a fossil crinoid. The hard parts of this marine animal are made of calcite plates and discs. It comprises a 'holdfast' that anchored it to the seabed, a stem, and the body cavity with 'arms' that trapped floating debris for food. The arms branch out into finer and finer feather-like structures (not shown here).

cross-section of stem

stem

distinguished, even with the hand lens. The fossil crinoid fragments are made of calcite – calcium carbonate. Hence this sedimentary rock is a type of limestone.

There are no comments on this task.

Task 5 The acid test (optional)

Warning: This optional test will remove some of the polished surface from your specimen.

One way of confirming that the fossils in this rock are indeed made of calcite is to place the specimen in an old jam jar (or similar container) with a small amount of vinegar, which is a weak acid. The acid will react with the calcium carbonate, dissolving it away and liberating carbon dioxide gas.

Use enough vinegar to cover about half the specimen. Label the jar clearly 'NOT TO BE EATEN' and put it out of the reach of children and animals where it will not be knocked over. You may be able to see bubbles of carbon dioxide around the specimen. To get much of an effect you will need to leave the specimen standing in vinegar for about 4 hours, or overnight; after this time, take the rock specimen out of the jar and wash it under a tap. The acid treatment will remove the shiny polished surface from the rock and will dissolve away some of the fossil material, leaving the dark muddy matrix standing slightly proud of the fossil material. The muddy material in the matrix does not react with the acid. With your hand lens, you may be able to see that the matrix has become slightly pitted, indicating that it contained some tiny calcite fragments that have dissolved away.

■ You may see some small particles of sediment at the bottom of the jar; what do you think this is?

☐ This sediment is mud from the matrix that has been released when the calcite holding the particles together dissolved in the acid.

When you have finished with the vinegar, pour it down a sink and wash the jar and specimen thoroughly.

The reaction of calcium carbonate with acid releases carbon (in the form of CO_2 gas) into the atmosphere that has been locked up in this particular part of the geochemical carbon cycle (Book 1, Section 7.4) for over 300 Ma (i.e. 300 million years; the Ma notation was introduced in Book 1 Box 3.3) – the time since this rock formed at the bottom of a long-vanished sea.

Summarise your observations and interpretation of Specimen 3 in Table 5.1.

You have now looked at two sedimentary rocks, both of which have a fragmental texture. The remaining three rocks (Specimens 4, 5 and 6) are crystalline – they consist of crystals of different minerals and of different sizes that are arranged either randomly or in alternating bands. The difference between a fragmental texture and examples of **crystalline textures** are shown in Figure 5.6 and are due to the different processes by which rocks are formed.

There are no comments on this task.

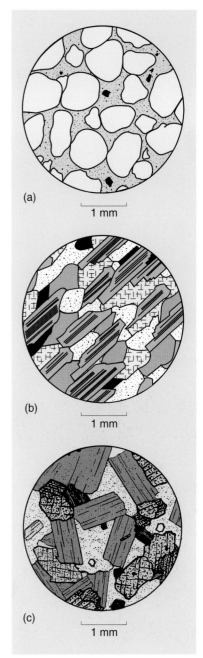

(a)   1 mm

(b)   1 mm

(c)   1 mm

Figure 5.6 Sketches illustrating examples of (a) fragmental, and (b) and (c) crystalline rock textures. The different minerals in each rock are distinguished by different shading. Each sketch represents a magnified piece of rock a few millimetres across.

Task 6 Describing Specimen 4

Look carefully at Specimen 4, examining it from different angles and using your hand lens to see the detail. Make a note of the colour, grain size and any other features, such as the colours and shapes of mineral grains, and any banding within the specimen. Then compare your notes with those in the comments on Task 6 at the end of this book.

The largest grains in this rock are about 2–3 mm across and have a reddish or orange colour, with a glassy appearance on broken surfaces. These are crystals of the mineral garnet. More abundant are the smaller shiny mineral flakes, best seen glinting in the light on the rough uncut surface of the specimen using the hand lens. These are flat, platy crystals of the mineral mica and they are arranged in roughly parallel layers that give this rock a banded appearance and allow it to split along uneven planes between the flakes of mica. You might be able to see this by prising away parts of the specimen with your fingernail.

Interpreting Specimen 4

A banded crystalline rock owes its texture to the effects of crystal growth in the solid state during a time when the rock was subjected to great pressure and heat many kilometres down inside the Earth. Because of the high pressure and high temperature, the atoms within pre-existing minerals become rearranged into a set of new minerals that grow in an interlocking three-dimensional arrangement of crystals. This process occurs in the solid state and is called **metamorphism**, which means 'changing form'. Specimen 4 was formed by metamorphism, so it is called a **metamorphic rock**. When rocks are being compressed more strongly in one direction than another, minerals that form flat, platy crystals (e.g. mica) tend to grow in roughly parallel bands at right angles to the compression, rather than in random orientations. The banded alignment of minerals is typical of metamorphic rocks formed in this way, and produces the texture sketched in Figure 5.6b.

Specimen 4 is representative of the metamorphic rock type known as schist (pronounced 'sh-ist'). The reddish garnet it contains is a mineral found in many metamorphic rocks. Other types of metamorphic rock have different minerals, or the banding can be coarser or finer than in Specimen 4.

Summarise your observations and interpretation of Specimen 4 in Table 5.1.

Task 7 Describing Specimen 5

Note the texture, colour, grain size, and any distinctive features of this specimen. Although each specimen is slightly different, it is likely that your Specimen 5 will have some brown or orange staining on some surfaces. These stains were caused by chemical reactions between water and the rock long after the rock formed, so they are a distraction that is unrelated to the origin of the rock, and can be ignored here.

Compare your notes with those given in the comments for Task 7 at the end of this book.

Interpreting Specimen 5

Like the schist you looked at in Task 6, Specimen 5 has a crystalline texture. But it does not show any banded alignment of crystals or tendency to break into flakes. This suggests that Specimen 5 did not form by metamorphism.

■ Can you suggest how these crystals may have grown, in contrast to the crystals in the schist, which grew in the solid state?

☐ The crystals might have grown from a liquid state.

The crystals in this rock grew from a molten magma while it cooled down. The crystals were free to grow in any direction, whereas in metamorphic rocks the crystals usually grow aligned in bands. Rocks formed from the solidification of magma are called **igneous rocks**. (The word igneous is derived from the Latin word *ignis*, meaning 'fire'.)

You may have noticed round holes or voids in the specimen. They can be up to several millimetres across. These holes represent gas bubbles that got trapped in the solidifying magma during a volcanic eruption, so this is a volcanic igneous rock.

Specimen 5 is an example of the volcanic rock, basalt. Basalt is the most common igneous rock on the Earth's surface, largely because the ocean floor is made of basalt. Volcanic rocks such as this are called extrusive igneous rocks, because they have been extruded onto the Earth's surface.

A volcanic rock such as Specimen 5 would have started to cool slowly in a magma chamber underground, allowing a few large crystals to grow. Then, when the magma was erupted, gas bubbles fizzed out of the magma, as they do when a bottle of fizzy drink is opened. As the magma cooled quickly at the surface, solidification became complete with the rapid growth of tiny crystals which trapped some of the gas bubbles in the volcanic rock.

Summarise your observations and interpretation of Specimen 5 in Table 5.1.

Task 8 Describing Specimen 6

The final specimen to examine is another crystalline rock. Use the hand lens to look at a flat face of this specimen, which shows a mosaic of quite large interlocking crystals. The rock is a three-dimensional jigsaw. Each grain joins up and interlocks with every other grain around it so there are absolutely no empty spaces between.

There are three different types of crystal in this specimen distinguishable by colour. Note their colour, and estimate their size (but note that several crystals of the same mineral may be joined together, giving the impression of a larger size).

Check your descriptions with the comments on Task 8 before continuing.

Interpreting Specimen 6

■ Do you think that this crystalline rock is metamorphic or igneous?

☐ The arrangement of crystals in approximately parallel bands is a feature of many metamorphic rocks. In Specimen 6, the crystals make up an interlocking mosaic with no obvious banding present, so it is unlikely to be metamorphic and more likely to be igneous.

Indeed, this is another igneous rock, this time made of crystals that are large enough to be seen without the hand lens. When this rock solidified from molten magma, the crystals were able to grow to relatively large sizes before the whole rock was completely solid, yielding a texture similar to the one sketched in Figure 5.6c. The longer the cooling time, the larger the crystals (all else being equal).

■ In what environment do you think slow cooling of magma might occur to give the large crystals seen in Specimen 6?

☐ Slow cooling would occur when magma cooled deep underground – for instance, in a magma chamber.

This rock was formed when molten magma was intruded into existing rocks and cooled very slowly. It is therefore called an intrusive igneous rock. The name of this particular type of intrusive igneous rock is granite. Granite is defined as an intrusive igneous rock containing the minerals quartz (the grey glassy crystals) and feldspar (the white, sometimes rectangular crystals), with smaller amounts of mica (the black flakes). These three minerals account for virtually all of the rock, and you should have distinguished them by colour.

When you are holding Specimen 6, you are holding the solidified product of a magma that cooled from about 800 °C at a depth of several kilometres below the Earth's surface.

Summarise your observations and interpretation of Specimen 6 in Table 5.1.

Review of Activity 5.1

To conclude this activity, you can reflect that you have been able to inspect a hand specimen and deduce a rock's texture, and relate your observations to how the rock formed. This revealed the three main ways in which rocks form. In the first case, the sandstone and limestone are sedimentary rocks, with fragmental textures (Figure 5.6a), that form by the accumulation of sedimentary grains in layers (for example, sand on a beach, or mud in the estuary of a river) at the Earth's surface. Metamorphic rocks are existing rocks that have 'changed form' (metamorphosed) in a solid state by the action of high pressure and/or temperature, for example after burial deep in the Earth. The specimen of schist is a metamorphic rock. It has an interlocking, intergrown, crystalline texture formed by recrystallisation under pressure that caused new crystals of platy mica to grow in uneven bands (Figure 5.6b). These allow the rock to break apart along these planes of weakness. Igneous rocks are formed from molten rock (magma) that becomes solid when it cools, either after a volcanic eruption at the Earth's surface or deep underground. Igneous rocks also have an interlocking, intergrown, crystalline texture, but the crystals have grown in random orientations (Figure 5.6c). Intrusive igneous rocks such as granite form by the slow cooling of magma at depth, resulting in large grain sizes. Extrusive igneous rocks such as basalt are formed when volcanic eruptions bring magma to the Earth's surface where it cools quickly. They have smaller grain sizes, and sometimes contain holes once occupied by escaping volcanic gases.

Your completed Table 5.1 (compare it with Table 5.3 in the comments on this activity) provides a record of your observations and a summary of the main features of the different rock types from the Practical Kit.

Activity 5.1 involved you in two aspects of science, and in particular geology, a branch of Earth Science. These are (i) making observations of rock specimens, a skill that takes time to develop and which comes with experience, and (ii) interpreting these observations by making connections between observable features of the rocks and the processes that produced them. There has been an element of detective work – piecing together observations and then explaining them.

5.2　Rocks and rock-forming processes

The rest of this chapter develops some of the ideas you met in Activity 5.1 and shows how the Earth's natural processes yield some other rock types, such as marble and slate.

5.2.1　The formation of igneous rocks

Igneous rocks are defined as having solidified from a molten state, either inside the Earth or on the surface. The lavas and pyroclasts produced by volcanoes are called extrusive igneous rocks, because they are formed by the extrusion of magma onto the Earth's surface. Other igneous rocks, such as granite, however, are formed deep underground; these are called intrusive igneous rocks, formed where magmas have cooled within the Earth (Figure 5.7).

When magma cools, crystals of different minerals start to grow from the liquid. The number and size of the crystals depend on the amount of time available for their growth (Figure 5.8). In the case of extrusive rocks, the amount of time is short – anything from a few seconds for a lump of volcanic ash flying through the air, to a few years for the interior of a thick lava flow. Rapid cooling results in small crystals (as in the specimen of basalt in the Practical Kit). For intrusive

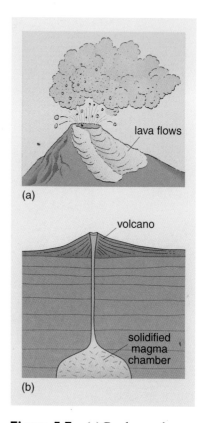

Figure 5.7　(a) Rocks, such as lava flows, formed when magma erupts onto the Earth's surface from a volcano are called extrusive rocks. (b) Rocks, such as granite, that form where magmas cool underground are called intrusive rocks. Note that the magma chamber is several kilometres below the Earth's surface.

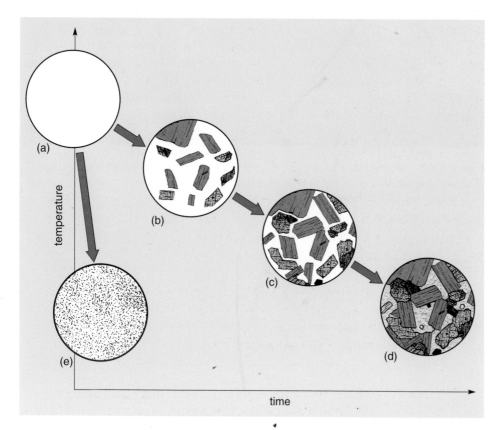

Figure 5.8　The number and size of crystals that grow in a magma depend on the temperature and the cooling rate. Starting with a hot liquid (a) that cools very slowly, the magma solidifies by the gradual growth of crystals of different minerals (indicated by different patterns of shading) to produce an igneous rock with randomly oriented large crystals (cooling path (a) to (d)). When cooling is fast, many very tiny crystals, rather than a few large crystals, grow with the result that a fine-grained igneous rock is formed (cooling path (a) to (e)).

rocks, the cooling rate is much slower and the magma has time to grow larger crystals and become completely crystallised (see the specimen of granite in the Practical Kit and Figure 5.2). (The magma at depth cannot be observed in the way that volcanic eruptions can, so the time required for intrusive rocks to crystallise is not known for sure, but may be up to several thousand years.) Generally speaking, the slower the cooling rate, the bigger the crystals.

Intrusive igneous rocks form several kilometres below the Earth's surface, so how is it that intrusive rocks such as granite can be found at the surface, for example as the Red Hills of Skye (Scotland), tors on Dartmoor, or Yosemite National Park in California (Figure 5.9)? The explanation is that all the rocks originally on top of the granite have been gradually worn away and removed as sedimentary grains, to be deposited elsewhere. This process can lead to the formation of sedimentary rocks.

Figure 5.9 Stretching to the horizon, all of the rocks in this view of Yosemite National Park (USA) are composed of granite, a pale-coloured intrusive igneous rock that crystallised slowly from a hot molten liquid several kilometres below the Earth's surface.

5.2.2   The formation of sedimentary rocks

Sedimentary rocks have been formed by the deposition of layers of sedimentary grains. For example, when sediment is transported by flowing water in rivers or seas, it can settle to the bottom in the same way as tea leaves or coffee grounds settle to the bottom of a pot. Sedimentary grains are produced in the first place when rocks at the Earth's surface are slowly broken up by exposure to rain, wind and frost in the processes collectively termed **weathering**. It is weathering that causes the facing on stone monuments and buildings to degrade slowly over time, making ancient gravestones more difficult to read than newer ones. Once a rock has been broken up by weathering into small rock fragments and individual mineral grains, these small particles can be picked up and removed by flowing water, wind or glaciers – a process known as **erosion**. The sediment can then be carried for great distances before being deposited, usually as roughly horizontal layers of sediment.

With time, these accumulations of sediment may themselves get washed or blown away. Alternatively, they may become compacted under the weight of overlying sediment and new minerals may grow in the spaces between grains. In this way, loose sedimentary grains become cemented together, forming a solid sedimentary rock; this is the process of lithification that you met in Book 1 (Section 7.4.3). The layers of sedimentary rock are called beds or strata (Figure 5.10) and are the result of a sequence of processes that go on all around the Earth – weathering, then erosion, transportation, deposition and lithification.

Figure 5.10   Layers of sedimentary strata, Dorset, England.

■ Are all sedimentary rocks composed of fragments of rock and minerals eroded from pre-existing rocks?

☐ No, some sedimentary rocks also contain fossils of plants or animals that had lived at the same time the sedimentary material was deposited (e.g. Practical Kit, Specimen 3).

Many limestones form from the accumulation of shells and calcite skeletons of certain marine organisms. Chalk is a well-known type of limestone that is found extensively across southern England, parts of France and other areas of northern Europe; much of it is almost pure calcite, and consists mostly of minute shells of countless billions of phytoplankton (Book 1, Section 7.4.3) fossils. Limestones are, however, rarely so pure; usually some sand, silt or mud is deposited along with calcite, as you found with the limestone sample in the Practical Kit. Limestones can form attractive ornamental stones, especially when containing fossils of large organisms, such as shells and reef-building corals.

Sedimentary rocks are useful in other ways. For example, limestones are an important source of calcium carbonate for making cement and fertiliser. Fragmentary rocks are often porous, with the individual pores between the grains being connected together. This lets liquids and gases move through the rock, so sedimentary strata often end up being underground reservoirs of water, oil and gas.

5.2.3 The formation of metamorphic rocks

Any type of rock can undergo a change of form to become a metamorphic rock if it is heated to temperatures of several hundreds of degrees Celsius, and/or if subjected to high pressure because of the weight of overlying rocks. An increase in pressure and temperature will come about if a rock becomes more deeply buried in the Earth as a result of earth movements, or if it is covered by a deepening layer of sedimentary deposits. Igneous and metamorphic rocks both have a crystalline texture and both form at high temperatures, but an important distinction is that metamorphism occurs in the solid state, whereas igneous rocks form from liquid rock.

During metamorphism, the atoms in the minerals making up the rock become reorganised, sometimes resulting in the regrowth of existing minerals, but more often in the formation of new minerals. As a result of recrystallisation, the new metamorphic rock may look very different from the original rock. The overall chemical composition of the rock normally remains about the same, however, with elements just rearranging themselves into new minerals that are more suited to the new temperature and pressure conditions. Metamorphic recrystallisation can often result in banding or alignment of platy or elongate crystals in the rock. An example is the schist specimen (Specimen 4) in the Practical Kit.

You may already know of two other metamorphic rocks – slate and marble. Although the terms slate and marble are often used for construction and ornamental stones, the colloquial use of 'slate' and 'marble' can apply to a much wider range of materials than those covered by the strict definitions of these metamorphic rocks. Slate is a metamorphic rock with an extremely fine grain size; it is almost impossible to make out any individual crystals even with a hand lens. It was originally laid down as a soft mud, but it has been recrystallised and the result is a hard, water-resistant rock that can be split into thin sheets. The flat surfaces often have a reflective sheen due to the alignment of many small mica crystals, rather like those of the schist. Marble is a metamorphic rock formed from limestone but, unlike schist and slate, marble doesn't often have a banded structure. This is because marble usually contains only one mineral, calcite, which has simply recrystallised from the calcite grains that made up the original limestone, so there cannot be alternating bands of different minerals. This means that marble doesn't break along preferred directions like metamorphic rocks that contain platy minerals arranged in parallel bands. It therefore makes a good material for sculptors to use, because smooth surfaces can be carved in any direction. Impurities in the marble often result in an attractive mottled appearance.

Although slate and marble are both crystalline, an important textural difference is that slate is banded (on a very fine scale) whereas marble is not banded. Banding occurs in metamorphic rocks only when there is an abundance of minerals with the right shape to form aligned bands – typically these are flat flakes, or plates, of mica.

5.2.4   Rocks as records of the past

The features that can be observed within a rock do much more than allow it to be classified as sedimentary, igneous or metamorphic; they are records of the dynamic processes within the Earth's interior and on its surface. So, although there are no active volcanoes in Britain, both intrusive and extrusive igneous rocks are to be found – for example, the famous landmarks of the Dartmoor granite tors, the Red Hills of Skye, the Giant's Causeway in Co. Antrim, and Arthur's Seat in Edinburgh – and these are evidence that Britain was volcanically active in the geological past. Similarly, the presence of metamorphic rocks (for example in much of the Scottish Highlands) indicates periods of past earth movements that buried rocks to great depth followed by considerable erosion that eventually exposed these rocks at the surface. Sedimentary rocks record the existence of ancient oceans, lakes, rivers, deserts and glaciers. The insights into past conditions on the Earth provided by rocks, and also by fossils (Book 1, Section 3.4), indicate how the Earth has changed over time, a theme that will be taken up in Book 6.

Activity 5.2   Summarising the distinguishing features of different rock types

We expect this activity will take you approximately 15 minutes.

Sedimentary, metamorphic, extrusive igneous and intrusive igneous rocks have their own distinguishing features. Summarise these features by completing Table 5.2.

Table 5.2 Summary of features that distinguish sedimentary, metamorphic and igneous rocks.

	Sedimentary	Metamorphic	Extrusive igneous	Intrusive igneous
Texture (fragmental or crystalline)				
For rocks with a crystalline texture, do the crystals have random orientations or are they arranged in bands?				
Can fossils be present?				
For igneous rocks, describe the grain size and how it relates to cooling rate				

Now compare your table with Table 5.4 in the comments on this activity at the end of this book.

5.3   Summary of Chapter 5

Rocks are classified into three types according to how they were formed. Igneous rocks are formed by solidification of molten magma; sedimentary rocks are deposited at the Earth's surface from water, air or ice; and metamorphic rocks are rocks of any origin that have been subsequently transformed (metamorphosed) by heat and/or pressure, often several kilometres down in the Earth.

Rocks are generally either crystalline (formed of interlocking mineral crystals), or fragmental (formed of mineral or rock fragments compacted and cemented together by later mineral growth). Most igneous and metamorphic rocks are crystalline, whereas most sedimentary rocks are fragmental. Metamorphic rocks can usually be distinguished from igneous rocks because they show a characteristic banding or alignment of minerals. The presence of fossils usually indicates a sedimentary rock. The appearance and texture of a rock thus allows the processes that formed it to be deduced.

In studying this chapter, you have made and recorded observations of the rock specimens, interpreted these specimens and summarised that information in table form. These are important aspects of doing observational science, something you started in Activity 2.1 of Book 1.

Chapter 6
Inside the Earth

Our investigation of the Earth has, in the last four chapters, concentrated on its surface features and the activity that affects its surface – earthquakes, volcanism, and the various igneous, sedimentary and metamorphic processes that form the rocks seen at the surface. It is now time to turn our attention to the interior of the Earth. Starting with the rocks that are known at the surface, how much of the Earth do these rocks represent – the whole Earth or only the surface? If they do not reach to the centre, what does? These are the questions that will be investigated in this chapter, in developing a model of the Earth's interior. As with the models you met in Book 1, this model of the Earth's interior is a simplified description of reality that fits the observations.

6.1 How is the inside of the Earth investigated?

There is one technique that can be used to investigate the interior of the Earth directly, that is, drilling into it and bringing up samples of the rock to the surface. Oil companies have drilled holes up to 8 km deep on land in their search for oil. Deeper holes have been drilled for research purposes; the deepest hole penetrates to 12 km in Russia. The deepest drill hole under the deep oceans is just over 2 km. All these drill holes have found rocks that are similar to the sedimentary, igneous and metamorphic rocks found at the Earth's surface, so these familiar rocks extend at least to those depths.

■ The mean radius of the Earth is 6371 km. What percentage of this radius has been penetrated by the deepest drilling?

□ A 12 km drill hole reaches only $\dfrac{12}{6371} \times 100\% = 0.19\%$ (to 2 significant figures) of the distance to the centre of the Earth.

So samples from drill holes are very limited in what information they can provide about the Earth's interior – drilling can only be used to investigate the rocks close to the surface. All the other techniques that can be used to investigate the interior of the Earth are indirect techniques which use observations or measurements made at the surface to interpret what is inside the Earth.

■ Imagine that you were given a parcel, and wanted to find out as much as you could about what was inside it without actually opening it. What might you do?

□ One of the simplest investigations would be to weigh the parcel, which would tell you whether any object inside was heavy or light and, depending on the size of the parcel, this might indicate whether it had high or low density.

A similar investigation can be made for the Earth. Is the overall density of the Earth similar to the density of the rocks at the surface of the Earth? If not, this would indicate that the interior of the Earth is different from the surface. From astronomical observations, the mean density of the Earth has been calculated to be 5.52×10^3 kg m^{-3}. How does this mean density compare with the density of surface rocks? Ocean floor rocks have a mean density of 3.0×10^3 kg m^{-3} and continental rocks 2.8×10^3 kg m^{-3} (Section 2.3), so the mean density of the Earth is almost twice the density of the surface rocks. An initial interpretation of this difference is that the interior of the Earth must be denser than the surface rocks, but before going any further with this interpretation, consider what the density of surface rocks would be if they were under the high pressure conditions inside the Earth. The pressure at the centre of the Earth is over a million times that at the surface, for example. Results from laboratory experiments in which surface rocks are subjected to high pressures indicate that their density does increase at high pressures, but the increase is not sufficient to produce the calculated mean density of the Earth. So the interior of the Earth must be made of materials that are different from the surface rocks.

But how do we find out what these materials might be? One useful clue comes from volcanoes that have erupted magma containing exotic lumps of a green rock brought up from inside the Earth (Figure 6.1). These lumps are crystalline rocks called **peridotite** ('per-id-oh-tight'; they contain the olive-green mineral olivine, which is an impure variety of the gemstone peridot, hence the name peridotite). Peridotite is somewhat more dense (3.3×10^3 kg m^{-3}) than the rocks normally found at the Earth's surface. Although peridotite is not dense enough to account for the higher mean density of the Earth, at least part of the Earth's interior must be made of peridotite.

Figure 6.1 Fragments of green peridotite up to 10 cm in size, surrounded by basalt. The peridotite was carried to the surface by a volcanic eruption of basalt on Lanzarote (Canary Islands) which lasted from 1730 to 1736.

To summarise, the main conclusions about the interior of the Earth that can be obtained from drilling, density measurements, and the occurrence of peridotite at the Earth's surface are:

- Drilling indicates that the surface rock types extend to a depth of at least 12 km on the continents, and at least 2 km under the oceans. This only 'scratches the surface' of the Earth.

- Density measurements indicate that some of the Earth's interior must have a much higher density than surface rocks.

- Because some volcanoes erupt magmas containing lumps of peridotite, this rock must be a part of the Earth's interior.

6.2   The seismic structure of the Earth

Drilling, density measurements and the occurrence of peridotite provide useful information about the interior of the Earth, but the information is not very specific. What would also be useful is a technique that makes it possible to look inside the Earth in the way that X-rays reveal the interior of the human body. X-rays cannot penetrate far into rock, however, so cannot be used to look inside the Earth, but the vibrations generated by earthquakes – seismic waves – do penetrate through the Earth, and can be used to investigate its deep interior. Seismic waves provide the most important source of information about the interior of the Earth. Because of this, some time will be spent in this section on the technique itself, as well as on discussing the results obtained.

6.2.1   Seismic waves

There are two main types of seismic waves – body waves and surface waves. **Body waves** are seismic waves that travel within the body of the Earth, spreading out from an earthquake focus in all directions, like sound waves in air. **Surface waves** are seismic waves that travel at and near the Earth's surface, like ripples spreading out from the point of entry when a stone is thrown into a pond. Surface waves usually shake the ground surface more than body waves, and are the most destructive waves in an earthquake. Body waves, however, are more useful than surface waves for investigating the Earth's interior because they travel within the Earth. Before learning how seismic waves are used to investigate inside the Earth, it is necessary to find out more about them, which you will do in Activity 6.1.

Activity 6.1   Investigating seismic waves

We expect this activity will take you approximately 30 minutes.

This activity will develop your understanding of the differences and similarities between the different types of seismic waves that travel through the Earth. The computer-based activity *Journey to the centre of the Earth* has an introduction and three main sections. For this activity, you should study the introduction and the first of the main sections, 'Seismic waves'. The other two main sections will be used in Sections 6.2.2 and 6.2.3.

Take notes of the principal conclusions or points in the activity as you are doing it, either electronically or on paper. When you have completed this activity, look at the comments at the end of this book.

So how are seismic waves used to investigate the Earth's interior? First of all, they must be recorded at the Earth's surface by a seismometer after they have travelled through the Earth (Section 3.4). Figure 6.2 is the seismogram from the 2005 Pakistan earthquake that was described in Chapter 3, with the arrivals of the different seismic waves added. Before the seismic waves arrive at the seismometer, the ground is still, and the seismogram trace shows little or no motion (the far left-hand side of Figure 6.2). **P waves** travel faster than the other types of seismic waves, so arrive earliest at the seismometer. **S waves** arrive next (about 10 minutes later on this seismogram) and **Love waves** and **Rayleigh waves** (both surface waves) arrive last of all. The four types of seismic wave differ in the size of the ground motion they produce and the time between peaks and troughs on the seismogram.

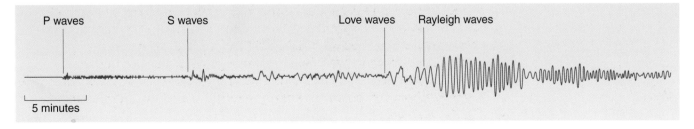

Figure 6.2   A seismogram of the 8 October 2005 Pakistan earthquake, recorded at Sutherland, South Africa (as in Figure 3.9) with the first arrival of each type of seismic wave marked.

■ Which waves produce the largest ground motion?

☐ The Rayleigh waves. The ground motion caused by the Rayleigh waves is about 6 times the ground motion caused by S waves and about 10 times more than the P-wave ground motion.

■ Which of the waves would be used to calculate the Richter magnitude of the earthquake?

☐ The wave producing the largest ground motion (Section 3.4), which is the Rayleigh wave.

Using a Richter magnitude based on the largest ground motion is not appropriate for all earthquakes at all locations. Instead there are various types of other magnitude scales that are more commonly used, and you may come across these in reports or data tables so for completeness some of them are mentioned here. Notice that they are given different symbols (either upper-case or lower-case M, followed by a subscript). Surface wave magnitude (M_s) is based on the maximum ground motion of the surface wave. M_s is used for observations of shallow earthquakes near the epicentre where the surface wave is larger than the body wave. Body wave magnitude (m_b) is calculated from the body waves and is usually calculated from data recorded at larger distances from the epicentre (P waves die out less than surface waves with increasing distance from the earthquake). Moment magnitude (M_w) is considered the best scale to use for larger earthquakes above about magnitude 8. Moment magnitude is measured over the broad range of waves present in the earthquake rather than the single waves that the other magnitude scales use. Finally, the local magnitude (M_L) is defined to be used for 'local' earthquakes up to 600 km away, and is the magnitude scale used by the British Geological Survey (BGS) when locating UK earthquakes.

The largest earthquake Richter magnitude ever recorded is 8.9 (Figure 3.10), whereas what is regarded as the world's largest instrumentally recorded earthquake (Chile, 1960) had Richter magnitude of 8.25, but an M_w magnitude of 9.5.

Question 6.1

Mark on the seismogram in Figure 6.3 the points where the P waves, S waves, Love waves and Rayleigh waves first arrive.

So the times when seismic waves arrive at a seismometer can be picked out on a seismogram. However, a seismogram does not show the time at which the earthquake occurred; it only records when the seismic waves reached the

5 minutes

Figure 6.3   Another seismogram of the 8 October 2005 Pakistan earthquake, recorded at Marble Bar, Australia. Time elapsed increases from left to right.

seismometer. Nevertheless, it is possible to use a number of seismograms, recorded at different locations, to determine both when and where an earthquake occurred.

Armed with this information, it is then possible to work out the time taken for a seismic wave to travel from the earthquake focus to a seismometer. This is called the **travel time**. The travel times for one type of wave (e.g. a P wave) arriving at a number of seismometers up to a few hundred kilometres from a shallow-focus earthquake increases with the distance of the seismometer from the epicentre. This is because the seismic waves have to travel farther (Figure 6.4). Plotting the travel time against the distance from the epicentre gives a series of points that lies close to a straight line (Figure 6.5). This graph can be used to calculate the mean P-wave speed in the parts of the Earth through which the waves have travelled. **Speed** is generally defined by:

$$\text{speed} = \frac{\text{distance travelled}}{\text{time interval}} \tag{6.1}$$

The speed of seismic waves turns out to be very informative, because the speed depends on the type of material through which the waves pass on their journey through the Earth. Calculating seismic wave speed involves measuring the slope, or gradient, of the line on the graph (see Box 6.1).

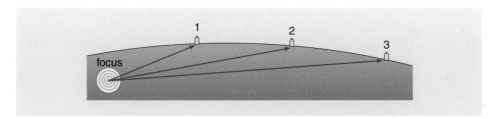

Figure 6.4   The paths of P waves from a shallow-focus earthquake to seismometers (1, 2 and 3) up to a few hundred kilometres away.

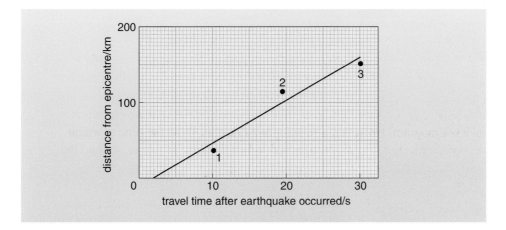

Figure 6.5   A travel time–distance graph for P waves from a shallow earthquake. Points 1, 2 and 3 correspond to the seismometers in Figure 6.4. The line is the best-fit straight line to the data points.

Box 6.1 The gradient of a straight-line graph

In everyday speech, the **gradient**, or slope, of a road is the amount the road goes up (or down) in a given distance. For example the gradient of a road might be signposted with a sign saying 'gradient 1 in 10', meaning that a change of 1 m in height occurs for every 10 m of horizontal distance. This definition is equally appropriate to describing the gradient of a straight line on a graph where the quantity (in mathematical terms this is called the **variable**) plotted on the vertical axis changes for a given change in the value of the variable plotted on the horizontal axis (Figure 6.6).

The gradient of a straight line is therefore defined as:

$$\text{gradient} = \frac{\text{change in vertical value}}{\text{change in horizontal value}} \qquad (6.2)$$

A useful way to remember this is to think of it as:

$$\text{gradient} = \frac{\text{rise}}{\text{run}}$$

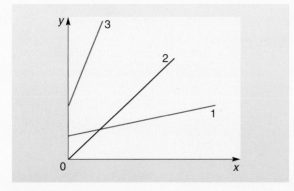

Figure 6.6   A graph of three lines with different gradients. Note that only one line passes through the origin (i.e. where the axes cross).

■   Which of the lines in Figure 6.6 has the largest gradient and which has the smallest gradient?

☐   Line 3 has the largest gradient – this is the steepest slope. Line 1 has the smallest gradient – it has the smallest change in the vertical direction for any particular change in the horizontal direction.

To work out the gradient of a straight line on a graph, the procedure is as follows. Two points on the line of

interest will be referred to as P and Q (Figure 6.7). Now any point on a graph can be specified by its coordinates, the values of the point plotted on the horizontal axis (called the x-axis) and on the vertical axis (called the y-axis). The coordinates of point P are (x_1, y_1) and the coordinates of point Q are (x_2, y_2). Note that the coordinates are written in brackets, separated by a comma, and with the x, or horizontal, coordinate placed before the y, or vertical, coordinate. In moving from P to Q, when the value of x changes from x_1 to x_2, the value of y changes from y_1 to y_2. The gradient of the line joining them is defined, therefore, as:

$$\text{gradient} = \frac{\text{change in value of } y}{\text{change in value of } x} \qquad (6.3)$$

The change in y is $y_2 - y_1$ and the change in x is $x_2 - x_1$, so:

$$\text{gradient} = \frac{y_2 - y_1}{x_2 - x_1} \qquad (6.4)$$

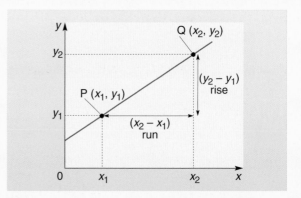

Figure 6.7   A line on a graph, showing the two points P and Q from which a gradient can be calculated (equal to rise divided by run).

Note that P and Q can be any points on the line. To increase the precision of the calculation, they should be quite well separated. It is also important to remember to read values *from the line you have drawn*, rather than using the original data used to draw the graph, since the original data will not necessarily lie on the 'best-fit' line to the data. The uncertainty in locating the exact distances on Figure 6.5, for example, and uncertainties in measuring exact travel times, mean that the position of each point in Figure 6.5 carries some uncertainty. An average description of the data is given by drawing a best-fit line to the points. The **best-fit straight line** is chosen to give the best representation of the data as a whole, so it need not necessarily go through *any* of the data points and should be drawn in such a way that there are approximately the same number of data points above and below the line. You might like to check that the line in Figure 6.5 has these properties. Generally, a best-fit straight line need not pass through the origin of the graph. (The origin has coordinates (0,0).)

To work out the gradient, the numerical values of x_1, x_2, y_1 and y_2 are substituted into this equation. For example, if the coordinates of P were $x_1 = 15.0$ s, $y_1 = 51.7$ km, and the coordinates of Q were $x_2 = 35.0$ s, $y_2 = 99.8$ km, these values would be used in Equation 6.4:

$$\text{gradient} = \frac{y_2 - y_1}{x_2 - x_1}$$

$$= \frac{99.8\ \text{km} - 51.7\ \text{km}}{35.0\ \text{s} - 15.0\ \text{s}}$$

$$= \frac{48.1\ \text{km}}{20.0\ \text{s}}$$

$$= 2.41\ \text{km s}^{-1} \text{ (to 3 significant figures)}$$

The straight line in Figure 6.5 does not go through the origin; it reaches the horizontal x-axis at a time of 2 s. This is called the **intercept** of the graph. It occurs in this case because it takes time (2 s in this case) for a P wave to travel from the earthquake focus to the epicentre on the Earth's surface.

What is the gradient of the line in Figure 6.5? For the greatest precision in the calculation, it is useful to choose $(x_2 - x_1)$ to be as large as possible, for example $x_1 = 2$ s, $x_2 = 30$ s.

■ What are the values of y_1 and y_2 in Figure 6.5, corresponding to $x_1 = 2$ s and $x_2 = 30$ s?

□ The values are $y_1 = 0$ km and $y_2 = 160$ km.

$$\text{gradient} = \frac{y_2 - y_1}{x_2 - x_1}$$

$$= \frac{160\ \text{km} - 0\ \text{km}}{30\ \text{s} - 2\ \text{s}} = \frac{160\ \text{km}}{28\ \text{s}} = 5.7\ \text{km s}^{-1} \text{ (to 2 significant figures)}$$

The gradient has the unit of km s^{-1}, which is a unit of speed. Distance (on the vertical axis) has been divided by time (on the horizontal axis).

So the gradient of the graph in Figure 6.5 is the mean P-wave speed of the seismic waves along the paths through the Earth shown in Figure 6.4.

Figure 6.5 has the travel time plotted on the horizontal axis and the distance plotted on the vertical axis. This was done because the gradient is then the speed of the seismic waves. However when scientists draw graphs, they usually follow the convention of plotting the variable that is fixed by the investigator, called the **independent variable**, on the x-axis, and the variable that depends on this, called the **dependent variable**, on the y-axis. Thus, travel time–distance graphs are normally plotted, as shown in Figure 6.8, with distance on the x-axis, as it is the independent variable (a seismometer distance), and travel time on the y-axis, as it is the dependent variable (the measured time at a seismometer).

Figure 6.8   A travel time–distance graph (usually just called a travel time graph) for P waves. The graph is plotted according to scientific convention, with time on the vertical *y*-axis and distance on the horizontal *x*-axis. The data and best-fit line are the same as in Figure 6.5 and the points 1, 2 and 3 correspond to the seismometers in Figure 6.4.

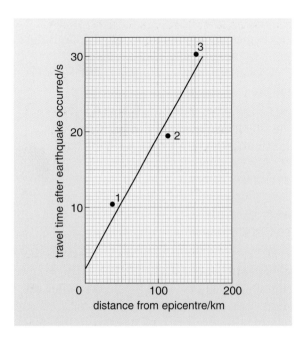

How can wave speed be calculated from the travel time graph in Figure 6.8?

First the gradient has to be calculated:

$$\text{gradient} = \frac{28\,\text{s}}{160\,\text{km}} \text{ or } 0.175\,\text{s km}^{-1}$$

The unit of the gradient just found is s km^{-1}. Recall that this can be written as $\frac{\text{s}}{\text{km}}$. Now (for reasons that will become obvious shortly) find the *inverse* of the unit, i.e. 'turn it upside down'. This gives $\frac{\text{km}}{\text{s}}$ which can be written as km s^{-1}. This, as you know, is a unit of speed. So the inverse of the unit of the gradient of the travel time graph in Figure 6.8 has the unit of speed. This gives a strong hint that to find the value of speed, the *inverse* of the value found for the gradient of the graph must be found, i.e.

$$\begin{aligned} \text{speed} &= \frac{1}{\text{gradient}} \\ &= \frac{1}{0.175\,\text{s km}^{-1}} \\ &= 5.7\,\text{km s}^{-1} \text{ (to 2 significant figures)} \end{aligned}$$

(6.5)

This value of 5.7 km s^{-1} is typical of the speed in continental crust. As would be expected, this value of speed is the same as that calculated using Figure 6.5.

So speed on a travel time graph is the *inverse* of the gradient, i.e. $\left(\dfrac{1}{\text{gradient}} \right)$.

All seismic travel time graphs used subsequently in this section will have distance on the *x*-axis, so remember that:

$$\text{speed} = \frac{1}{\text{gradient}}$$

Now that you know how to determine seismic wave speeds from travel time graphs, you can use them to investigate the structure of the Earth.

6.2.2   The crust

Drilling has failed to reach rocks that differ from those found at the surface, but the great density of the Earth implies that if deeper depths are searched then different (denser) materials will be found. A study of travel time graphs offers a way of doing this.

Activity 6.2   Travel time graphs

We expect this activity will take you approximately 45 minutes.

In this activity, you will use earthquake travel time graphs to measure the P-wave speed in the upper layer of the Earth, and to determine how deep this layer extends. You should work through 'Travel time graphs', the second main section of the computer-based activity *Journey to the centre of the Earth*. The section is divided into a number of stages in which you will interpret travel time graphs, model the Earth's crust, and investigate a deeper layer of the Earth.

Take notes of the main conclusions or points in the activity as you are doing it either electronically or on paper. When you have completed this activity, look at the comments at the end of this book.

Your investigation of the Earth's structure in Activity 6.2 revealed a change in the properties of the Earth at a boundary called the **Mohorovičić discontinuity**, or **Moho**. This is a global **seismic discontinuity**, existing all around the Earth, but not always at the same depth. The layer above this discontinuity is the Earth's **crust** and the region below it is the **mantle**. The Moho occurs at about 7 km below the ocean floor. But beneath continents its depth is very variable, from 20 km to 80 km, averaging 35 km, and it is deepest below mountain belts and high plateau regions (Figure 6.9). You should recall from Section 2.3 that the division between oceanic and continental crust is not the same as the coastline; it occurs offshore, generally beneath the continental rise (see the hypsometric plot in Figure 2.7). A summary of information about the properties of the crust is given in Table 6.1.

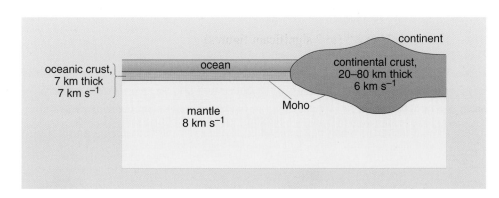

Figure 6.9   Seismic structure of the oceanic and continental crust and mantle. The seismic wave speeds shown are the mean P-wave speeds, to 1 significant figure.

Table 6.1 Characteristics of oceanic crust and continental crust.

Characteristic	Oceanic crust	Continental crust
Thickness	7 km	20–80 km, average 35 km
Mean P-wave speed	7 km s^{-1}	6 km s^{-1}
Mean density	3.0×10^3 kg m^{-3}	2.8×10^3 kg m^{-3}
Main rock types	basalt	sedimentary (e.g. sandstone, limestone) and metamorphic rocks, granite and some other igneous rocks

6.2.3 The mantle and core

To investigate the mantle requires looking deeper into the Earth, using the travel times from seismometers at greater distances from the epicentre – thousands of kilometres instead of the hundreds of kilometres that we used to investigate the crust and Moho. Figure 6.10 is a travel time graph extending to 10^4 km.

Figure 6.10 Travel time graph for earthquake P waves at distances up to 10^4 km from the epicentre. These are the times for the first P waves to arrive; other P waves arrive later. The label 'distance/10^3 km' means that each value on this axis should be multiplied by 10^3 km to obtain the actual distance in kilometres. The two boxes show enlargements of parts of the graph at distances of 2×10^3 km and 8×10^3 km; they show that for small distance intervals the graph is approximately a straight line. The 'epicentral angle' scale will be explained later.

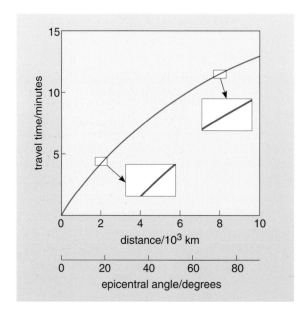

■ What is the main difference between the travel time graph to 10^4 km (Figure 6.10) and the travel time graph to 200 km (Figure 6.8)?

☐ The graph to distances of 10^4 km is a curve, whereas the graph to 200 km is a straight line.

If the data from the 200 km travel time graph (Figure 6.8) were plotted on Figure 6.10, they would occupy just a small part of the line in the bottom left-hand corner of the graph. This small part of the curve will appear as an approximately straight line when enlarged – hence Figure 6.8 is a straight-line travel time graph.

There are a number of reasons for the curved shape of the travel time graph in Figure 6.10.

1 The wave speed changes with depth.

2 The wave paths change by **refraction** due to encountering materials with different wave speeds.

3 The Earth's spherical shape affects travel times at greater distances.

■ Does the gradient of the graph in Figure 6.10 increase or decrease with increasing distance? (Look at the two box enlargements.)

□ It decreases. The gradient at a distance of 8×10^3 km is smaller (i.e. the curve is less steep) than the gradient at 2×10^3 km.

As the gradient of the travel time graph decreases with distance of the seismometer from the earthquake, this suggests that the P-wave speed increases with distance (remember that $\text{speed} = \dfrac{1}{\text{gradient}}$). Waves that have travelled greater distances have usually travelled deeper into the Earth, so this suggests that P-wave speed generally increases with depth inside the Earth.

An alternative measure of the distance of a seismometer from an earthquake epicentre is the **epicentral angle**, the angle between two radius lines drawn from the centre of the Earth to the epicentre and to the seismometer (Figure 6.11). The maximum epicentral angle is 180° for a seismic wave that has travelled right through the centre of the Earth. Epicentral angle, instead of distance around the Earth's surface, is usually plotted on the *x*-axis of travel time graphs.

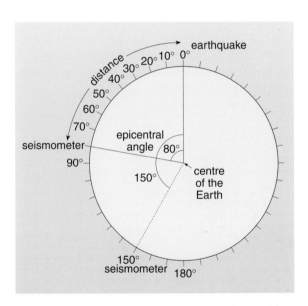

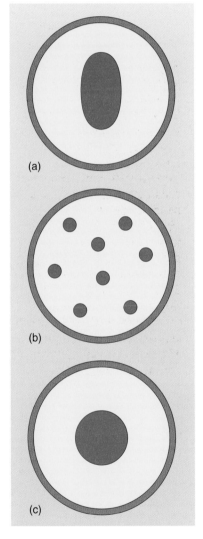

Figure 6.11 A cross-section of the Earth, showing that the distance between an earthquake epicentre and a seismometer can be represented by the epicentral angle. The locations of seismometers at epicentral angles of 80° and 150° are indicated.

The travel time graph in Figure 6.10 is the same for *all* earthquakes (after correction for different focal depths), wherever the earthquake takes place, and wherever the seismometers are distributed. This fact provides useful information about the interior of the Earth, because if the position of an earthquake makes no difference to travel times, then the Earth's interior structure must be radially symmetrical. This means that the seismic properties at all points at a given distance from the centre of the Earth are the same. In other words, the variations in seismic properties are concentrically arranged.

■ Which of the models (a)–(c) in Figure 6.12 has a concentric seismic structure?

□ Model (c). Models (a) and (b) are not concentric about the Earth's centre. These are therefore not possible models for the Earth's interior, since they are not consistent with seismic observations.

Figure 6.12 Hypothetical models of the Earth's interior seismic structure. The red areas have higher seismic wave speeds than the yellow areas. The brown outer layer is the crust (not to scale).

Activity 6.3   Down to the centre

We expect this activity will take you approximately 30 minutes.

In this activity, you will use travel time graphs to investigate deeper inside the Earth, to model the rock type of the mantle, and to investigate down to the centre of the Earth. You should work with the last main section of the computer-based activity *Journey to the centre of the Earth*, which is itself in two parts: 'Modelling the mantle' and 'Down to the centre'.

'Modelling the mantle' investigates travel time graphs at greater distances than the previous section (Activity 6.2), corresponding to greater depths in the Earth. 'Down to the centre' investigates what happens below the mantle, at still greater distances on travel time graphs.

Take notes of the main conclusions or points in the activity as you are doing it either electronically or on paper. When you have completed this activity, look at the comments at the end of this book.

Travel time graphs for the whole Earth, shown in Activity 6.3 and Figure 6.13, provide additional clues to the Earth's structure. From them it can be deduced that the mantle is formed of peridotite, and that there is a liquid outer **core** about 2900 km below the surface. You have therefore now located two major seismic discontinuities within the Earth, the Moho and the mantle–core boundary. There is one more, the outer core–inner core boundary. The study of seismic waves indicates that the inner core (unlike the outer core) is solid.

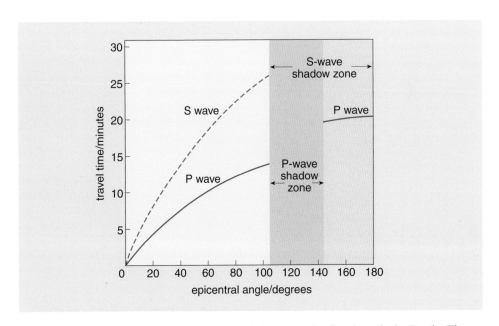

Figure 6.13   P-wave and S-wave travel time graphs for the whole Earth. There is a **P-wave shadow zone** from epicentral angles of 105° to 143°, and an **S-wave shadow zone** from 105° to 180°.

From travel time graphs like Figure 6.13, Earth scientists have developed models for the way in which seismic wave speed and density vary with depth in the Earth, and Figure 6.14 summarises the results. There is a lot of information in this graph, so spend a few minutes studying it and its caption before answering the questions that follow.

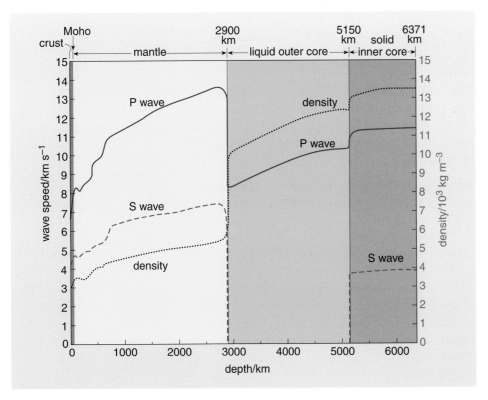

Figure 6.14 The variation of wave speed (left vertical axis) and density (right vertical axis) with depth inside the Earth. The graph has two vertical axes, for wave speed and density, so that the changes in wave speed and density can be compared. The blue continuous line is P-wave speed, the black dotted line is S-wave speed and the purple dashed line is density. S waves cannot travel in the liquid outer core, but are known to exist in the inner core, since part of the P waves can transform into S waves on entering the inner core at the outer core–inner core boundary and back again to P waves on leaving the inner core.

■ What is the depth of the outer core–inner core boundary?

☐ 5150 km. (At this depth there are changes in both P-wave speed and S-wave speed.)

■ What happens to the P-wave speed at the mantle–core boundary, and at the outer core–inner core boundary?

☐ The P-wave speed decreases significantly at the mantle–core boundary, and increases slightly at the outer core–inner core boundary.

6.3   Density, magnetism and meteorites

In this section, other observations that can be used to provide information about the Earth's interior will be looked at briefly. Figure 6.14 summarises how density varies with depth in the Earth. In Section 6.1, it was noted that the mean density of the Earth is 5.52×10^3 kg m^{-3}. Various techniques indicate that the density of the core is greater than this, varying between 1.00×10^4 kg m^{-3} and 1.36×10^4 kg m^{-3}, with a large difference in density between the mantle and the core; the core is over twice as dense as the mantle (Figure 6.14). This suggests that the core has a composition that is very different from that of the mantle.

The Earth's magnetism (which causes a compass needle to point towards the North Pole) can also provide information about the interior of the Earth. Current theories for the origin of the Earth's magnetism (which lie outside the scope of this course) suggest that the Earth has a liquid outer core of a metallic composition.

Additional evidence for the interior composition of the Earth comes from a source you might not have expected: space. More than a million kilograms of extraterrestrial rock fall towards the Earth from space each year. Many of these rocks, which are leftovers from the formation of the Solar System, vaporise completely as they pass through the atmosphere, but some survive to reach the Earth's surface, and are then called **meteorites**. Meteorites allow material from *inside* an Earth-like planet to be studied. Their compositions are either peridotite or an iron–nickel metal combination, suggesting that these materials may be important parts of the Earth's interior. The impact of large meteorites on the Earth's surface produces an impact crater, which may be of significant size. One of the most dramatic meteorite impact craters is Meteor Crater in Arizona (Figure 6.15).

Figure 6.15   An aerial view of Meteor Crater, Arizona. This is believed to have been formed by the impact of a meteorite about 50 000 years ago. It is 1.2 km across and 173 m deep.

At this point, all these lines of evidence for the structure and composition of the Earth can be drawn together in order to produce a model of the Earth's interior that is consistent with each bit of evidence (Figure 6.16). The upper part of the mantle is similar to the specimens of peridotite that are seen at the Earth's surface, but deeper in the mantle there is a higher-density form of peridotite. The predominant element in the core is iron; Earth scientists are fairly certain of that, but the more detailed composition is much less certain. The solid inner core may be pure iron, or it may be iron with a small amount of nickel. The liquid outer core is mainly iron with a small amount of nickel, and around 10% of a lighter element, probably oxygen.

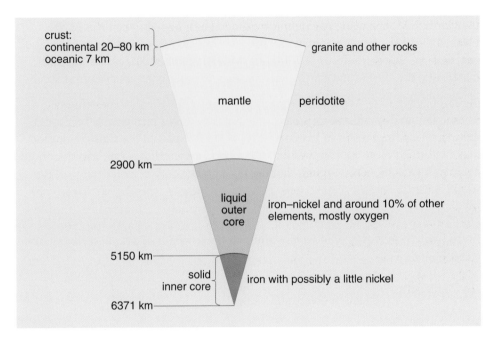

Figure 6.16   A model for the structure and composition of the Earth.

Question 6.2

Consider the following statements on Earth structure and composition and, for each, list which sources of evidence (seismic, density, magnetism and meteorites) would have been used to make or support the statement. A statement may be based on more than one line of evidence.

(a) The mantle–core boundary is at a depth of 2900 km.

(b) The outer core is liquid.

6.4   Summary of Chapter 6

There are a number of lines of evidence that are used to develop a model of the Earth's interior: drilling, density, seismic waves, magnetism and meteorites.

Drilling has found rocks similar to those at the Earth's surface extending down to a depth of 12 km.

The mean density of the Earth is about twice the density of crustal rocks, which indicates that part (at least) of the Earth at depth must be much denser than the crust.

There are major discontinuities in seismic wave speeds with depth in the Earth. The first of these is at a depth that varies between 7 and 80 km. This discontinuity is called the Mohorovičić discontinuity (the Moho). The surface layer of the Earth above it is called the crust, and the layer below it is called the mantle. The next seismic discontinuity is at 2900 km, which is the boundary between the mantle and the core of the Earth. There is also an outer core–inner core seismic discontinuity. The outer core is in a liquid state, whereas the inner core is solid.

These seismic discontinuities are accompanied by major changes in the Earth's density. The composition of meteorites suggests that part of the Earth's interior may be formed of peridotite, and that other parts are an iron–nickel combination. The Earth's magnetism suggests that the liquid outer core is metallic.

Figure 6.16 is a model for the structure and composition of the Earth's interior that is consistent with these lines of evidence.

In studying this chapter, you have learnt that the gradient of a straight-line graph is calculated from:

$$\text{gradient} = \frac{\text{change in vertical value}}{\text{change in horizontal value}}$$

For a graph of earthquake travel time (on the vertical y-axis) against distance (on the horizontal x-axis), the speed is $\frac{1}{\text{gradient}}$.

Chapter 7
The Earth's changing face: continental drift and sea-floor spreading

In the last chapter, you saw that the Earth consists of concentric layers. In this chapter you will start to investigate evidence that the outer layer is slowly changing and moving. Later chapters will show how this slow process explains many aspects of the Earth's activity.

7.1   Continental drift

You may have noticed that, on a map of the world, the Atlantic coastlines of western Africa and eastern South America have similar shapes (Figure 2.4). If you could move the two continents, they would fit together remarkably well. And if the true border between continental and oceanic crust – such as the edge of the continental rise at a depth of 1 km below sea level (Section 2.3) – is used instead of the coastlines, then the fit is even better. It looks as if the two continents might once have been joined. Do you think this is possible?

If you do, then you wouldn't be the first person to think so. As long ago as 1620 the English philosopher Francis Bacon (1561–1626) recognised the similarities of the continental outlines but it was not until the 1910s and 1920s that scientists became excited by the possibility that the continents were once joined together and have since drifted apart. Foremost among this group of innovative thinkers was the German meteorologist Alfred Wegener (1880–1930) who built up a body of evidence that convinced him that the continents had drifted across the globe through time:

> The continents must have shifted. South America must have lain alongside Africa and formed a unified block which was split in two [which became] increasingly separated over a period of millions of years like pieces of a cracked ice floe in water.
>
> (Wegener, 1928)

Using the evidence he had gathered, Wegener argued that all the continents had at one time been joined together as one large land mass (Figure 7.1) – a

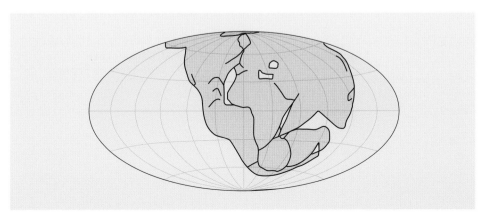

Figure 7.1   Wegener's map of the supercontinent Pangaea as he considered it to be about 300 Ma ago. The approximate outlines of the present continental land masses are included in order to show how they have broken off from the larger supercontinent.

supercontinent which he named Pangaea (pronounced 'pan-jee-ah', and meaning 'all land') – that had started to break apart about 165 Ma ago.

Wegener made a strong case for **continental drift** but his hypothesis troubled many of his contemporary scientists. Those who didn't dismiss it out of hand subjected his evidence and arguments to closer scrutiny – the proper but sometimes difficult response of scientists to radical new ideas. Wegener's work stood up to these tests, and more recent lines of evidence have given still further support to the idea of continental drift. One of the arguments for continental drift relies on evidence contained in sedimentary rocks found on the continents.

7.2   Evidence for continental drift: ancient climates

Alfred Wegener fitted the continents together like pieces of a jigsaw (Figure 7.1), making a plausible reconstruction of the shape of a huge continental land mass. But solving a jigsaw puzzle is more than a case of just fitting the shaped pieces together. The pattern or picture on the jigsaw has to fit together as well. On the Earth, this 'picture' is defined by the distribution of different rock types, so the rock types on, say, the east side of South America should be the same as those on the west side of Africa. If reconstructions such as the one in Figure 7.1 are correct, you would predict that the rocks would match up across the joins between continental blocks. You will see shortly that this is the case, but extra lines of evidence for the movement of the continents come from the rocks themselves. This involves the record in certain sedimentary rocks of the climate at the time they were deposited. In particular, red sandstone is often formed in arid desert environments; tropical swamps, such as those found in the Amazon Basin, can generate extensive coal deposits (Book 1, Section 7.4.3); and the erosion of surface rocks by the ice sheets found in polar regions leads to deposits of rock debris with grain sizes ranging from mud to house-sized boulders. This glacially deposited sediment is known as **till** (Book 1, Section 3.4.2).

At the present day, each type of climate is more or less restricted to a distinct range of latitudes. For example, Figure 7.2 and Table 7.1 show that regions with a hot and dry desert climate are generally restricted to between 30° N and 30° S. Places with a hot and wet tropical climate are also found between these latitudes, but they are generally confined to a more equatorial band between 20° N and 20° S. The cold polar climate is found in the latitudes 60° to 90° N and 60° to 90° S.

Table 7.1 Climates identified in Figure 7.2 and their corresponding environments, approximate latitude ranges, and the sediments they can produce.

Climate	Environment	Approximate latitude range	Characteristic sedimentary deposit
hot desert	hot and arid	30° N to 30° S	red sandstone
tropical	hot and wet swamp	20° N to 20° S	coal
polar	cold ice sheets	60°–90° N and 60°–90° S	till

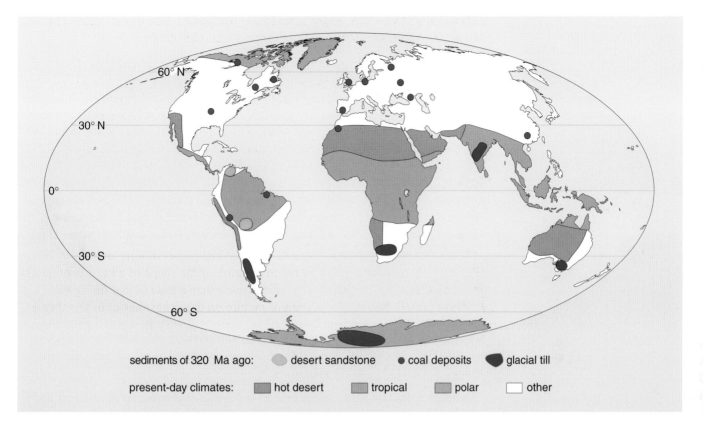

Figure 7.2   The distribution of three modern climate zones across the world, and the locations of desert sandstones, coal deposits and glacial tills that formed about 320 Ma ago.

A region's climate plays a crucial role in determining which type of sediment is formed there. If these sediments are not eroded away, they form strata of sedimentary rock, which provide a geological guide to the climate prevailing at a particular time and place. Therefore, if the climate zone indicated by ancient sedimentary rock is different from the present-day climate zone where the rocks are found, then either the climate zones have moved or the location has moved with respect to the fixed distribution of the global climate zones. It is hard to imagine how major shifts in the pattern of global climate zones could happen, for example equatorial regions becoming very cold at the same time as polar regions becoming hot. (Indeed, you will remember from Book 1, Activity 8.1 *Global warming and cooling* that the amount of solar radiation received at the poles is much less than near the Equator, and so it would be impossible to have hot poles and cold equatorial regions.) The more likely alternative is that the land has moved between different latitudes.

Figure 7.2 shows where desert sandstones, coals and till deposits were deposited about 320 million years ago.

■ After studying Figure 7.2 carefully, do you think that the climate-sensitive sediments of 320 Ma ago each occur in their appropriate present-day climate zone?

☐ Apart from a few cases, most of the 320 Ma old sediments are not found in their appropriate present-day climate zones.

In fact, they appear to be arranged across the world in quite a different way compared with the current climate patterns. The record of 320 Ma old glacial tills is not restricted to the latitude ranges of 60°–90° N and S; they also occur at lower latitudes in South America, Africa, India and Australia. This implies that these regions were, for some reason, subjected to much colder climates 320 Ma ago than they are today. The coal deposits that imply hot and humid conditions mostly occur at much higher latitudes than one would expect from modern climate patterns. Most of the coal deposits appear to be outside the tropics – in Europe, North Africa, North America and Russia. Only the desert sandstone deposits occur in their correct latitudinal range – between 30° N and 30° S – although in regions that have a tropical climate today.

Continental drift offers an explanation for mismatches between the ancient and modern climates of particular places. Thus, South Africa must have moved from a polar region where glacial tills were deposited around 320 Ma ago, to its current position where desert sands are now being deposited on top of the 320 Ma old tills. Similarly, India has moved from polar latitudes to tropical latitudes. In contrast, the presence of numerous coalfields in Europe suggests that Europe lay within about 20° of the Equator 320 Ma ago and has since moved to its present position in temperate latitudes. The pre-drift configuration of the continents 320 Ma ago is shown in Figure 7.3.

Question 7.1

Use Figure 7.3 to decide whether the 320 Ma old climate-sensitive sediments fall into their correct climate zones.

As well as fitting the continental jigsaw pieces together, Figure 7.3 also places the jigsaw in a particular orientation and a particular position on the Earth, in order to have the climate zone indicators in their appropriate latitudes. Together, this amounts to compelling evidence that the continents have moved around during vast stretches of time.

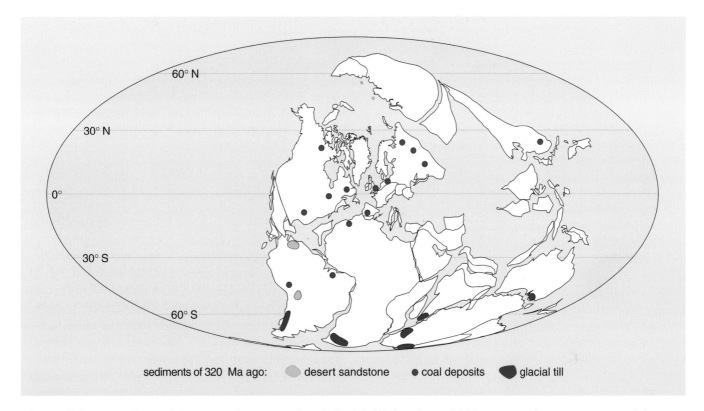

Figure 7.3   Locations of desert sandstone, coal and glacial till that formed 320 Ma ago shown on a map of the continents at the time when these sediments were deposited.

Since Wegener's day, new technologies have added to the evidence for continental drift, and today, careful measurements using the satellite-based global positioning system (GPS) have been successful in detecting directly the slow migration of the continents. Wegener's hypothesis has stood the test of these further observations and the scientific community now accepts that the continents drift over the Earth, and that the familiar position of the continents is just a snapshot from a continually running movie of continents in motion. But, as many of Wegener's detractors were quick to point out, there is no immediately obvious driving mechanism for continental drift, and the theory says nothing about how the ocean floor that lies between the drifting continents behaves. Even Wegener admitted that these gaps in the continental drift theory were problematical, although he believed that one day they would be resolved. The solution was provided by the more all-encompassing theory of plate tectonics which emerged later in the 20th century, on the heels of another theory – that of sea-floor spreading, which is explained in the next section.

7.3   Sea-floor spreading and the origin of ocean basins

The previous section gave compelling evidence that the Earth's continental masses are on the move and drift across the Earth. But how do the ocean basins fit in with this? It would help if we had more information about what the ocean floor is like. This is easier said than done because the ocean floor is obviously much less accessible than the continents, making it difficult to observe. For example, at the mean ocean depth of 3700 m the pressure is 370 times greater than atmospheric pressure, and the temperature is between –l and 4 °C. No light penetrates to this inhospitable place. It is a measure of this inaccessibility that it was only in the late 19th century that the Mid-Atlantic Ridge, one of the Earth's greatest mountain ranges and clearly visible in Figure 2.3, was discovered by accident during the laying of trans-Atlantic telephone cables. Some of the mid-ocean ridges in the Pacific Ocean were not discovered until the 1950s. In the mid-20th century, knowledge of the mid-ocean ridges accumulated very slowly; shallow earthquakes were found to occur beneath ridge crests (Chapter 3) and volcanic eruptions of basalt lava were observed on islands such as Iceland that lie on mid-ocean ridges (Chapter 4). To get a much fuller picture of mid-ocean ridges required specialised submersible craft, and these were developed in the 1950s and 1960s. A submersible can descend much deeper than submarines, and can take one or two scientists, crammed into a space no bigger than the inside of a small car, to the ocean floor. Submersibles provided the ability to carry out 'fieldwork' on the ocean floor for the first time. The views of this hidden world amazed the intrepid submariners and gave a host of new observations that begged to be explained.

These dives revealed that the mid-ocean ridges are an alien world where plumes of hot acidic water gush from the sea floor (Figure 7.4a) and bacteria living off the chemicals in the hot springs are eaten by animals that were previously unknown. The rocks there are volcanic lava flows, erupted from long cracks and fissures extending along the length of the mid-ocean ridge. They occur as thin sheets of lava and jumbled networks of interconnected pillow-shaped pods of lava that formed as the outer skin of slowly advancing lava froze on contact with cold seawater, like wax dribbling from a candle (Figure 7.4b). **Pillow lavas** like these are characteristic of basalt lava that has erupted slowly under water. The mid-ocean ridges are places where there is intense volcanic, thermal, biological and seismic activity.

The many shallow earthquakes at mid-ocean ridges are evidence that the crust there is frequently breaking and moving along faults. At the same time, the ocean crust is growing by the addition of lavas erupted along the length of the ridge. In contrast, the abyssal plains are remarkably inactive and are covered in hundreds

(a)

(b)

Figure 7.4   Views of a mid-ocean ridge seen by illuminating the pitch-black depths. (a) Clouds of mineral particles form 'black smoke' that billows upwards as very hot (up to 400 °C) mineral-rich water jets into cold seawater at the crest of the East Pacific Rise. This is the first picture ever to be taken of black smokers, and dates from 1979. Crabs and other animals have colonised the rocky surface of lava flows and minerals deposited from the black smokers. (b) Pillow lavas on the Mid-Atlantic Ridge, 3150 m below sea level. Each large 'pillow' is about 0.5 to 1 m in diameter.

of metres thickness of sediment which must have taken time to accumulate, so these parts of the ocean floor must be older than the sediment-free mid-ocean ridges. These observations are best accounted for by the theory of **sea-floor spreading** (Figure 7.5), which states that the ocean floor on either side of a mid-ocean ridge is moving away from the ridge, allowing hot magma to be intruded from below the ridge, where it solidifies to form new ocean floor. In turn, this new crust gets split apart, moved aside, and replaced by still-younger volcanic ocean-floor rocks. After many, many repetitions of this process, the lavas that were originally erupted at the ridge crest become more and more distant from their birthplace and an ocean basin grows.

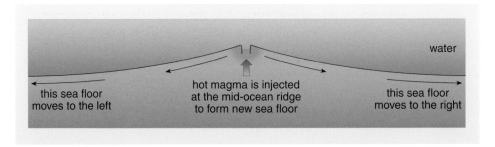

Figure 7.5   A simple cross-section through a mid-ocean ridge, showing how sea-floor spreading accounts for the origin of the ocean floor.

7.3.1   How fast does sea-floor spreading happen?

This section investigates the rate, or speed, at which sea-floor spreading is splitting the Earth's surface apart, the so-called **sea-floor spreading rate**. The first step is to decide what to measure in order to work out the rate of spreading.

■   Which two variables need to be measured in order to calculate the speed at which something moves?

☐   The distance moved and the time taken (Equation 6.1).

Consider an analogy of sea-floor spreading provided by two conveyor belts, arranged end to end but moving in opposite directions (Figure 7.6). In this analogy, two crates are placed onto the conveyors at the point where they diverge and get carried farther and farther apart as time goes on, just as the igneous rocks at a mid-ocean ridge are split apart and carried off in opposite directions by sea-floor spreading. The rate at which the two crates become separated is given by measuring the distance separating them and dividing by the time since they were put onto the diverging conveyor belts. Thus, to find the rate at which the ocean floor spreads requires a way of labelling two points on the ocean floor that were once side by side at the ridge but are now some distance apart. You also need to know how long ago they were at the ridge. It turns out that these critical pieces of information are provided by invisible 'magnetic labels' on the ocean floor.

These invisible labels are held by magnetic minerals within the rocks of the ocean floor, and are read by a sensitive instrument known as a magnetometer, which is towed from a ship or plane. The magnetometer measures the magnetism in the

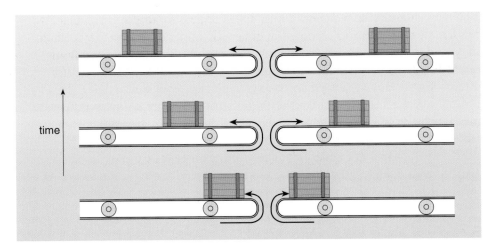

Figure 7.6   An analogy of sea-floor spreading given by two moving conveyor belts.

Earth below it. The results of a magnetic survey in the North Atlantic Ocean (Figure 7.7) are typical of what has been found in the ocean basins worldwide: there are areas where the magnetism is either stronger than average (labelled as black areas) or weaker than average (labelled as white areas). These magnetic anomalies were quite a surprise when they were first discovered, given that the rocks on the ocean floor are monotonously basalt with a covering of sediment. Equally impressive is the fact that the **marine magnetic anomalies** are arranged in bands, or stripes (albeit with ragged edges), several kilometres wide. These bands are sometimes known as magnetic stripes.

■ From Figure 7.7, can you see a relationship between the orientation of the magnetic stripes and the orientation of the crest of the mid-ocean ridge?

☐ The magnetic stripes are parallel with the ridge crest.

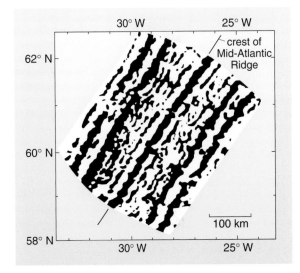

Figure 7.7   A map of marine magnetic anomalies southwest of Iceland shows a pattern of magnetic stripes. The Mid-Atlantic Ridge runs from northeast to southwest across the middle of the survey area.

What is the origin of these marine magnetic anomalies? To answer this question, the Earth's magnetism in the distant past needs to be considered. Imagine that you embark on a voyage back in time, holding a compass. Today, at the start of the voyage, the compass needle points roughly towards the North Pole, and the Earth's magnetism is said to have **normal polarity**. Travelling back through recorded history to 1900 years ago, when the first compasses were invented in China, the same familiar situation applies. But, 800 000 years ago, you'd find that the compass needle was pointing towards the South Pole! In this case, the Earth's magnetism is said to possess **reversed polarity**. One million years ago the compass points to the North Pole again, and four million years ago to the South Pole. In fact, the north and south magnetic poles have reversed at apparently random intervals of several million years or less.

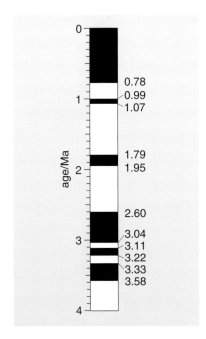

Figure 7.8 The geomagnetic polarity timescale for the last 4 Ma. By convention, black denotes normal polarity and white denotes reversed polarity.

You may naturally be wondering what the evidence for this is. The polarity of the Earth's magnetism is recorded by magnetic minerals in lava flows when they cool, so by measuring the polarity and age of a great many lava flows, mainly from the continents, it has been possible to establish the pattern of alternating periods of normal and reversed polarity over the last 600 Ma. The switches between normal and reversed polarity are called **polarity reversals** and happen quickly. The pattern and dates of the polarity reversals define what is known as the **geomagnetic polarity timescale**; the most recent 4 Ma of this timescale is shown in Figure 7.8. (The word geomagnetic means 'relating to the Earth's magnetism'; the prefix *geo*, as in geography, geology, and so on, means 'Earth'.)

Question 7.2

Use Figure 7.8 to answer the following questions:

(a) How many times in the last 4 Ma has the Earth's magnetic polarity reversed?

(b) What was the polarity of the Earth's magnetism 0.5, 1.5 and 2.5 Ma ago?

(c) When did the polarity last change from normal to reversed?

(d) A rock sample is known to have been formed sometime within the last 2 Ma and has normal polarity. Within what range of ages could it have been formed?

(e) What is the age of the most recent reversal?

It is the division into normal and reversed polarity that accounts for the marine magnetic anomalies seen in Figure 7.7. Where the rocks beneath the magnetometer have reversed polarity, their magnetism partially cancels out the normal polarity of the Earth's present-day magnetism, so the total magnetic signal there is relatively weak. In contrast, rocks with normal polarity complement the Earth's magnetism, and the magnetometer detects a relatively strong total magnetic signal. At the ridge itself, the rocks have been formed relatively recently, so they have normal polarity (shaded black in Figure 7.7). Moving away from the ridge crest, the magnetic survey detected a polarity reversal; the rocks in the white stripe have reversed polarity. (Note that this coding of black stripes to label normal polarity and white stripes to label reversed polarity is a standard convention.) With increasing distance from the ridge, the pattern of stripes on the northwest side of the ridge is the same as the pattern on the southeast side. To see this symmetry most clearly, compare the two broad black stripes and the intervening white stripe near the ends of the surveyed region. Comparing the pattern of reversals revealed by marine magnetic surveys with the pattern in the geomagnetic polarity timescale, they are found to match (Figure 7.9).

The symmetrical magnetic stripes are strong evidence in support of the sea-floor spreading theory. Each black (or white) stripe represents half of the ocean floor produced at the ridge during one of the periods when the Earth's magnetism had normal (or reversed) polarity. The two halves have been split apart by sea-floor spreading, which is analogous to the separation of the two crates on the diverging conveyor belts in Figure 7.6.

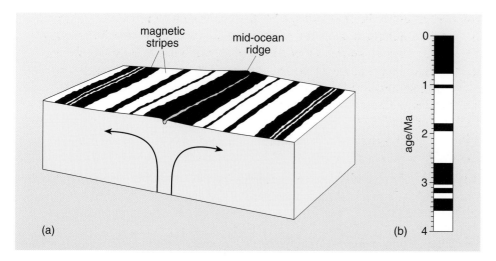

(a)   (b)

Figure 7.9   (a) The pattern of magnetic stripes on either side of a mid-ocean ridge, moving away from the ridge, is the same as (b) the pattern of reversals on the geomagnetic polarity timescale, moving back in time.

■ How can the marine magnetic anomaly pattern help in working out the spreading rate at the Mid-Atlantic Ridge?

☐ If an ocean-floor polarity reversal can be matched with a reversal on the timescale in Figure 7.8, then you know how long it took for the rocks associated with that polarity reversal to travel from their site of origin at the ridge crest to their present positions. The spreading rate can therefore be worked out if the distance travelled is known.

Consider the most recent polarity reversal; according to Figure 7.8 it took place about 0.78 Ma ago. Rocks of this age on the ocean floor southwest of Iceland were originally erupted at the ridge but have since been split apart and moved aside, as younger rocks were intruded, and are now found about 8.5 km away from the ridge, i.e. some 17 km apart.

Because the separation distance is 17 km and the time elapsed is 0.78 Ma, the speed of separation is:

$$\text{speed of separation} = \frac{\text{separation distance}}{\text{elapsed time}}$$

$$= \frac{17 \text{ km}}{0.78 \text{ Ma}} = 22 \text{ km Ma}^{-1} \text{ to 2 significant figures.}$$

A speed measured in kilometres per million years (km Ma^{-1}) is perhaps difficult to visualise and for this reason sea-floor spreading rates are conventionally reported in the more easily imagined units of millimetres per year (mm y^{-1}, or mm a^{-1} in some books), or very often centimetres per year (cm y^{-1}).

■ What is 22 km Ma^{-1} in units of mm y^{-1}?

☐ To convert a speed of 22 kilometres per million years into a speed with units of millimetres per year, you need to convert 22 km into millimetres, and 1 Ma into years. 22 km is 22×10^3 m, which is $22 \times 10^3 \times 10^3$ mm; this is

22×10^6 mm, which is 2.2×10^7 mm when written in scientific notation. A million years is 1×10^6 y, so 22 kilometres per million years is 2.2×10^7 mm per 1×10^6 y. This can be written as:

$$22 \text{ km Ma}^{-1} \; = \; \frac{2.2 \times 10^7 \text{ mm}}{1 \times 10^6 \text{ y}}$$

= 22 mm y^{-1} (You might want to check that you can get this answer with your calculator.)

Notice that the numerical value of the spreading rate in km Ma^{-1} is the same as the value in mm y^{-1} (this is because both parts of the unit are scaled down by the same factor, 10^6). A rate of 22 mm y^{-1} is similar to the rate at which fingernails grow.

Information about all of the reversals near the Mid-Atlantic Ridge southwest of Iceland is given in Table 7.2 and is plotted as a graph in Figure 7.10. The data show some scatter around a best-fit straight line that passes extremely close to the origin (i.e. the point (0, 0)). As you discovered in Chapter 6 (Box 6.1), some scatter in the data is to be expected because the values of the measurements that are being plotted inevitably have some experimental uncertainty. Each distance measurement has some uncertainty, and the ages of the reversals will also have some uncertainty. The result that the best fit line in Figure 7.10 passes very close to the origin is re-assuring because it means that rocks that lie side by side at the centre of the ridge (i.e. with a separation of 0 km) have an age of 0 Ma, which would be expected if the rocks at the ridge were erupted very recently, as the theory of sea-floor spreading predicts. Nonetheless, if the distance measurements or the age measurements had large uncertainties it is possible that the best-fit line wouldn't go near the origin, even though it might be expected to. When drawing best-fit lines, avoid the temptation to draw the line exactly through the origin, even if you expect it to, unless the data truly justify it.

Table 7.2 Positions of dated polarity reversals on the Mid-Atlantic Ridge southwest of Iceland.

Age of reversal/Ma	Separation distance/km
0.78	17
0.99	18
1.07	21
1.79	32
1.95	39
2.60	48
3.04	58
3.11	59
3.22	62
3.33	65
3.58	66

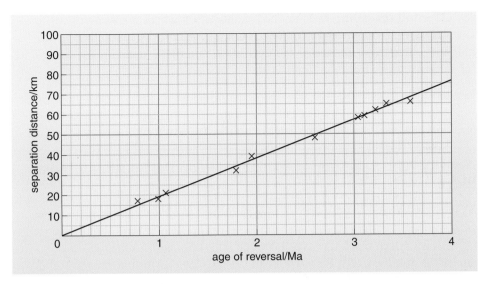

Figure 7.10   Graph of data in Table 7.2 and the best-fit straight line through the data.

- What does the gradient of the line in Figure 7.10 represent?

☐ It is the average speed at which points on either side of the Mid-Atlantic Ridge move away from each other.

To determine the average speed of sea-floor spreading at the Mid-Atlantic Ridge, the first step is to find the gradient of the best-fit line in Figure 7.10. In general, and recalling what you learned in Chapter 6 (Equation 6.4), the gradient is found from:

$$\text{gradient} = \frac{\text{rise}}{\text{run}} = \frac{y_2 - y_1}{x_2 - x_1}$$

where (x_1, y_1) and (x_2, y_2) are two points on the line whose gradient you wish to calculate.

The x and y coordinates of any two points on the best-fit line will do, but it is best to choose points that are quite far apart. It's also useful to choose points that are easily read – for example where one of the grid lines crosses the best-fit line. For instance, selecting 4.0 Ma for x_2 gives a value for y_2 of 76 km. The point (0.5, 10) also lies on the line. Therefore:

$$\text{gradient} = \frac{\text{rise}}{\text{run}} = \frac{76 \text{ km} - 10 \text{ km}}{4.0 \text{ Ma} - 0.5 \text{ Ma}} = \frac{66 \text{ km}}{3.5 \text{ Ma}} = 19 \text{ km Ma}^{-1} \text{ (to 2 significant figures)}$$

Question 7.3

Express 19 km Ma^{-1} in units of mm y^{-1}.

The earlier estimate of the spreading rate (22 mm y^{-1}) was based on just one piece of information, whereas the estimate from the graph, which uses all the data, should be more representative of the spreading rate at the Mid-Atlantic Ridge. The spreading rate of 19 mm y^{-1} for the Mid-Atlantic Ridge is properly called the **full spreading rate**, defined as the rate at which points on opposite sides of the ridge move away from each other. This contrasts with the **half spreading rate**, defined as the rate at which a single point on one side of the ridge moves away from the ridge crest.

You have discovered that the sea-floor spreading rate on the Mid-Atlantic Ridge is 19 mm y^{-1}, but do all mid-ocean ridges spread at this rate? To answer this question, you will need to complete the following activity.

Activity 7.1   Sea-floor spreading rates on the Southeast Indian Ridge

We expect this activity will take you approximately 1 hour.

The Southeast Indian Ridge is a mid-ocean ridge that extends southeast across the Indian Ocean, passes between Australia and Antarctica, and enters the southwestern Pacific Ocean (Figure 2.6). Information about the distribution of marine magnetic anomalies at two points along the ridge is shown in Table 7.3 and one set of data is plotted in Figure 7.11. This provides the information you will need to work out the sea-floor spreading rates at these locations.

Table 7.3 Positions of dated polarity reversals at two locations on the Southeast Indian Ridge.

Age of reversal/Ma	Separation distance at 70.2° E /km	Separation distance at 118.7° E /km
0.78	48	55
0.99	52	81
1.07	63	86
1.79	100	130
1.95	115	156
2.60	140	190
3.04	170	227
3.11	178	239
3.22	185	248
3.33	187	258
3.58	207	274

Task 1 Drawing a best-fit straight line and determining its gradient

The data for longitude 70.2 °E (given in Table 7.3) are plotted in Figure 7.11 (also available on the course website, which may be more convenient if you want to work with an enlarged graph or with paper that isn't bound into a book).

(a) Using a ruler (a transparent one is best), draw by eye a best-fit straight line, remembering the guidance from Box 6.1 to try to have as many points above the line as below; don't force the line through the origin (a best-fit straight line may or may not happen to go through the origin); it is not necessary for the line to pass through any of the points.

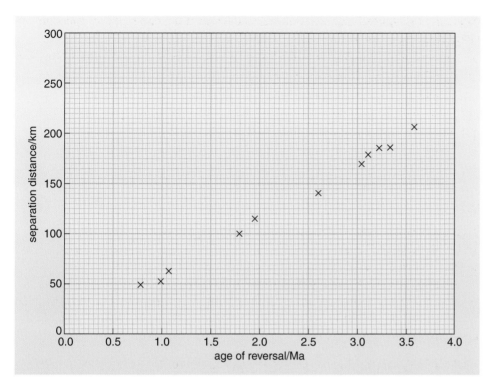

Figure 7.11   Graph showing the age and separation distances of magnetic reversals near the Southeast Indian Ridge at 70.2° E (the plotted data are given in Table 7.3).

(b) Then use your best-fit line to calculate the sea-floor spreading rate, in units of mm y^{-1} and to an appropriate number of significant figures, taking into account how accurately you can read points off your graph.

(c) How does the rate you calculated compare with the rate for the Mid-Atlantic Ridge near Iceland that was given in the text (19 mm y^{-1})?

Now look at the comments on this task at the end of this book.

Task 2 Plotting data, drawing the best-fit straight line and determining its gradient

The data for the second location on the Southeast Indian Ridge, at longitude 118.7° E, are listed in Table 7.3.

(a) Plot these on Figure 7.12 (or another version of this figure on the course website) using a sharp pencil (this will allow you to plot the points accurately and correct any mistakes). Plot each point as an X-shaped cross (as you did in Book 1, Activities 3.1 and 7.3).

(b) Using a ruler, draw a best-fit straight line by eye. Before calculating the sea-floor spreading rate, write a couple of sentences explaining whether you think the plotted data (and the best-fit line) indicate that the sea-floor spreading rate at longitude 118.7° E is faster, slower or the same as at longitude 70.2° E.

(c) Use the best-fit line to calculate the sea-floor spreading rate, in units of mm y^{-1} and to an appropriate number of significant figures.

Now look at the comments on this task at the end of this book.

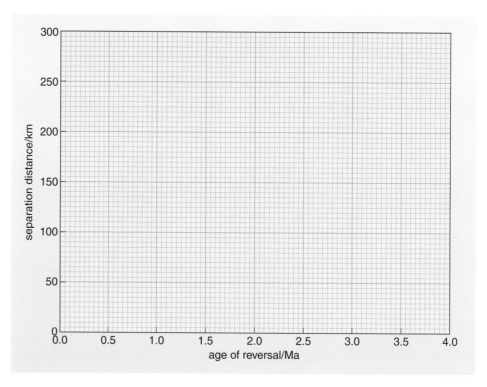

Figure 7.12   For use with Task 2.

Task 3 Explaining your results

You should have found that the sea-floor spreading rate on the Southeast Indian Ridge at longitude 70.2° E is less than at longitude 118.7° E. Were you expecting this? How can the result be explained? Have a think about this for a few minutes and then read the comments on this task at the end of this book.

7.4   Continental drift and sea-floor spreading: examples of scientific discovery

Looking back at the evidence, there seems to be little doubt that the continents have drifted over the face of the Earth and that the ocean floor is created at mid-ocean ridges by the process of sea-floor spreading. In the past, however, many scientists could not accept these theories because the most compelling evidence had not been discovered or its true importance had not been realised. The way in which continental drift was established was very different from the discovery of sea-floor spreading. The stories of how these discoveries came about illustrate that scientific knowledge and theories only sometimes develop in an ordered, logical progression. In other cases, their development involves the inspired pulling together of what seemed previously to be unconnected facts. Science's exploration of the unknown is often an unpredictable voyage.

In the case of continental drift, it was the good jigsaw fit of continental coastlines that led Alfred Wegener to hypothesise that the continents had drifted apart at some distant time in the past. He then went on to find other types of evidence that backed up the idea that continental drift really had happened.

The discovery of sea-floor spreading came about very differently. Unlike the observations that led Wegener and others to pursue ideas about continental drift, the observations that were to lead to the idea of sea-floor spreading were less visible and came from unlikely quarters. By the late 1950s, the superpowers had developed sophisticated military submarines, but the floor of the oceans in which submarine warfare might have to be waged was largely unknown. This drove the US Navy secretly to map the ocean floor and, unknown to the rest of the scientific world, to discover mid-ocean ridges in the Pacific. Independently, mid-ocean ridges in the Indian and Atlantic Oceans were being surveyed in curiosity-driven expeditions of discovery by scientists from the UK and USA.

While this was going on, other scientists were occupied in trying to discover as much as possible about the Earth's magnetism and the magnetic properties of rocks. Although the possibility of magnetic polarity reversals had been proposed at the beginning of the 1900s, it wasn't until the 1950s that this became a popular topic of study and reversed and normally magnetised rocks became widely recognised in volcanic rocks across the Earth. By the 1960s, advances in the methods used for measuring the age of volcanic rocks made it possible to date precisely when the magnetised basalt lavas had been erupted, allowing polarity reversals to be dated and the geomagnetic polarity timescale to be defined. Meanwhile, scientists studying the ocean were persuaded to do magnetic surveys. This led, in 1958, to the discovery of marine magnetic anomaly patterns off the Pacific coast of North America. But no one at the time understood how these magnetic stripes were formed or what they meant.

Excited by the results from the explosion in ocean research, and influenced by contemporary ideas about continental drift, Harry Hess of Princeton University, USA, speculated, in 1960, that the ocean floors were formed at mid-ocean ridges by the intrusion and extrusion of basalt magma and grew by being carried away from the ridge by slow-moving currents flowing in the mantle. It was not until 1961 that Bob Dietz, a scientist at a US Navy laboratory, coined a term for this hypothetical process. He called it sea-floor spreading. But conclusive evidence that sea-floor spreading actually occurred seemed to be elusive, and the idea was regarded as controversial.

Unknown to everyone, all the pieces of the puzzle that were needed to substantiate the theory of sea-floor spreading were available in the early 1960s. Then, the light dawned. At Cambridge University, a young research student, Fred Vine, and his supervisor Drummond Matthews, realised the connection between spreading and magnetic stripes. They published their ideas in the 7 September 1963 issue of the weekly science journal *Nature*. In the same year, a Canadian geologist, Lawrence W. Morley, realised independently how magnetic stripes fitted in with the theory of sea-floor spreading and he too submitted his work for publication, but to a different peer-reviewed journal. In Morley's case, the journal editor failed to be impressed:

> Such speculations make interesting talk at cocktail parties, but it is not the sort of thing that ought to be published under serious scientific aegis.

(Powell, 2001)

In the end, all the credit went to Vine and Matthews, but the episode created a classic (and extreme) example of the occasional pit-falls of the peer-review system.

Now that sea-floor spreading appeared to be a reality, it became feasible to anticipate its consequences and seek them out. Further magnetic surveys over mid-ocean ridges and refinements to the geomagnetic polarity timescale showed that sea-floor spreading, at rates of tens of millimetres per year, operated in all of the ocean basins. Drilling into the deep ocean floor from a moored drilling ship became possible in the 1960s and a consortium of five oceanographic institutions in the USA initiated a new phase of exploration by organising a dedicated research vessel and a drilling programme. Drilling into the ocean floor showed that the rocks on the floor of the South Atlantic Ocean become older with increasing distance from the Mid-Atlantic Ridge, just as sea-floor spreading theory had predicted. In the 1970s, submersible craft began to be taken to the mid-ocean ridges, notably discovering new organisms and hot mineralised springs (black smokers) at ridge crests, the 'factories' where new ocean crust is forged. Research has continued to the present day, providing many major advances in knowledge and understanding: the sea floor has been mapped in great detail using measurements from orbiting satellites; military seismometers originally designed to listen for enemy submarines have located earthquakes and volcanic eruptions from bursts of sea-floor spreading on the Juan de Fuca Ridge (Figure 2.6); and GPS measurements are providing new ways of measuring the motion of drifting continents.

A century ago, few scientists believed in continental drift. Now, faced with so much convincing evidence, all agree that the imperceptibly slow processes of continental drift and sea-floor spreading really are happening. Although one deals with the continents and the other with the ocean floor, it was realised in the late 1960s that they are expressions of the single process that was to become known as plate tectonics, and this is the subject of the next two chapters.

7.5   Summary of Chapter 7

The theory of continental drift is based on evidence for the hypothesis, originally put forward by Alfred Wegener, that continental land masses have moved across the surface of the Earth through time.

250 Ma ago, the continents as we know them today were arranged next to each other, constituting a super-continent called Pangaea. The subsequent break-up of Pangaea, and the drifting apart of the separated continental blocks, can be recognised from several lines of evidence, including:

- The coastlines of certain continents fit together. This can be explained by the break-up of a super-continent.

- Certain sedimentary rocks, such as desert sandstone, coal and glacial till, form only under particular climatic conditions and hence, by analogy with today's global distribution of climate belts, are likely to have formed in particular ranges of latitude. However, these rocks can be found in places well outside these ranges of latitude. This can be explained if the rocks formed in the appropriate latitudes but have since drifted to other latitudes.

The theory of sea-floor spreading accounts for evidence that the age of the ocean floor increases with distance away from mid-ocean ridges. New ocean floor is created at mid-ocean ridges, by the intrusion of basaltic magma. This activity produces the volcanic rocks, hot black smokers, faults and shallow earthquakes found at mid-ocean ridges.

Sea-floor spreading also explains the symmetrical striped pattern of marine magnetic anomalies that is revealed by magnetometer surveys of the oceans. The stripes identify sections of ocean floor formed at a mid-ocean ridge during timespans when the Earth's magnetism had either normal or reversed polarity. The Earth's magnetic polarity has randomly switched between normal and reversed through time.

The rate of sea-floor spreading can be determined by comparing the spacing of magnetic polarity reversals with the time sequence of reversals given by the geomagnetic polarity timescale. A graph of these two quantities gives a set of points arranged close to a best-fit straight line. The gradient of this line gives the average sea-floor spreading rate. Rates are a few tens of millimetres per year, but vary from one mid-ocean ridge to another and along the length of an individual ridge.

In studying this chapter, you have added to your knowledge of the Earth and theories of how it operates. You have also developed your skills of interpreting and plotting graphs, including drawing a best-fit straight line through scattered data and calculating the gradient of a straight line to estimate speed.

Chapter 8
The theory of plate tectonics

Once sea-floor spreading had become an established theory in the mid-1960s, it was soon realised that it was the long-sought mechanism for explaining continental drift. The continents were carried around by sea-floor spreading rather than mysteriously ploughing through or gliding over a solid surface. By combining evidence for continental drift with the mechanism of sea-floor spreading, a wide-ranging theory for the dynamics of the Earth's surface could begin to be formulated. This was the theory of **plate tectonics**. It revolutionised scientists' understanding of how the Earth works because it became possible to link together previously unrelated features of the Earth, such as the distribution and shape of mountain belts, the location of seismic zones, volcanism and the shape of the ocean floor. That all of these diverse observations could be explained by just one theory spoke of an elegance that is often the hallmark of great science. Because of their importance, plate tectonics have already been mentioned, but now it is time to describe the theory more fully. 'Tectonics' involves the movement and deformation of solid rock within and at the surface of the Earth. But what, in this context, is a plate?

8.1　Plates, lithosphere and asthenosphere

To understand what a plate is, you first need to consider the layered structure of the Earth. You saw in Chapter 6 that the Earth's layered structure includes a thin crust, of granitic (parts of the continental crust) or basaltic (oceanic crust) composition, overlying a mantle made of peridotite. These layers have different compositions and are separated by the Moho, a major seismic discontinuity (Section 6.2.2).

However, the Earth can also be divided into layers based on the strength of the materials in them (Figure 8.1). These layers are quite distinct from the compositional or seismic layers discussed in Chapter 6. The outer layer is strong and rigid, and is called the **lithosphere** (*lithos* being the Greek word for 'rock'). The lithosphere incorporates not only the crust but also part of the mantle. Below the lithosphere is a layer that is weaker and more easily deformed, the **asthenosphere** (*asthenia* being Greek for 'weak'). Earthquakes occur within the strong lithosphere, but not within the more easily deformed asthenosphere, which tends to flow (very sluggishly) rather than break. The boundary between the lithosphere and asthenosphere is therefore defined by a change in strength between the two layers.

The base of the lithosphere lies within the mantle (Figure 8.1). The lithosphere is about 100 km thick, but its thickness is variable; oceanic lithosphere (lithosphere with oceanic crust) is generally thinner than continental lithosphere (lithosphere with continental crust).

But what determines the thickness of the lithosphere? The marked difference in strength between the lithosphere and the asthenosphere is caused by temperature increasing with increasing depth below the Earth's surface. At the base of the

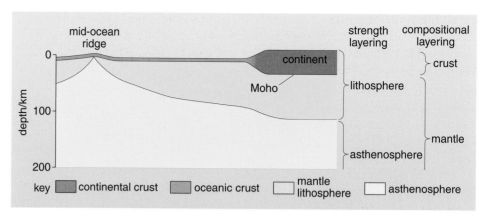

Figure 8.1   The strong outer layer of the Earth, the lithosphere, includes the crust and top of the mantle. The asthenosphere is the weaker layer beneath the lithosphere. The lithosphere and asthenosphere are distinguished by their different strengths, whereas the crust and mantle differ in composition.

lithosphere, the temperature is close to the melting temperature of the mantle rock at this depth. Under these conditions, the minerals in the mantle are more easily deformed. The depth to the top of the asthenosphere (i.e. the thickness of the lithosphere) depends on the rate at which temperature increases with depth. At spreading mid-ocean ridges, temperatures are high close to the surface so the lithosphere is thinner. Beneath continents, temperatures increase only slowly with depth, so the lithosphere is thicker (Figure 8.1).

Question 8.1

Separate each of the following pairs of properties into the one that applies to the lithosphere, and the one that applies to the asthenosphere:

weaker/stronger

rigid/more easily deformed

higher temperature/lower temperature

crust and top of the mantle/within the mantle

earthquakes occur/no earthquakes occur

Now we can return to considering the question 'What is a plate?' A plate is an area of the Earth's lithosphere. The global map of earthquake epicentres (Figure 3.6) provides information about the location and extent of individual plates. This figure shows that most earthquakes occur in narrow seismic zones (Section 3.3), which are zones of faulting in the lithosphere. These zones surround areas of lithosphere in which there is relatively little evidence of active deformation, but there is much faulting and deformation at their edges, suggesting movement. Such areas of lithosphere, separated by seismic zones, are called **lithospheric plates** (or more usually within Earth sciences, just **plates**). Plates are relatively thin in comparison with their horizontal dimensions; they are only about 100 km thick (the thickness of the lithosphere) but thousands of kilometres in width. The Earth's surface comprises seven major plates (the Pacific Plate is the largest) and numerous smaller plates (Figure 8.2).

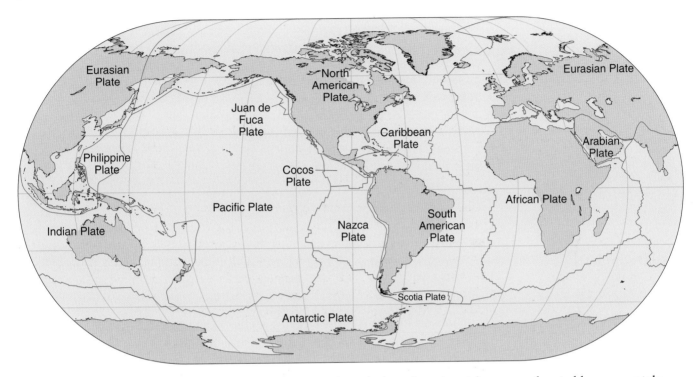

Figure 8.2   The Earth's lithospheric plates. The plate boundaries of continental areas are located less accurately than those in the oceans as seismic zones in continental lithosphere are broader than in oceanic lithosphere. Plate boundaries in the far north are uncertain.

■ Do plate boundaries coincide with the boundaries between continental and oceanic crust? (Remember that this boundary is beneath the continental rise, not at the land–sea boundary; Section 2.3 and Section 6.2.2.)

☐ In general no, except for the western edge of North, Central and South America.

■ Do all plates contain areas of both oceanic and continental lithosphere?

☐ No, but most plates do. (Some plates have just oceanic lithosphere, e.g. the Cocos and Nazca Plates. There are no plates that have just continental lithosphere.)

Having dealt with the question 'What is a plate?', the next step is to consider what plates do. The lithospheric plates move around the Earth over the weaker asthenosphere and this is where the 'tectonics' comes into plate tectonics. The plates do not all move in the same direction; instead they move in different directions. So when a plate containing one continent moves relative to a plate containing another continent this produces the effect of continental drift. For example, the North American continent is part of the North American Plate, whereas Europe is part of the Eurasian Plate (Figure 8.2). As the plates move relative to each other, so do the continents that are part of those plates. Continental drift is therefore explained by plate tectonics.

Because the plates move in different directions, they jostle each other at their edges. There the rocks of one plate are moving relative to the rocks of another plate, causing faulting and earthquakes, which is why plate boundaries are characterised by seismic zones. One way of visualising this is to think of the analogy of a frozen pond, with a layer of ice at the surface and water below. Suppose the ice is cracked, and the pieces of ice are equivalent to plates. If you were to push an ice plate, the ice would move easily over the underlying water (equivalent to the asthenosphere) but would crash into the surrounding ice plates at its edge. The interior of the ice plate would not be deformed by such collisions, only the edges.

8.2   Plate boundaries

■   Do plate boundaries (shown on Figure 8.2) coincide with any of the major topographic features of the Earth's surface (shown on Figure 2.3 and Figure 2.6)?

☐   Yes. All mid-ocean ridges are plate boundaries. For example, the plate boundary in the Atlantic Ocean is a mid-ocean ridge (the Mid-Atlantic Ridge). All ocean trenches are also plate boundaries; an example is the Peru–Chile Trench off the west coast of South America. Some mountain belts are plate boundaries, for example the Himalayas.

The most prominent topographic features on the Earth are associated with plate boundaries. However, the essence of plate tectonics concerns the relative movement of the plates, and plate boundaries can be classified into three types, depending on the direction of relative motion between the plates on each side of the boundary.

At **divergent plate boundaries**, plates are moving away from each other (Figures 8.3a and 8.3d). The conventional symbol for a divergent plate boundary on a tectonic map is a double line. New lithosphere is added to the plates at the boundary. This is what happens during sea-floor spreading at mid-ocean ridges, so mid-ocean ridges are divergent plate boundaries. The direction of motion of the plates is usually perpendicular to the plate boundary, as in Figure 8.3a, but it does not have to be so; if it is not, then the ridge is said to be spreading obliquely.

The theory of plate tectonics incorporates sea-floor spreading. But the creation of new lithosphere by sea-floor spreading must be balanced by the destruction of lithosphere elsewhere, otherwise the lithosphere would increase in area and

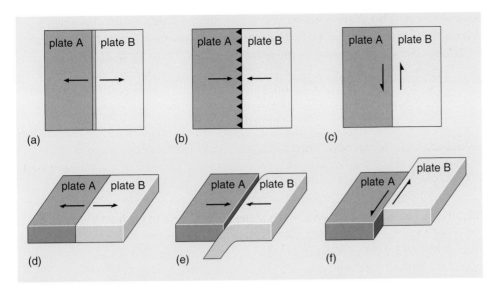

Figure 8.3   The three types of plate boundary, between plates A and B. The motion of each plate is shown by the arrows. (a), (b) and (c) are plan (map) views, and (d), (e) and (f) are block diagrams that give a three-dimensional view of the motion. (a) and (d) show a divergent plate boundary, indicated by the conventional double line map symbol. (b) and (e) show a convergent plate boundary, with plates A and B moving towards each other. In this type of convergent boundary, plate B is descending beneath plate A. On a map, this is indicated by barbs on the overriding plate (plate A). (c) and (f) show a transform fault plate boundary. The single line is the conventional symbol for a transform fault on a map.

the Earth would expand! Since the Earth is not expanding, lithosphere must be destroyed at the same overall rate as it is being created. This must occur at another type of plate boundary, a convergent plate boundary.

Along **convergent plate boundaries**, plates are moving towards each other. You may be able to predict what will happen in this case by thinking again about the plates of ice; if two ice plates are pushed towards each other, either one plate will move under the other, or the plates will crumple up. Similar situations occur with lithospheric plates. Figures 8.3b and 8.3e illustrate one form of convergent boundary, where plate B descends below plate A. The conventional symbol for a convergent plate boundary on a tectonic map is a barbed line, with the barbs pointing in the direction of the overriding plate.

Where one plate descends beneath another, an ocean trench is formed. A convergent plate boundary of this type may develop a volcanic island arc when the overriding plate is of oceanic lithosphere or a line of volcanoes along the edge of a continent when the overriding plate is of continental lithosphere. Alternatively the plates will crumple up and thicken into a mountain belt where they converge if both plates are of continental lithosphere. As with divergent plate boundaries, the direction of motion does not have to be perpendicular to the plate boundary; oblique convergence is fairly common.

At **transform fault plate boundaries**, plates move past each other in opposite directions (Figure 8.3c and 8.3f). The conventional symbol for a transform fault boundary on a tectonic map is a single line.

Figure 8.4 shows where the different types of plate boundary occur.

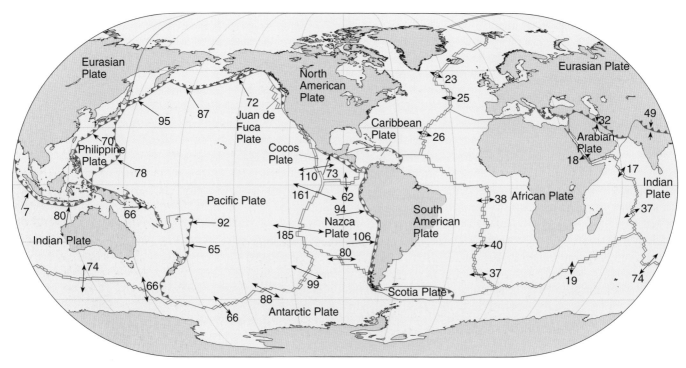

key   // divergent plate boundary   ⟋ convergent plate boundary   / transform fault plate boundary

Figure 8.4   The Earth's lithospheric plates and plate boundaries. Plate boundaries in the far north are uncertain. Refer to Figure 2.6 for names of topographic features associated with plate boundaries. The black arrows and numbers give the direction and speed of relative motion between plates and are discussed in Section 8.4. Speeds of motion are given in mm y^{-1}, and for divergent plate boundaries these are full spreading rates. The length of each arrow is proportional to the speed of relative motion, so the longest arrows show the highest speeds of relative motion.

Activity 8.1   Completing a table of plate boundary features

We expect this activity will take you approximately 30 minutes.

To help you distinguish between the different types of plate boundary, this activity requires you to summarise their important features in a table. Complete Table 8.1 using information from this section and from earlier chapters. This is another example of a summary table, which will help you to identify, remember and revise the key features of different types of plate boundary. This table is also available in electronic form on the course website. Now look at the comments on this activity at the end of this book.

Table 8.1 The characteristics of each type of plate boundary.

Characteristic	Divergent	Convergent	Transform fault
Direction of motion of plates with respect to plate boundary			
Depth of earthquake foci (shallow, intermediate, or deep)			
Destruction or creation of lithosphere, or neither			
Physical features associated with boundary			

8.3 Plate motion

The motion of plates on the Earth involves motion over the surface of a sphere, which sounds fairly complex. However, you can still learn a lot about plate motion by considering a simpler situation – two plates moving on a horizontal surface (a 'flat Earth' model). This is a tactic often used in science; taking a potentially tricky situation and simplifying it to something more familiar or more manageable in order to start understanding the more complex situation.

Consider the motion between two plates A and B on a horizontal surface, with plate B completely surrounding plate A (Figure 8.5a). The plate boundary between plates A and B is made up of four straight lines, and the relative motion between the plates is shown at the eastern boundary.

■ Which type of plate boundary is the eastern boundary in Figure 8.5a?

☐ It is a divergent boundary as the relative motion between the two plates is away from each other.

How about the other boundaries? As plates are rigid, if plate A is moving west with respect to plate B at the eastern boundary, it must also be moving west at the other boundaries. At the western boundary this means that the plates are converging (plate A is moving west, towards plate B here) so this is a convergent boundary. At the northern and southern boundaries, which run east–west, the relative plate motion must be parallel to the boundaries, so they are transform faults. These plate boundaries are marked on Figure 8.5b using the standard symbols that you met in Figure 8.3.

Activity 8.2 Using a physical model to help understand plate motion

We expect this activity will take you approximately 15 minutes.

This activity uses a physical model of plate motion. Draw an enlarged version of Figure 8.5a on a sheet of paper, and cut out plate A along the plate boundaries.

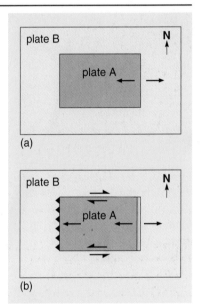

Figure 8.5 The relative motion between two plates on a flat Earth. These are plan views. Plate A is totally surrounded by plate B. The relative motion between the plates is shown by the arrows in (a), and the types of plate boundary deduced from this motion are shown in (b). Plate boundary symbols are as in Figure 8.3. The western boundary, showing plate A descending beneath plate B, is one of a number of possibilities for this convergent boundary; other possibilities are that plate B descends beneath plate A, or the plates crumple together.

Now place plate A back inside plate B, and move A in the direction shown by the arrow on A, towards the left. Observe what happens at each of the edges of rectangle (plate) A. Which type of plate boundary is each edge of A analogous to?

Compare your observations with those in the comments on this activity at the end of this book.

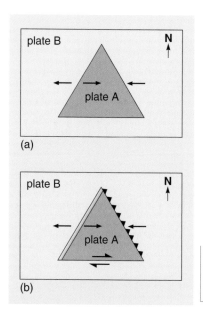

Figure 8.6   The relative motion between two plates on a flat Earth. Two of the plate boundaries are oblique to the direction of motion. Plate boundary symbols are as in Figure 8.3.

Now consider another plate-tectonic situation, where the motion between the plates is not perpendicular to the plate boundaries (Figure 8.6a). Plates A and B have plate boundaries in a triangular shape. What are the types of plate boundary in this situation? The southern boundary is the simplest to work out, as here the plate boundary is parallel to the relative plate motion, so the plates slip past each other at a transform fault. At the western boundary, the plates are moving away from each other so this is a divergent plate boundary (this is an example of an obliquely spreading divergent boundary of the type mentioned in Section 8.2). The plates are moving towards each other (obliquely) at the eastern boundary, so this is a convergent plate boundary (Figure 8.6b). If this is not clear, try the paper-cutting technique of Activity 8.2.

Question 8.2

Work out which type of plate boundaries will be present between the two plates A and B in Figure 8.7 and draw them on the figure using the conventional symbols (see Figures 8.3–8.6).

Question 8.3

The triangular plates in Figures 8.6 and 8.7 may seem unrealistic, but if you look at the Cocos Plate (Figure 8.4) you will see that it is approximately triangular. As a simplification, assume that the Cocos Plate is triangular in shape and that it is surrounded by only one other plate, then draw the Cocos Plate and the surrounding plate in the style of Figure 8.6b, showing the types of plate boundaries.

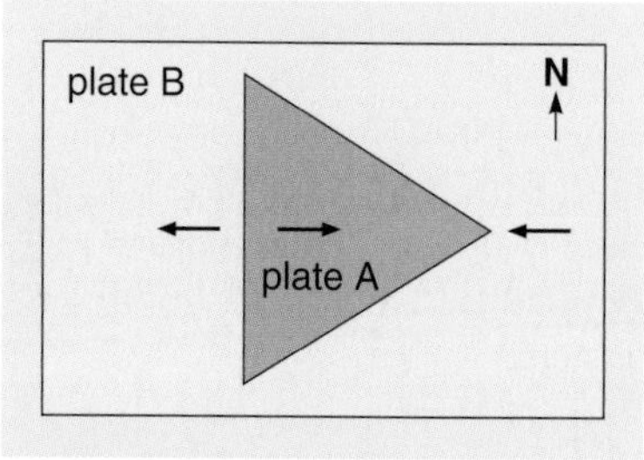

8.4   The speed of relative plate motion

How do we determine the speed of relative plate motion at plate boundaries? There are a number of methods for doing this, some involving plate movements over geological time periods (millions of years) and others involving present-day rates of motion. In Section 7.3, average rates of sea-floor spreading were calculated, which were several tens of millimetres per year. This is the typical long-term rate of relative movement between plates at divergent plate boundaries. Present-day ('instantaneous') rates of relative plate motion can be determined by methods that involve monitoring small changes in the distance between fixed points on two or more plates. The relative speeds of plates are shown in Figure 8.4, which you should look back at now.

Figure 8.7   The relative motion between two plates on a flat Earth. For use with Question 8.2.

Question 8.4

Using the information about relative plate speeds from Figure 8.4, and using Figure 2.6 to identify topographic features:

(a) Which neighbouring plates have the highest relative speeds of motion, and which type of plate boundary separates them?

(b) Where is the highest relative speed for a different type of boundary from that in (a)?

(c) Where is the lowest rate of sea-floor spreading?

You can use the directions of relative plate motion shown in Figure 8.4 to consider how common it is for plates to move obliquely at divergent and convergent plate boundaries, and how oblique the motion is. Consider first the motion at divergent plate boundaries.

■ Are there examples of obvious oblique motion, or is the motion mainly perpendicular to the diverging ridge segments? (Remember to look at the motion relative to individual ridge segments, denoted by the double lines, rather than the overall alignment of the mid-ocean ridge.)

☐ In general, the motion is perpendicular or nearly perpendicular to the double lines identifying the position of divergent boundaries, with no very oblique motion.

At convergent boundaries, there are a number of places where the motion is distinctly oblique, such as the northwest edge of the Pacific Plate and the northern boundary between the Indian and Pacific Plates.

So transform faults are parallel to the plate motion, divergent plate boundaries are usually perpendicular or nearly perpendicular to the plate motion, but convergent plate boundaries are quite often oblique to the plate motion.

■ Which of Figures 8.5, 8.6 and 8.7 therefore represents a geologically unlikely situation?

☐ Figure 8.6, which shows a ridge spreading very obliquely.

To conclude this section, consider for a moment just how fast plates are travelling in everyday terms. The fastest sprinter can run 100 m in about 10 s, which is 10 m s^{-1}. A reasonable walking pace is about 5 km h^{-1}, which is about 1.4 m s^{-1}. In contrast, the fastest relative plate speed is 185 mm y^{-1}, which is around 6×10^{-9} m s^{-1}. So plates travel very slowly. The fastest ones move at a relative rate similar to the rate at which hair grows. The slower ones move only at fingernail growth rates. However insignificant that seems, it is enough to release energy in the form of major earthquakes, and, over millions of years, to have separated Europe and North America by thousands of kilometres.

Question 8.5

(a) How far will two plates have moved relative to each other in a million years if their relative speed is 185 mm y^{-1}?

To calculate the distance travelled over a certain time at a given speed you have to rearrange Equation 6.1 so that it has the form 'distance travelled = …'. You will learn how to do this in Book 3. In the meantime, you are given the result, which is:

$$\text{distance travelled} = \text{speed} \times \text{time interval} \tag{8.1}$$

(b) Roughly how long will it take for the distance between London (on the Eurasian Plate) and New York (on the North American Plate) to increase by 1 km at current sea-floor spreading rates? You will need to use an equation that is also related to Equation 6.1:

$$\text{time interval} = \frac{\text{distance travelled}}{\text{speed}} \tag{8.2}$$

8.5   Divergent plate boundary processes

Divergent plate boundaries are sites of sea-floor spreading. It is here that new oceanic lithosphere is made, so divergent plate boundaries are sometimes referred to as constructive plate boundaries. Whatever term is used, the challenge facing the Earth scientist is to work out how new oceanic lithosphere is produced at divergent boundaries. The first step is to find out in more detail what the oceanic lithosphere is made from.

8.5.1   The structure and composition of oceanic lithosphere

By exploring the ocean floor, scientists have discovered that the top of the oceanic lithosphere consists of a layer of fine-grained sediment overlying basaltic lava flows (Section 7.3). But what lies beneath the basalt lavas? To answer this question, and so gain a complete picture of the 100 km or so thick oceanic lithosphere, we draw on two lines of evidence.

Seismology

One of the conclusions about the interior structure of the Earth that comes from seismology is that the oceanic crust is a layer of rock about 7 km thick (Section 6.2.2). Seismology can be used to find out even more about this layer, and detailed seismic investigations have revealed that the oceanic crust is itself composed of layers, each with a different seismic wave speed. The uppermost seismic layer corresponds to the layer of sediment that covers the ocean floor, and the top of the next seismic layer corresponds to the lava flows of basalt. But identifying the composition of deeper layers requires another approach.

Rock samples from the oceanic lithosphere

You have already been introduced to the lava flows and sediment that lie on the ocean floor (Section 7.3). These surface rocks normally hide the deep interior of the oceanic crust, but sometimes erosion or the movement of rocks on either side of a transform fault exposes the deeper portions of oceanic crust (Figure 8.8a). The faces of the transform faults shown in Figure 8.8a are vertical, but these rock faces commonly collapse, resulting in an irregular sloping surface that exposes deep parts of the ocean crust at the foot, and rocks from the ocean floor at the top. At the Vema transform fault, located at 11° N on the Mid-Atlantic Ridge, French scientists used a submersible to traverse down one such slope. What they found there led them to draw Figure 8.8b, based on their observations of the different rocks encountered as they traversed down the slope and their interpretation of the continuation of the rock layers beneath the surface.

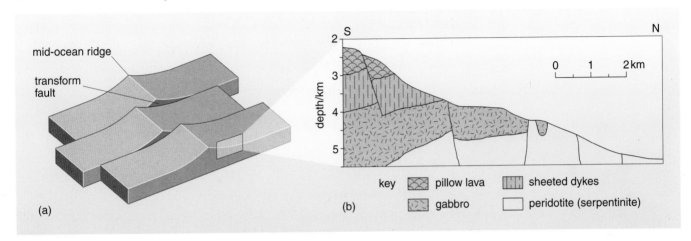

Figure 8.8   (a) Schematic block diagram of a mid-ocean ridge that has been cut by two transform faults, exposing the interior of oceanic lithosphere (the purple faces). (b) A cross-section showing nearly horizontal layers of rock near the Mid-Atlantic Ridge.

At the shallowest depth in the cross-section are basaltic pillow lavas, much as would be expected for the ocean floor. Below these are two layers which, although of the same chemical and mineral composition as the basaltic lavas, are very different in appearance. The shallower layer comprises near-vertical sheets of basaltic rock a metre or so wide. Each sheet of rock is a dyke. The dykes seen in the Vema transform fault are packed closely together, and this portion of oceanic crust consists of little else than parallel vertical sheets of dykes; it is called a **sheeted dyke complex**. The structure is analogous to a pack of playing cards standing vertically, each card representing a single dyke.

At greater depth, the rock is **gabbro**, a coarse-grained intrusive rock with the same mineral and chemical composition as basalt. This rock formed by the slow cooling of basaltic magma deep underground. The deepest rocks contain the mineral serpentine, which is formed when peridotite becomes chemically altered by reacting with heated seawater. This deepest rock, called serpentinite, is therefore regarded as the altered top of the mantle.

A complementary view of the oceanic lithosphere has been obtained by the Integrated Ocean Drilling Programme, the international scientific endeavour to investigate the ocean floor by drilling into it from a ship. The deepest penetration into oceanic crust (up to the end of 2006) was achieved in 1993 by drilling

2.1 km into the Nazca Plate, some 200 km south of the divergent plate boundary with the Cocos Plate in the eastern Pacific Ocean (see Figure 8.2 for the locations of plates). After drilling through 275 m of sediment, the drill passed through about 600 m of pillow lavas before entering slightly coarser-grained basalt, which was interpreted as a sheeted dyke complex.

8.5.2   The formation of oceanic lithosphere

How can the observations you have just read about be used to explain how oceanic lithosphere is formed? First, the major crustal layers will be considered.

Question 8.6

Each of the processes A–C below accounts for one of the components (1–3) of the oceanic crust. Which process is responsible for each component?

A   Transport of basalt magma along vertical cracks in the crust

B   Slow crystallisation of basalt magma

C   Volcanic eruption onto the ocean floor

1   Gabbro

2   Pillow lavas of basalt

3   Sheeted dykes of basalt

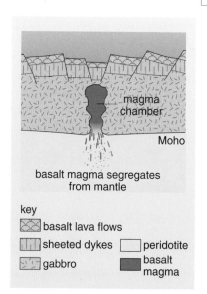

basalt magma segregates from mantle

key

basalt lava flows

sheeted dykes   peridotite

gabbro   basalt magma

Figure 8.9   A cross-section of a mid-ocean ridge showing the transfer of basalt magma from the mantle into the crust, which accounts for the structure and composition of oceanic lithosphere.

Piecing together the origins of the separate components of oceanic crust, the first conclusion we can reach is that, apart from the relatively thin covering layer of sediment, the rocks of the oceanic crust have an igneous origin. This means that they were ultimately derived from a magma – but where did this magma come from? By carrying out experiments in which different types of rock are heated at high pressure and temperature, to simulate conditions within the Earth, it has been found that basalt magma is produced by melting mantle peridotite. So, considering the whole of the oceanic lithosphere, we can think of it as being the product of a 'factory' that produces, stores, transports and delivers basaltic magma from the mantle to the crust at mid-ocean ridges (Figure 8.9). Once basalt magma has been formed by melting of mantle peridotite, it embarks on an upward journey, but it also starts to cool and crystallise. The basalt may stop rising, and accumulate in a magma chamber within the crust where it slowly crystallises to produce gabbro. Some magma escapes through fissures above the magma chamber and flows to the surface where it erupts as lava on the ocean floor. The magma left in the fissure cools and solidifies, forming a dyke. At a later date another fissure opens up and another dyke is intruded between its predecessors, much as an extra playing card might be forced into the end-on pack of playing cards you imagined earlier. As more and more dykes are intruded, the crustal 'pack of cards' is widened, perpetuating the process of sea-floor spreading. The arrival of hot magma at and near the surface causes seawater that has percolated into the oceanic crust to be heated and then discharged as hot mineral-enriched water that forms black smokers (Figure 7.4a).

When the lavas and dykes cool, they become magnetised, providing a record of the polarity of the Earth's magnetism. The resulting magnetic stripes (Figure 7.9a) allow the rate of sea-floor spreading to be estimated, as described in Section 7.3.

In summary, sea-floor spreading can account for the origin of oceanic lithosphere at divergent plate boundaries. It explains the layered structure of oceanic lithosphere, the basaltic composition and rock types of the oceanic crust, striped marine magnetic anomaly patterns, and the shallow-focus earthquakes, volcanic eruptions and metal-rich hot springs (black smokers) at mid-ocean ridges.

8.6   Convergent plate boundary processes

Although divergent plate boundaries give rise to volcanic eruptions (mainly below the ocean surface) and shallow earthquakes, the catastrophic volcanic eruptions and devastating earthquakes that are reported on the news usually occur at convergent plate boundaries, where two plates are moving towards each other. That these differences exist suggests that the processes that occur at convergent plate boundaries are very different from those at divergent plate boundaries. To find out about the processes occurring at convergent plate boundaries, we can consider some specific examples.

■   The edge of a plate may be made of continental or oceanic lithosphere, so what combinations of lithosphere types might be present at convergent boundaries?

☐   There are potentially three types of convergent plate boundary: where both edges are oceanic lithosphere, where both edges are continental lithosphere, and where one edge is oceanic and the other is continental lithosphere.

Question 8.7

According to Figure 8.4, there are convergent plate boundaries along (a) the Izu–Bonin Trench in the western Pacific (see Figure 2.6), (b) the western side of South America and (c) in the Himalayas. In each case, identify the two plates involved and decide whether only continental, or oceanic or both types of lithosphere are involved.

Having identified these three types of convergent plate boundaries, you will now have a look at what processes are going on there, and see whether they are dependent on the specific type of convergent boundary. Because earthquakes are caused by movement within the Earth, one way to find out more about the motion of the plates is to locate where the earthquakes occur. The earthquake foci at each of the plate boundaries considered in Question 8.7 are shown in Figure 8.10. This diagram is similar in style to the diagram showing activity on the San Andreas Fault associated with the Loma Prieta earthquake (Figures 3.5b and c), only here a much larger region is being considered.

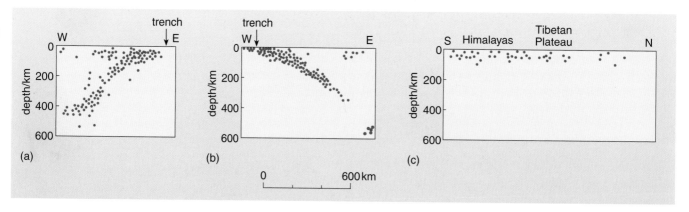

Figure 8.10   Cross-sections perpendicular to convergent plate boundaries showing the distribution of earthquake foci near (a) the Izu–Bonin Trench in the western Pacific, (b) the northern Chilean Andes (20° S) near the Peru–Chile Trench on the western side of South America, and (c) Tibet (85° E). Note that these cross-sections have no vertical exaggeration.

■   What is the depth of the deepest earthquake in each region shown in Figure 8.10?

☐   The deepest earthquakes in the region of the Izu–Bonin Trench and the Peru–Chile Trench are at a depth of almost 600 km, whereas below Tibet the deepest is at about 100 km.

The Tibetan example is different from the other two in having mostly shallow-focus earthquakes (i.e. less than 70 km; Section 3.3), whereas the others have many intermediate and some deep-focus (more than 300 km) earthquakes.

■   How are the earthquake foci in Figure 8.10 distributed?

☐   In Tibet, the earthquakes are distributed fairly evenly across the plate boundary. Near the Izu–Bonin Trench and in Chile the earthquakes are mostly confined to an inclined zone, about 100 km thick, which reaches depths of several hundred kilometres.

Inclined zones of earthquakes such as those near the Izu–Bonin Trench and in Chile were first discovered beneath Japan by Kiyoo Wadati in 1934, but their origin was a puzzle. Twenty years later, an American, Hugo Benioff, found similar inclined earthquake zones elsewhere around the Pacific rim and he realised that each one defined an enormous inclined fault zone that reached far into the Earth. Then, when the theory of plate tectonics was put forward in the 1960s, it suddenly became obvious that these earthquakes occurred where one plate was descending into the mantle beneath another plate, as in Figure 8.11. The intermediate and deep-focus earthquakes occur within and at the edges of the descending plate. The inclined zone of earthquakes is now known as a **Wadati–Benioff zone** (or sometimes just a Benioff zone). If you refer back to

Figure 3.6, you can identify some of the larger Wadati–Benioff zones around the Pacific because they are the only regions where deep-focus earthquakes occur. The descending plate is said to be subducting, and the general area of the Earth where this happens is called a **subduction zone**. Subduction zones may also be referred to as destructive plate boundaries because here one of the plates is being lost from the Earth's surface as it descends into the mantle.

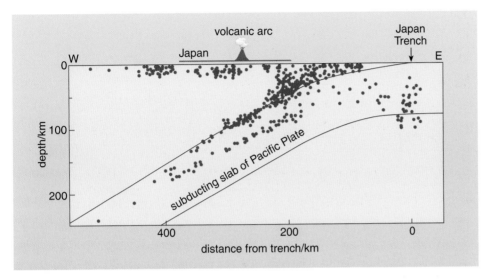

Figure 8.11   The distribution of earthquake foci defining the Wadati–Benioff zone beneath Japan marks the position of the Pacific Plate as it descends beneath the Eurasian Plate.

■ What major features are present on the Earth's surface in the vicinity of subduction zones? (Use the plate boundary map, Figure 8.2, in conjunction with Figures 2.3 and 2.6 to answer this question.)

☐ Volcanic arcs are found on the crust that overlies the Wadati–Benioff zone, and deep ocean trenches occur parallel to the arc. If two oceanic plates are converging, then a volcanic island arc forms on the overriding oceanic plate (e.g. the Izu–Bonin arc); if an oceanic plate is subducting beneath continental lithosphere, then the volcanic chains form near the edge of the continent (e.g. the volcanoes of the Andes).

The association of volcanic arcs and ocean trenches, which was noted in Section 4.3, is a characteristic feature of subduction zones, but how are they explained by the subduction process? The trench can be thought of as a deep notch running along the length of a plate boundary where subducting oceanic lithosphere bends beneath the edge of the overriding lithospheric plate (either oceanic or continental). As the oceanic plate passes under the leading edge of the overriding plate, the layer of oceanic sediment may be scraped off. So, instead of descending into the mantle with the rest of the oceanic plate, this sediment may be forced to pile up on the edge of the overriding plate, as illustrated in Figure 8.12. In extreme cases, the trench may become completely filled and the accumulated sediment reaches sea level. This is what has happened at the subduction zone in the Caribbean, where the island of Barbados is the tip of a wedge of sediment several kilometres thick.

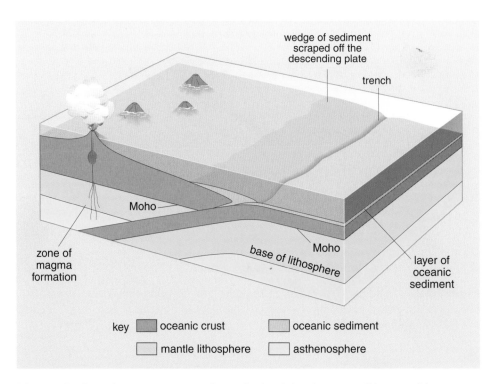

Figure 8.12   The components of a typical subduction zone illustrated in a block diagram. Although not drawn to scale, the diagram represents a region about 150 km high, 500 km long and 100 km wide.

You observed previously that explosive volcanoes tend to be found near ocean trenches rather than at mid-ocean ridges (Section 4.3). The relatively high water content of the magma required to cause an explosive eruption is critical here and is linked to the subduction process itself. The descending oceanic lithosphere carries water into the mantle at the subduction zone, so when this mantle melts to produce magma, the magma contains a lot of water. Being at great depth and therefore under high pressure, the water stays dissolved within the liquid magma. But when the magmas rise to high levels in the crust the water escapes from the magma (as steam), producing dangerously explosive volcanic eruptions. The magmas can also solidify as intrusive igneous rocks within the crust, and may release metal-rich fluids into cracks, fissures and veins underground, to form ore deposits. Many of the large copper, tin and gold deposits in the Andes were formed in this way.

You will now broaden your view of subduction zones and consider what happens when continental lithosphere is attached to oceanic lithosphere that is

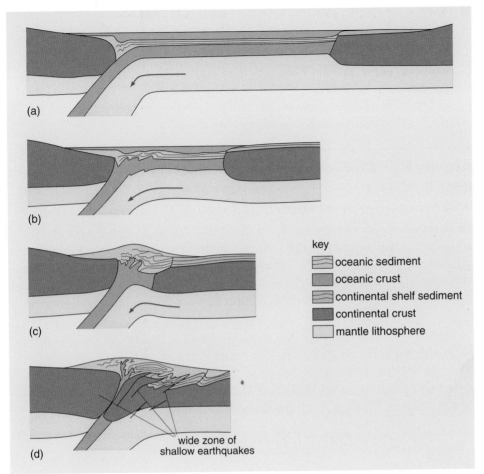

Figure 8.13   The sequence of events, seen in cross-section, that starts with subduction of oceanic lithosphere (a) and ends with the collision of two blocks of continental lithosphere, forming a continent/continent convergent plate boundary. Note that the sedimentary layers are part of the crust.

key

oceanic sediment

oceanic crust

continental shelf sediment

continental crust

mantle lithosphere

wide zone of shallow earthquakes

subducting under another continent. This is the situation shown in Figure 8.13a. As subduction proceeds, the ocean that lies between the continents becomes narrower (Figure 8.13b). Eventually all the oceanic lithosphere is consumed (Figure 8.13c) and the two continental masses collide (Figure 8.13d). This produces the third type of convergent boundary – the type where two plates of continental lithosphere are on opposite sides of the boundary.

The continents crumple together and subduction stops because the continents have a sufficiently low density to remain buoyant; they remain floating at the surface rather than sinking into the mantle. Fragments of oceanic lithosphere can be trapped in the collision and the colliding continents become buckled into a major mountain belt (Figure 8.13d) where oceanic sedimentary rock may be elevated to the tops of mountains. The faulting that accompanies the collision generates earthquakes, but not volcanoes. This is the series of events that led to the Himalayan Mountains and the broad region of shallow- and intermediate-focus earthquakes across Tibet shown in Figure 8.10c. The crumpled and thickened crust provides the deep burial and heating required to recrystallise the rocks, so metamorphism occurs in the deep roots of mountain belts formed by continental collision.

■ Look at the map of plate boundaries (Figure 8.4) and Figure 2.3 to see if you can identify one other convergent plate boundary where colliding continents have produced a mountain belt along the plate boundary.

☐ Collision of the Arabian Plate with the Eurasian Plate is associated with the mountain belt running northwest to southeast from Turkey to the Gulf of Oman (the Zagros Mountains). This plate boundary is characterised by shallow-focus earthquakes. Volcanoes are absent.

Activity 8.3   Compare and contrast different types of convergent plate boundary

We expect this activity will take you approximately 45 minutes.

There are three types of convergent plate boundary, depending on the types of lithosphere at the boundary. In this activity, you will write a brief account to compare and contrast these three types of convergent plate boundary. It will consolidate your understanding of this topic, as well as providing practice in producing a short account in which you make comparisons and contrasts between different things.

Note the 'compare and contrast'. This is different from being asked to 'describe' or 'explain'. It is very important to do what you've been asked to do in a question (and not doing so is a frequent cause of substantial loss of marks in assessments). 'Describe', 'explain', 'compare', 'contrast' are sometimes known as 'process words', and others include 'criticise', 'define', 'illustrate', 'discuss'. They all have (sometimes subtly) different meanings. Typical definitions of compare and contrast are:

compare – give an account of the extent of similarities between two (or more) items, referring to both (all) of them throughout.

contrast – give an account of the extent of differences between two (or more) items, referring to both (all) of them throughout.

So on this occasion you need to look for similarities and differences between the three types of convergent boundary. This is not quite the same as what you did in Activity 5.2 and Activity 8.1. There you simply put information about different features into a table, but here you need to point out explicitly the ways in which the plate boundaries are similar to each other and the ways in which they are different. However, you might find it helpful to start by producing a table with three rows, one for each type of convergent boundary, and with different features noted in each column. You can then use this information as you write up an account with a logical flow, probably concentrating on one feature (e.g. the presence or absence of earthquakes) at a time. You should discuss surface features, earthquakes and volcanic activity, and should aim for an account that is about 200 words long.

When you have completed your account, compare it with the example given in the comments on this activity at the end of this book.

8.7   Transform fault plate boundary processes

Transform fault plate boundaries occur when plates slide past each other in opposite directions, causing shallow earthquakes, but without creating or destroying lithosphere and without generating volcanoes. The San Andreas

Fault, illustrated in Figures 3.3 and 3.5, is one example. It involves part of California (on the Pacific Plate) sliding northwest along the fault past the rest of North America (on the North American Plate). There are potentially three types of transform faults: those that link a convergent boundary with a divergent boundary, two divergent boundaries and those that link two convergent boundaries. Figure 8.14 shows an example of each type.

Are there real-life examples of these plate boundaries? Transform faults linking two divergent boundaries, as in Figure 8.14a, are the most common, and account for the displacements between adjacent segments of mid-ocean ridges seen in Figure 2.3. For example, the Cocos–Nazca Ridge (also known as the Galápagos Spreading Center) is a divergent plate boundary that is split into several segments by transform faults (Figure 8.15). Transform faults associated with subduction zones are much less common, but a real example of the situation sketched in Figure 8.14b occurs at the eastern end of the Cocos–Nazca Ridge. Here, a heavily faulted seismic zone delineates a transform fault (the Panama Fracture Zone) connecting a divergent boundary (the eastern end of the Costa Rica Rift, which is the easternmost part of the Cocos–Nazca Ridge) with the eastern end of a convergent boundary (the Middle America Trench). An example of a transform fault linking two convergent boundaries passes through New Zealand (Figure 8.4).

It was stated previously that plate tectonics provides a comprehensive explanation of many diverse aspects of the Earth, such as its surface features, earthquakes, volcanism and certain mineral deposits. Figure 8.16 is a summary of all three

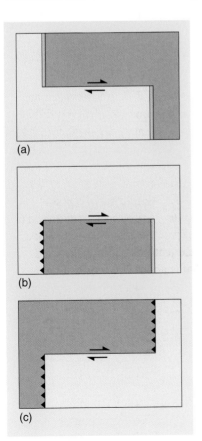

(a)

(b)

(c)

Figure 8.14   Sketches of three types of transform fault plate boundary. The single-headed arrows give the relative sense of movement on either side of the transform fault; other symbols used are the conventional ones for a divergent boundary (double lines) and convergent boundary (barbs). (a) Transform fault linking two divergent boundaries. (b) Transform fault linking convergent and divergent boundaries. (c) Transform fault linking two convergent boundaries.

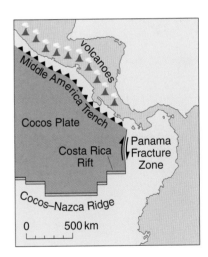

Figure 8.15   Map of plate boundaries around the eastern parts of the Cocos Plate, in the eastern Pacific Ocean near Central America. For simplicity, plate boundaries east of the Panama Fracture Zone (see Figure 8.4) have been omitted.

plate boundaries. To illustrate the success of plate tectonics in accounting for several aspects of the active Earth, Figure 8.17 illustrates how a great many of the features associated with the Pacific coast of western North America can be

Figure 8.16   Diagram showing the three major types of plate boundary.

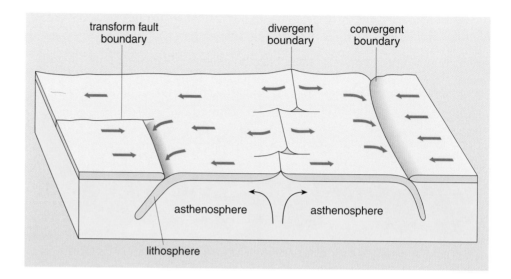

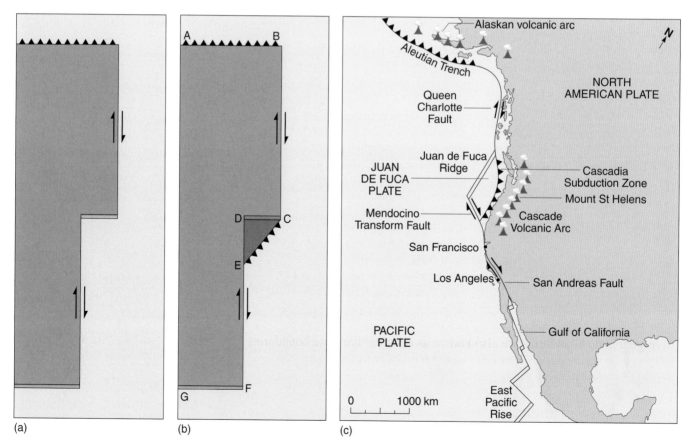

Figure 8.17   (a) Sketch of a plate boundary system. (b) Sketch of a plate boundary system similar to (a), which corresponds to the plate tectonics of western North America summarised in (c).

explained by plate tectonics. As a starting point, consider the plate boundaries in Figure 8.17a. This shows a transform fault linking a subduction zone with a divergent boundary, which is in turn linked to a second divergent boundary by another transform fault.

■ How many plates are present in Figure 8.17a?

☐ Two. Relative to the pink (paler shaded) plate, the purple (darker shaded) plate is moving towards the top of the page. (One way of visualising this is to cut a sheet of paper into the approximately 'P' shape defined by the plate boundaries, and to slide the left-hand plate past the right-hand plate. Spaces will open up in the positions of the divergent boundaries, and subduction will occur along the convergent boundary.)

With the addition of a small subduction zone (Figure 8.17b), this sketch contains all the essential elements of the plate-tectonic situation in western North America (Figure 8.17c).

Question 8.8

Name the features in Figure 8.17c that correspond to the following plate boundaries in Figure 8.17b: AB; BC; CD; EF; FG.

8.8   Summary of Chapter 8

The Earth's outer rigid layer, the lithosphere, is about 100 km thick. It overlies the weaker asthenosphere. The lithosphere is divided by seismic zones into fragments called plates. Plate tectonics is a theory that describes how plates interact and move. It incorporates the theory of sea-floor spreading and provides an explanation for continental drift.

There are three types of plate boundary, distinguished by the direction of relative motion between two plates. Divergent plate boundaries occur where plates are moving away from each other, and are found at mid-ocean ridges. Convergent plate boundaries occur where two plates are moving towards each other, and are characterised by an ocean trench and island arc, or an ocean trench and line of volcanoes along the edge of a continent, or a mountain belt. Transform fault plate boundaries occur where two plates move past each other in opposite directions.

The speeds of relative plate motion range from 10 to 200 mm y^{-1}.

Divergent plate boundaries are also known as constructive plate boundaries because new oceanic lithosphere is created here by the process of sea-floor spreading. The composition and structure of oceanic lithosphere can be discovered from several lines of evidence. These include seismological evidence for a layered lithosphere, including a crust of about 7 km thickness which is itself layered. Rock samples obtained by dredging and drilling indicate that oceanic crust comprises a thin layer of sediment overlying a layer of basaltic lavas overlying a sheeted dyke complex overlying gabbro.

The composition of all the igneous rocks in oceanic crust is basaltic; they differ only in their grain size, reflecting differences in the rate of magma cooling and the manner of emplacement. Basaltic magma is generated in the mantle beneath mid-ocean ridges (divergent plate boundaries) and rises into the crust. Within the crust it may cool slowly to form gabbro or may be transported in dykes to the ocean floor where it erupts to form lava. Sea-floor spreading generates new oceanic lithosphere by the injection of basaltic magmas into existing oceanic lithosphere at mid-ocean ridges.

Oceanic lithosphere is destroyed by subduction at a convergent plate boundary, also known as a destructive plate boundary. Subduction produces a deep ocean trench, a Wadati–Benioff zone of earthquake foci dipping beneath the overriding plate, and a volcanic arc above the Wadati–Benioff zone where explosive volcanic eruptions occur and metal-rich ore deposits may be formed. Subduction occurs when dense oceanic lithosphere sinks into the mantle. Continental lithosphere is not subducted because it is too buoyant to sink into the mantle.

Where two pieces of continental lithosphere collide at a convergent plate boundary, they produce a mountain belt. This is associated with shallow earthquakes but no volcanism; an example is the Himalayas.

Plates slide past each other at transform fault boundaries, producing shallow earthquakes but no volcanic activity. Transform faults are commonly associated with mid-ocean ridges, where they cut the ridge at right angles, linking ridge sections. Transform faults also occur on land; for example, the North American Plate slides southeast past the Pacific Plate along the San Andreas Fault in California.

In studying this chapter, you have increased your knowledge of the Earth, and gained experience in writing a short account comparing and contrasting different things (types of plate boundary). You have also used tables to summarise information.

Chapter 9
Plate movement and Earth history

Having found out that the plates *are* moving, this chapter aims to find out *why* the plates are moving – what drives their motion? Important clues that will lead to an answer to this question come from the speeds at which different plates move over the Earth's interior, and from certain volcanoes that are found in the middle of plates, for example those of Hawaii.

This chapter also investigates how the theory of plate tectonics helps us to understand the Earth as it is today and, because it describes how the Earth's oceans and continents slowly change over time, how plate tectonics can also be used to learn about the Earth in the past and indeed, possibly, in the future.

9.1   The Hawaiian hot spot

Situated in the middle of the Pacific Plate, the Hawaiian Islands are a popular tourist destination and home to some of the world's most intensively studied volcanoes. In Figure 2.3 the Hawaiian Islands are a cluster of barely discernable dots in the middle of the Pacific Ocean, but they are no mere specks of volcanic rock. The highest point on the largest island (the Big Island) is 4.2 km above sea level, making its height above the ocean floor (9–10 km) greater than the height Mt Everest is above sea level. The volume of the Big Island is a staggering 10^5 km^3. All of the Hawaiian Islands have been produced by basaltic volcanism but only the Big Island is still active and growing in size.

What can be made of this volcanism, situated in a plate interior, some 4000 km from the nearest plate boundary? After all, plate tectonics seems to do such a good job of explaining why volcanoes occur at plate boundaries. Does this mean that the plate-tectonics theory has failed, and that Earth scientists need to start again and come up with something better? The good news is that plate tectonics still stands, but to explain the volcanoes of Hawaii requires something extra – the mantle under Hawaii must be unusually hot in order to cause the melting needed to supply the volcanoes with basaltic magma. An anomalously hot zone such as this is called a **hot spot**. Hot spots are attributed to plumes of hot material upwelling from great depths in the Earth, probably from the bottom of the mantle. Other hot-spot volcanoes are dotted around the world (Figure 9.1); most of them are found far from plate boundaries but some, such as Iceland, coincide with divergent plate boundaries. This is probably coincidence since plumes are derived from the deep mantle, whereas plate boundaries are surface features; as plates move, some boundaries are inevitably in the path of ascending plumes.

Hawaii is part of a chain of islands and submarine mountain peaks (called seamounts) stretching almost 6000 km across the northwest Pacific, making the prominent 'L'-shaped feature that you noted in Figure 2.3 and in Section 2.2.3. Like Hawaii itself, these islands and seamounts are made of basaltic volcanic rocks. But, unlike Hawaii's Big Island, they are extinct volcanoes, and the ages of some are shown in Figure 9.2a.

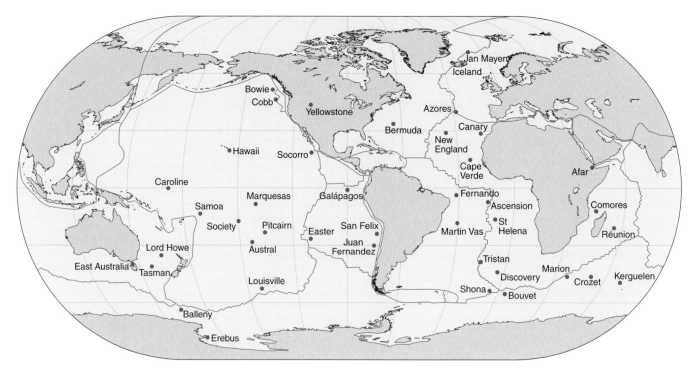

Figure 9.1   The global distribution of hot spots. Names are given for reference only; don't attempt to remember them all. Plate boundaries are shown as blue lines.

■   Do the ages of the extinct volcanoes show any relationship to their locations?

☐   Yes. The farther away from Hawaii, the older the volcanism.

To see this relationship more clearly, all the available data can be plotted on a graph of age versus distance along the chain, and this is done in Figure 9.2b.

Question 9.1

(a)   Use the best-fit straight line in Figure 9.2b to estimate the average rate at which volcanic activity has appeared to move along the Hawaiian–Emperor chain. Express your answer in mm y^{-1} to two significant figures.

(b)   In which direction has this movement been?

Your answers to Question 9.1 should lead you to expect that future volcanic islands will be built up to the southeast of Hawaii. Indeed, the foundations of the next island in the Hawaiian chain are already in place. About 30 km south of Hawaii lies a conical submarine mountain (Loihi), with volcanic craters and hot-water vents at its summit.

But, fascinating as these volcanoes are, how do they relate to plate movements?

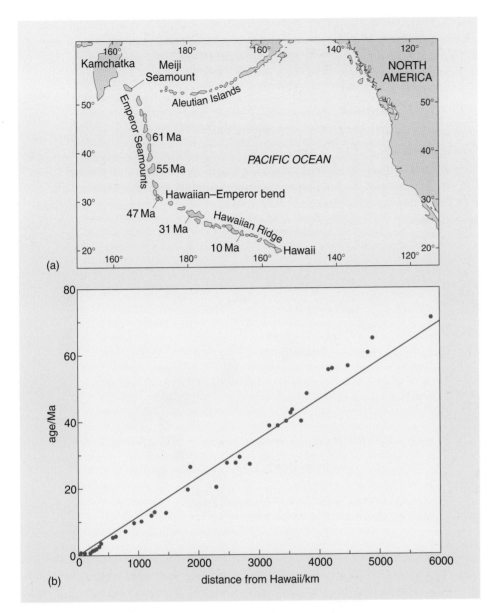

Figure 9.2 (a) The Hawaiian–Emperor chain extends from Hawaii to the Meiji Seamount off Kamchatka. The ages of selected islands and seamounts are indicated in millions of years. (b) Graph of age versus distance from Hawaii measured along the Hawaii–Emperor chain, and the best-fit straight line through the data.

9.2   Hot-spot trails and absolute plate motion

The trail of volcanoes along the Hawaiian Ridge could be caused by a hot spot moving beneath a stationary Pacific Plate, or by the plate moving over a static hot spot. It is not immediately obvious how these two possibilities can be distinguished. However, there are other hot spots beneath the Pacific Plate, and the chains of extinct volcanoes that they have produced are similar in shape and age progression to the Hawaiian chain (Figure 2.3). The simplest explanation of this is that all the hot spots are more or less fixed in place and the Pacific Plate moves over them. If each hot spot was moving independently, you would expect to find that each volcanic chain had a different shape or age progression. Thus, hot spots can be considered as fixed markers in the interior of the Earth. This is a very useful result because it allows the rates of plate motion relative to the interior to be found from the age progression along hot-spot trails.

One way of visualising the movement of the Pacific Plate over the Hawaiian hot spot is to imagine a sheet of paper moving over a candle flame (Figure 9.3). The candle flame singes the moving paper, leaving a trail of scorch marks that records the past positions of the hot flame. The marks furthest from the flame are the oldest and the paper has moved in the direction from the youngest to the oldest scorch mark.

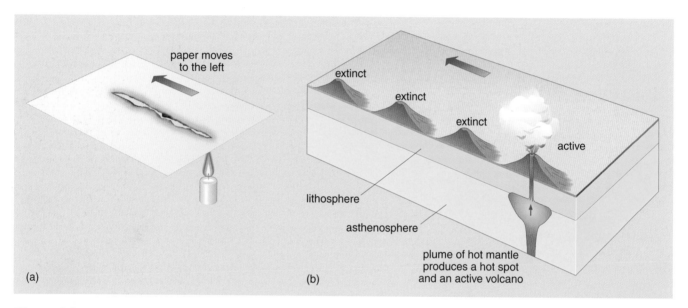

Figure 9.3   A sheet of paper moving over a flame (a) is analogous to a lithospheric plate moving over a hot spot (b).

■ If the Hawaiian hot spot is stationary and the Pacific Plate moves over it, then which one of the following two statements is correct?

(a) The Pacific Plate is moving northwest at 86 mm y^{-1} with respect to the Hawaiian hot spot.

(b) The Pacific Plate is moving southeast at 86 mm y^{-1} with respect to the Hawaiian hot spot.

☐ Statement (a) is the correct one, as can be verified by considering the candle-and-paper analogy.

■ The Hawaiian–Emperor chain has a bend, or kink, in it (Figure 9.2a). What do you think has caused this?

☐ Because the hot-spot trail records the direction of plate movement, a change in the direction of the trail (at the Hawaiian–Emperor bend) signifies a change in the direction of plate motion.

Thus, the Pacific Plate must have changed from moving north to moving northwest at the time of the bend, about 43 Ma ago.

When the age progressions along other hot-spot trails are worked out, the speeds and directions of plate motion relative to the fixed frame of reference given by the hot spots are found to be as shown in Figure 9.4. So you can see now that there are two ways of considering the rates at which the plates are moving. In Figure 8.4 it was shown how one plate moves relative to its neighbour, whereas Figure 9.4 shows how each plate moves relative to the interior of the Earth. The latter motions are called **absolute plate motions** because they do not rely on describing how a plate moves relative to something (another plate) that is itself moving.

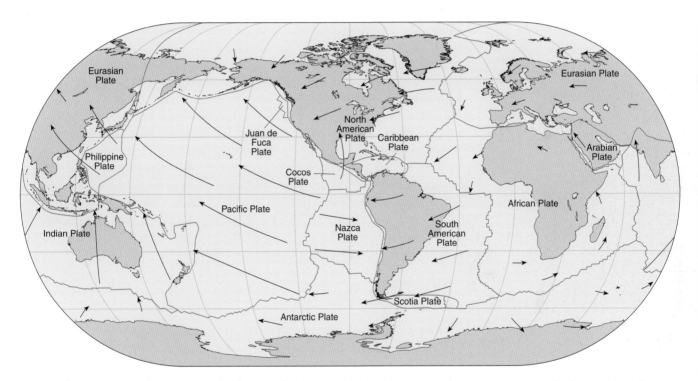

Figure 9.4   Present-day motion of lithospheric plates relative to hot spots (absolute plate motion) are shown by the arrows. These indicate the amount of movement that would occur in 50 Ma; the longer the arrow, the faster the speed.

To appreciate the confusion that can arise from considering relative plate motions, look at the relative plate motion on the southern Mid-Atlantic Ridge in Figure 8.4. The sea-floor spreading rates indicate that Africa is moving eastwards; but if you were standing on the Central Indian Ridge, Africa would appear to be moving to the west! This confusion is avoided if the static interior of the Earth is taken as the viewing point, allowing an absolute speed for each plate to be defined. It is these absolute speeds that can provide clues as to what determines how fast a plate moves.

Question 9.2

Which plate has the fastest absolute speeds, and which plate has the slowest absolute speeds?

9.3   Speed limits for plates

Why don't all plates have the same absolute speeds? There are a number of factors that can cause plates to move and other factors that can retard motion, with different speeds arising because the relative importance of these factors varies from plate to plate. To decide what these factors might be, consider first why oceanic lithosphere subducts.

The lithosphere floats on the asthenosphere because its mean density is less than that of the asthenosphere. This is because the crustal lithosphere contains many rock types that are less dense than the peridotite in the asthenosphere. However, the density of oceanic lithosphere also depends on how cold it is, and this depends on how old it is. Because oceanic lithosphere is produced by igneous activity at mid-ocean ridges, it is relatively hot when formed. But it cools gradually over many millions of years as sea-floor spreading carries it far from the mid-ocean ridge. As it cools, it becomes denser, and scientists are agreed that the subducting portion of oceanic lithosphere is slightly denser than the asthenosphere. (The reason that subduction starts in the first place has not yet been resolved. What is more certain is that once subduction has started, it will keep going.) Thus at least one factor contributing to plate motion could be the sinking of the denser subducting slab into the mantle, which pulls the rest of the plate with it – an effect called **slab pull**.

■ Can slab pull be the only factor causing plates to move? (*Hint*: are all moving plates attached to subducting slabs of lithosphere?)

☐ Plates such as the Antarctic and North American Plates have no subducting parts (see Figure 8.4), yet they are moving, so there must be some additional factor.

A factor associated with divergent, rather than convergent, plate boundaries is provided by the lithosphere sliding off the raised ridge – this is **ridge slide**. Counteracting these driving forces is the frictional **drag** acting on the underside of the plate (Figure 9.5). You can model these three effects by using a sheet of paper, as shown in Figure 9.6. A sheet of paper on a smooth table top provides a model of a lithospheric plate on the asthenosphere. If the paper is nudged gently along the table (Figure 9.6a), the paper will slow down and come to a halt because of the frictional drag between the table and the paper. This is analogous to the drag that acts to slow down the motion of lithospheric plates as they slide over the asthenosphere. To keep the plate moving, something must continue to drive it.

If the paper is allowed to hang over the edge of the table, analogous to a lithospheric plate subducting, then the weight of the 'slab' will pull the rest of the paper with it when there is insufficient paper in contact with the table for the drag to stop the motion (Figure 9.6b). This demonstrates the slab-pull effect.

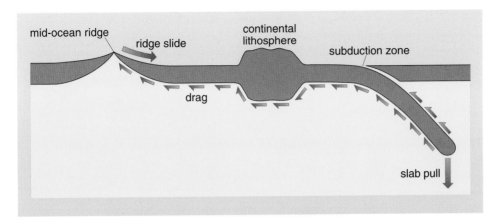

Figure 9.5 A schematic cross-section of a lithospheric plate, labelled with the effects that cause the lithospheric plate to move over the asthenosphere and the drag that retards motion.

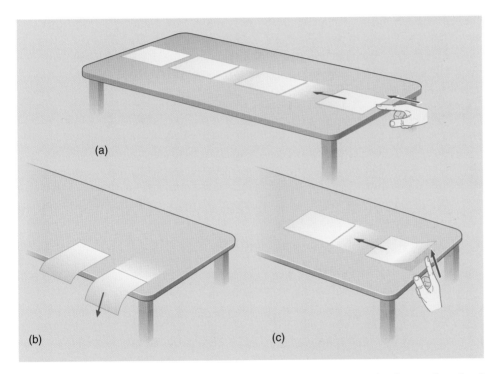

Figure 9.6 A sheet of paper moving over a table illustrates the factors involved when a lithospheric plate moves over the asthenosphere: (a) drag on the base of the plate; (b) slab pull; (c) ridge slide.

Ridge slide can be modelled by raising one end of the paper above the table to simulate the elevation of the oceanic lithosphere at a mid-ocean ridge. Given sufficient elevation, the paper slides over the table, just as a lithospheric plate might slide over the asthenosphere (Figure 9.6c).

To test whether these factors account for the motion of plates, consider how they might be expected to influence the absolute speeds of plates and then check those expectations against the available evidence from Figure 9.4. For example, if slab pull is important in causing a plate to move quickly, then you would expect to find that for fast-moving plates a large proportion of their outer edge would be undergoing subduction. Similarly, if ridge slide is important, then plates with a divergent plate boundary along one side should move rapidly.

Question 9.3

By comparing Figures 9.4 and 8.4, decide which of the following attributes describe (a) the plate with the fastest absolute speeds, and (b) the plate with the slowest absolute speeds:

1   The plate contains a large area of continental lithosphere.

2   The margins of the plate are attached to a subducting slab.

3   There is a divergent plate boundary on one side of the plate.

From the evidence, it appears that plates attached to subducting slabs do indeed move relatively rapidly, and plates with divergent boundaries also move rapidly, confirming slab pull and ridge slide as important driving factors. On the other hand, the low speeds of plates carrying continental lithosphere suggest that these exert a large drag, perhaps because the continental lithosphere is especially thick (as indicated in Figure 9.5) and this slows the plate's movement over the asthenosphere.

Although slab pull, ridge slide and continental drag can account for the main features of plate motion, this is not the whole story. There are additional effects at work such as the resistance where plates grind past each other at transform fault boundaries and where plates collide. There are also suggestions that the rocks in the mantle are sufficiently hot to be constantly flowing as a result of convection and that this gradual movement drags on the base of plates, contributing to their motion.

9.4   Plate tectonics and Earth history

The theory of plate tectonics helps us to understand the Earth's surface as it is today and, because it accounts for how the Earth's oceans and continents slowly change over time, it can also be used to interpret events in the Earth's past. The theory of sea-floor spreading, and the age of oceanic crust from ocean drilling, have shown us that the oceanic crust is relatively young (all less than about 180 Ma old; see Figure 9.7) in comparison with the 4600 Ma age of the Earth.

The continents are on average much older than the oceans, and include rocks up to almost 4000 Ma old. The difference in ages between continental crust and the younger oceanic crust is due to differences in how they form, and in the case of oceanic crust, how it is destroyed. As you saw in Section 8.5, new oceanic crust is formed at mid-ocean ridges (divergent plate boundaries), then spreads away from the ridge, before finally being subducted back into the mantle at subduction zones. Most oceanic crust exists only for a (geologically) short time before being recycled back into the mantle. This means that there is no very old oceanic crust around (with the exception of small pieces preserved on the continents).

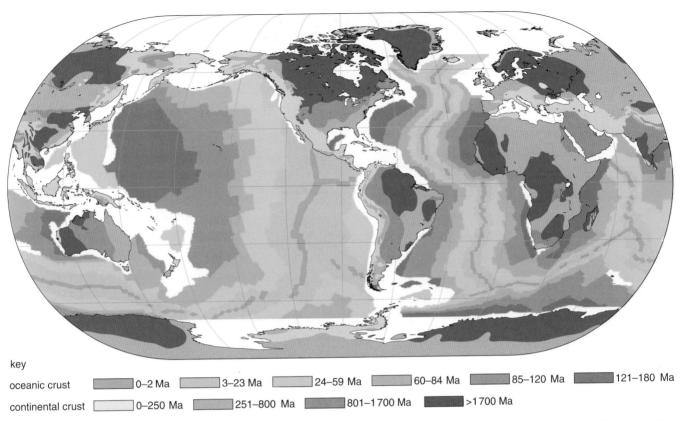

key

oceanic crust   ☐ 0–2 Ma   ☐ 3–23 Ma   ☐ 24–59 Ma   ☐ 60–84 Ma   ☐ 85–120 Ma   ☐ 121–180 Ma

continental crust   ☐ 0–250 Ma   ☐ 251–800 Ma   ☐ 801–1 700 Ma   ☐ >1 700 Ma

Figure 9.7 The ages of the oceanic and continental crust. The white areas are where data are too poor for accurate ages to be determined.

Continents are different – very old continental rocks are still around today. Continents can be eroded, and may change their shape by splitting or colliding, but they tend to be preserved. This is fortunate for Earth scientists, as it allows the Earth to be studied back to an early stage in its history. Later in this section, the continental crust, and how it has developed, will be considered, but first a more detailed look at the oceans.

9.4.1 The cycle of oceanic lithosphere creation and destruction

Although there is no oceanic lithosphere older than 180 Ma, individual oceans may be older. The Pacific Ocean, for example, first came into existence about 300 Ma ago. The oldest parts of the Pacific oceanic lithosphere have now been subducted, but it is known the ocean existed 300 Ma ago through various geological clues that have been left. For example, the tiny Juan de Fuca Plate in the northeast Pacific (Figures 8.2 and 8.17c) is the final remnant of a much larger and older oceanic plate that has been (and is still being) subducted beneath North America. At present, the Pacific Ocean is closing (reducing in size), but it will probably take another 200 Ma or so to vanish completely, so the overall lifetime of the Pacific Ocean could be about 500 Ma. If this is a fairly typical age for a large ocean, then there has been time in the Earth's history for many cycles of ocean creation and destruction.

The relationship between plate tectonics and the ocean cycle can be explored by considering a very much simplified model of the Earth. Figure 9.8a is a cross-section through this model with two oceans, separated by two continents. Ocean AD (i.e. the ocean between points A and D) has a spreading mid-ocean ridge, and is expanding. Ocean BC has subduction zones at both edges as well as a spreading ridge. Overall, because ocean AD is expanding, and because the model Earth must stay the same size, it follows that ocean BC must be contracting. At a later time (Figure 9.8b) the spreading ridge in ocean BC has been subducted and the ocean BC is now contracting faster than in Figure 9.8a.

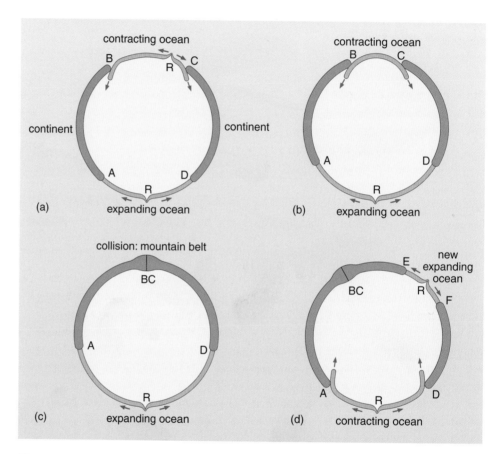

Figure 9.8   The ocean cycle. (a) Initially, both oceans have spreading mid-ocean ridges, R, and ocean BC has subduction zones at B and C. Ocean AD is expanding and ocean BC is contracting. (b) At a later time, the ridge in ocean BC has been subducted. (c) Later, the ocean BC has closed completely. (d) Later still, subduction has started in ocean AD and a new ocean EF has opened, splitting the continent.

■ Will the spreading rate of the ridge in ocean AD have changed (if the subduction rates do not change) between Figure 9.8a and Figure 9.8b?

☐ Yes; as ocean BC is contracting faster in Figure 9.8b, ocean AD must expand faster, so the ridge will have a higher spreading rate.

Figure 9.8c shows the situation at a later stage. Ocean BC has closed completely, and the continents have collided to form a mountain belt. There is now only one large continent (a 'supercontinent') and one large ocean.

■   What will happen to the spreading rate of ocean AD at this stage?

☐   The collision of the two continents will reduce their speed of convergence or even stop it, and so the spreading rate of ocean AD will reduce to match.

There are a number of different scenarios that could happen after this; one of them is shown in Figure 9.8d. The ocean AD, which had very old, cold and therefore dense lithosphere at its edges, has developed subduction zones at each edge, and is contracting. It will eventually close up completely, like ocean BC did. Because ocean AD is now contracting, spreading must start somewhere else to maintain the size of the model Earth. This is happening where the supercontinent has split, forming two new continents, AE and FD, separated by a new expanding ocean, EF.

Question 9.4

Draw, in the style of Figure 9.8, an alternative stage (d), where the supercontinent AD has not split apart.

The ocean cycle shown in Figure 9.8 is an illustration of one of the fundamental deductions from plate-tectonic theory that geological processes on one part of the Earth can affect processes a long distance away, on, or at the margins of, other plates. For example, the closure of ocean BC can cause a different ocean, AD, to stop expanding, develop subduction zones and begin to contract.

Question 9.5

Figure 9.9 is a simplified cross-section of the Earth at the present day, approximately through the Tropic of Capricorn (23.5° S), showing the continents and oceans, drawn in the same style as Figure 9.8 but without the mid-ocean ridges and subduction zones marked. Draw ridges and subduction zones on the cross-section, using information from this section and Figures 2.6 and 8.4, mark each ocean as 'expanding' or 'contracting', and name each ocean, mid-ocean ridge and trench.

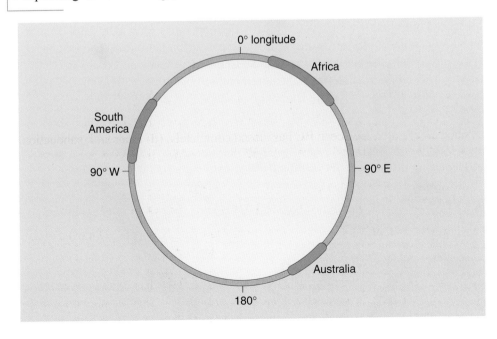

Figure 9.9   For use with Question 9.5.

9.4.2   Plate tectonics and the global increase of continental crust

You have seen that plate tectonics, and in particular sea-floor spreading, is responsible for the origin and growth of oceanic lithosphere (Section 8.5). And plate tectonics is responsible for the destruction of oceanic lithosphere through subduction, resulting in a relatively 'young' ocean floor and the operation of a cycle of ocean formation and destruction.

Plate tectonics also plays a role in the growth of continental crust but, as you will see, the history of the continents is different from that of the oceans. The first evidence of this is the much greater age of the continents (see Figure 9.7). A second indication is that a wide range of igneous, sedimentary and metamorphic rocks are present on the continents, in contrast to the essentially igneous oceanic crust. Together these indicate that the processes that form and destroy continental crust must be very different from those that form and destroy oceanic crust.

Continents can be considered to grow in two ways – by addition of new material from a different part of the Earth such as the mantle or the oceanic lithosphere, and by rearrangement of existing continental material.

New material can be added in two ways:

1   By igneous activity at subduction zones (Section 8.6). The continental crust of South America, for example, with volcanoes and intrusive igneous rocks along its western side, is increasing in volume, because magma from the mantle is being added to the overlying crust.

2   By the incorporation of oceanic lithosphere into continents (Figure 8.13d).

The processes through which existing continental material gets redistributed and rearranged are many and sometimes complex. For example, two continents can collide, forming a larger continent (Figure 8.13d). Continents can also grow not just by the collision of two substantial continents to give a larger continent, but by processes that add smaller areas onto continents. One of these processes is illustrated in Figure 9.10. Consider what will happen to a plate with both oceanic and continental lithosphere, with the oceanic part being subducted beneath an island arc. When the continent reaches the island arc, the arc and continent collide, and subduction stops, as the continent will not subduct beneath the arc because of its low density. The island arc is added to the edge of the continent so the continent increases in size (Figure 9.10b). This process is called **island-arc accretion**. The formation of western North America, for example, involved accretion of a number of island arcs that originally existed in an ancient Pacific Ocean and collided with the continent along convergent plate boundaries.

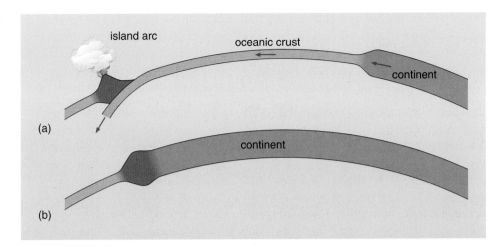

Figure 9.10   Island-arc accretion. (a) Oceanic lithosphere is being subducted at an island arc. The plate with this oceanic lithosphere also has continental lithosphere. (b) When the continent reaches the subduction zone, the arc and continent collide forming a larger continent.

So continental crust can be re-organised by plate tectonics, but continental material can also be redistributed by sedimentary processes. Consider what happens to continents when they are weathered and eroded by the action of wind, water or ice. The products are rock and mineral fragments and dissolved material that may end up either as new sedimentary rock on land or on the ocean floor. The new rock on land is still part of the continent, so it doesn't add material to the continental crust. How about the ocean-floor sediments, which are now part of the oceanic crust? The oceanic crust is recycled into the mantle at subduction zones, but much of the sediment is scraped off the descending oceanic plate, onto the upper continental plate, a process called **subduction-zone accretion** (Section 8.6 and Figure 8.13). This process adds oceanic sediment to the margin of an island arc or a continent. Although this creates 'new' continental crust at a particular locality, the materials involved are not new but were derived from existing continental crust – so subduction-zone accretion recycles continental crust.

Are there any processes that can remove continental crust, similar to the subduction of oceanic crust back into the mantle?

Unlike the oceanic lithosphere, very little continental crust is recycled into the mantle.

■   Why is continental crust prevented from being subducted when it reaches a subduction zone?

☐   Continental crust is less dense than the mantle (Section 8.6), so large volumes are too buoyant to be subducted.

Despite this, some of the sediment on the ocean floor (originally from the continents) is subducted with the igneous oceanic crust into the mantle. So it *is* possible to destroy at least some of the continental crust (after its erosion and deposition as oceanic sediment) by subduction.

Now consider the balance between the rate of creation of new continental crust by volcanic activity at subduction zones and the rate of destruction by subduction of sediment. If those rates were equal, the total amount of continental crust would not change. Most Earth scientists believe that more continental crust is being created than destroyed, so the amount of continental crust is increasing with time.

This does not necessarily imply that individual continents are growing. Some are, by the processes that have just been described, but others are in the process of splitting into smaller continents. To find an example of this, you need to look on Figure 8.4 for a mid-ocean ridge in a narrow ocean separating two continents, or parts of continents, to find areas where sea-floor spreading has recently started. The best example is the split between Africa and Arabia, occupied by the Red Sea. Another is the split of Baja California from the rest of Mexico (southwest North America).

It is worth remembering that all types of continental growth – from the joining of two large continents, to subduction-zone volcanism, subduction-zone accretion and island-arc accretion – and continental destruction are caused by plate tectonics. An Earth without plate tectonics would be very different indeed.

9.4.3   Plate motion in the past and future

Having studied the cycle of ocean creation and destruction (Section 9.4.1) and the growth and recycling of continental crust (Section 9.4.2), this knowledge can now be applied to investigate the plate-tectonic history of the Earth, with its past continents and oceans. Predictions can also be made about what will happen to present-day plates in the future.

The recognition of present-day plate boundaries, and measurement of the rates of absolute and relative present plate motion, are relatively straightforward, using earthquakes, volcanoes, hot spots and the Earth's major surface features. But how can we find out about plates in the past? The main evidence of a present-day plate boundary – earthquakes – does not generally produce features that are preserved in older rocks. However, the evidence from ancient climates and marine magnetic anomalies (Section 7.3) can be used to determine the position of continents or plates in the past.

As well as determining the past position of plates, it is also possible to predict what will happen to plates in the future – at least for the (geologically) near future of a hundred million years or so. The starting point for these predictions is present plate motion, which is known fairly accurately (Figure 8.4). Predictions for too far in the future, or in too much detail, are subject to greater uncertainty. Because the movement of any one plate is severely constrained by the movements of all the others, a major change in the direction or rate of motion of one plate (caused, for example, by a continental collision) usually causes the pattern of motion of plates to be rearranged globally (as in Figure 9.8, for example) into one of a number of different possibilities (Question 9.4). Several such rearrangements have occurred in the past. An exact prediction of what will happen cannot be made – only possibilities can be suggested. Predictions for the future are not certain: they are just best estimates based on the present data.

Question 9.6

Los Angeles, on the western side of the San Andreas Fault, is part of the Pacific Plate, and San Francisco, on the eastern side, is part of the North American Plate (Figure 8.17c). The cities are about 560 km apart at present but are moving together as the plates slide past each other. The relative speed of movement of the two plates along the fault is about 20 mm y^{-1}. At this present rate, how long will it take for Los Angeles to become a suburb of San Francisco?

9.5   Summary of Chapter 9

Certain volcanoes, such as those on Hawaii, are not associated with plate-boundary processes; instead they are formed from a rising plume of deep-mantle material – a hot spot. These plumes remain stationary, while plates move over them, creating a line of volcanoes that become older in the direction of absolute plate motion. The age of each volcano gives the time it was over the mantle plume, and allows the plate's absolute rate of movement over the asthenosphere to be calculated. Kinks in hot-spot island chains are evidence for past changes in the direction of absolute plate motion.

A world map of absolute plate motions reveals some slowly moving plates (Eurasian and African) and other fast-moving ones (Pacific and Indian).

The main factors responsible for plate motion are slab pull and ridge slide, and the main resistance to plate motion is the drag on the base of the plate, particularly beneath thick continental lithosphere.

All of the oceanic crust is less than 180 Ma old. There is no older oceanic crust still in existence as it has been recycled into the mantle by subduction. Continental crust is up to 4000 Ma old. It grows by volcanic activity at subduction zones and by incorporation of oceanic crust into continental crust at collision zones. The amount of continental crust on the Earth is increasing with time. Individual continents can increase in size by subduction-zone accretion and island-arc accretion, as well as by continental collision.

Plate movement has created and destroyed oceans; created supercontinents and also split them. Some countries or continents have moved large distances, changing latitude and climate.

Chapter 10
Plate tectonics and the whole Earth

Much of this book, so far, has been about plate tectonics and the processes by which the Earth's lithospheric plates are created, destroyed and interact with each other. This chapter gives the opportunity to review some of what you have learned and to build on your understanding of the Earth by incorporating some of the information you met in Book 1. All around us, the water and carbon cycles proceed, generating feedbacks that control the composition of the atmosphere, and through that the global mean surface temperature. At the same time, processes that form rocks are active in different parts of the Earth: rocks are being heated and squeezed beneath mountain belts at convergent plate boundaries to form new metamorphic rocks; other rocks beneath mid-ocean ridges and subduction zones are melting to form magmas that eventually cool as new igneous rocks. Also, right now, new sediments are being formed, with each grain of sand or mud in a river estuary being derived from weathering and erosion of rocks further upstream where particles were liberated by weathering and erosion, then transported by the river and eventually deposited (as in Figure 10.1). Over many centuries, these sediments may become deeply buried under more sedimentary material, becoming compacted and cemented to form a sedimentary rock (Section 5.2.2). Thus, the rocks of the mountains can be destroyed and remade as new sedimentary rocks. But what was the origin of the rocks that were eroded to produce the new sediments?

Figure 10.1 The mountains of North Wales, in the distant background, are the source of the mud deposits of the Mawddach Estuary, seen in the foreground.

The rocks making up the cliffs on a shoreline, or high mountain crags, are made from materials that were once parts of some other rocks. And, given time, these same cliffs and crags will themselves be transformed, a fact that will be only too familiar if you live in an area subject to the effects of coastal erosion. This suggests a cycle, analogous to the carbon or water cycles that you met in Book 1, in which any rock may become converted into other rock types. This is the **rock cycle**.

10.1   Moving around the rock cycle

Figure 10.2 illustrates the simplicity of the rock cycle: the three classes of rock are linked by arrows indicating that any type of rock can be converted into any other type of rock.

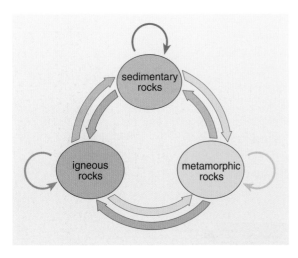

Figure 10.2   A schematic diagram of the rock cycle. The blue arrows represent formation of sedimentary rocks, red arrows formation of igneous rocks, and yellow arrows formation of metamorphic rocks.

■   How many arrows lead to each class of rock?

☐   Three. One arrow comes from each of the other rock classes, and one comes from within the class itself.

Each set of the three sets of coloured arrows in Figure 10.2 is associated with one general type of rock-forming process. For example, the blue arrows in Figure 10.2 represent the sedimentary processes by which sedimentary rocks form from pre-existing rocks of any type. Yellow arrows represent the formation of metamorphic rocks from any other rock, be it sedimentary, igneous or metamorphic, by recrystallisation during deep burial and/or heating. Igneous rocks form (red arrows) when magmas cool, and most magmas are produced by the incomplete melting of mantle peridotite, although some magmas form when existing metamorphic, sedimentary or igneous rocks become so hot that they melt.

At the start of this chapter, it was noted that one sedimentary rock may be broken down into sediment, redeposited, and potentially turned into a new sedimentary rock. However, the new sediment is not just the old sedimentary rock stuck back together again after having been broken apart and transported. Some of the original mineral grains will have been dissolved, and those that get transported will become deposited alongside grains originating from other rocks. If you examine some grains of sand from a beach, you'll generally find some broken fragments of sea-shells; these certainly weren't part of the rocks supplying the mineral grains. Likewise, magmas are formed by the incomplete melting of pre-existing rocks, so the original rock does not get entirely converted to magma. Of the processes that move material around the rock cycle, only metamorphism involves the conversion of one rock type to another without it gaining or losing any material.

Figure 10.2 is a purely schematic illustration of the important idea that all types of rock can be derived from, or lead to, another type of rock. A better way of illustrating the possible ways of moving material around the rock cycle is with a diagram that places the rock-forming processes into their geological contexts. Since the rock cycle involves processes occurring on the Earth's surface and also within its interior, a schematic cross-section through the Earth is used, as shown in Figure 10.3. This diagram shows only the most prominent processes within the rock cycle. Less significant processes, like the melting of igneous or sedimentary rocks to form new magmas, and the recrystallisation of metamorphic rocks to form new metamorphic rocks, haven't been included in Figure 10.3.

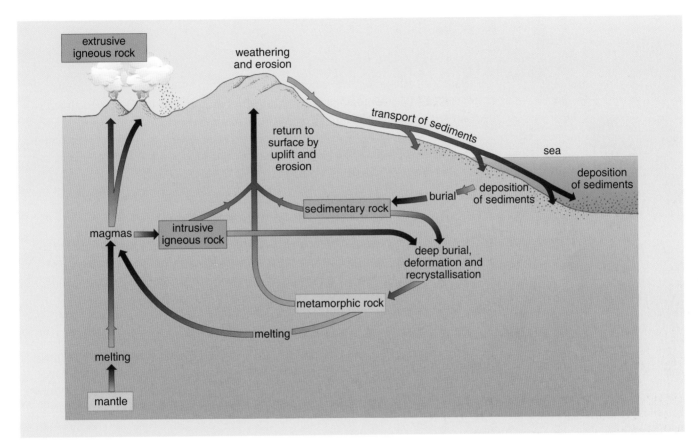

Figure 10.3   The rock cycle. The arrows show the processes involved in transforming one type of rock (contained in a box) to another type.

Activity 10.1   Travelling around the rock cycle

We expect this activity will take you approximately 20 minutes.

Use the information about the rock cycle summarised in Figure 10.3 and your knowledge of rocks from earlier chapters to do the following:

(a) Briefly describe how the minerals in sedimentary rocks exposed at the Earth's surface can be converted into metamorphic rocks.

(b) Briefly describe two different ways in which the materials in an intrusive igneous rock could be converted into a metamorphic rock.

(c) Briefly describe how an atom that was originally in the mantle could end up in a sedimentary rock.

(d) State which parts of the rock cycle involve the Earth's atmosphere.

Now look at the comments on this activity at the end of this book.

The rock cycle even has an influence on humankind. In the carbon cycle, volcanoes are a source of atmospheric carbon dioxide, which, through photosynthesis, can be extracted from the atmosphere by plants that are in turn eaten by animals such as humans. In Book 1 (Section 7.3), you learned that carbonate rocks and fossil fuels are enormous stores of the Earth's carbon and that the carbon in a lump of coal, barrel of crude oil or petrol tank, was once part of a living organism. Through the carbon cycle, rocks are intimately linked into life on the Earth.

10.2   The rock cycle, life and plate tectonics

It should be becoming apparent that some seemingly unconnected parts of the Earth are in fact linked together in ways that are important for humankind and other life. Some of these connections are explained here, to round off the picture of the Earth, before the last part of the book introduces you to other planets and the Universe as a whole.

10.2.1   The rock cycle and plate tectonics

The rock cycle operates because of the continuously active processes that affect the Earth's surface and interior. Many of these processes occur specifically at plate boundaries rather than being distributed evenly over the Earth.

■   Suggest a plate-tectonic setting where metamorphic processes are most likely to take place.

☐   At convergent plate boundaries. The increases in pressure and temperature needed to cause metamorphism in the crust occur in continental collision zones. Metamorphism also takes place in the crust within subduction zones where rocks descend to great depths and hence experience great pressure.

■   In which plate-tectonic settings do igneous processes take place?

☐   Melting takes place in the mantle beneath divergent plate boundaries, above the subducting plate at convergent plate boundaries, and far from plate boundaries at hot spots. (Occasionally, crustal rocks will melt to form magmas where metamorphism is particularly intense at continental collision zones.)

Sedimentary rocks form under a great variety of circumstances, such as in glacial environments, deserts and the coral reefs on continental shelves. Some great rivers, such as the Nile and Mississippi, transport sedimentary material many thousands of kilometres across plate interiors, laying down fertile, muddy sediments and modifying the coastline by forming deltas. Other great rivers, such as the Ganges, Indus and Brahmaputra, rise in the high mountain belts where plates are colliding. In these collision zones, plate convergence thrusts mountains upwards, but the steep mountain slopes and high rainfall encourage weathering and erosion, with the result that sites of mountain building are actually prodigious suppliers of sediment, which gets washed away and deposited elsewhere. Indeed, the Bay of Bengal contains several million cubic kilometres of sediment that has been removed from the Himalayan Mountains in the last 40 Ma by erosion and transported to the sea.

Plate tectonics thus maintains the rock cycle, not only by producing metamorphic and igneous rocks at plate boundaries, but also through its influence on sedimentary processes. Although the rock cycle moulds the geology of the crust, it does not operate independently of other parts of the Earth. For one thing, the rock cycle crucially involves the mantle, which is the source of most magma. Furthermore, subduction removes rocks from the crust and adds them to the mantle.

10.2.2   Life and the rock cycle

Life can be found nearly everywhere on the surface of the Earth – from the deepest ocean floor to the peaks of the highest mountains and into the atmosphere. Life has even been found in the pores of rocks 2 km below the surface. Anywhere, it seems, where there are water and nutrients, and where temperatures are not too extreme, life is possible.

An obvious example of life's influence on the rock cycle is the formation of limestones. For example, chalk is formed from sediments composed of the remains of countless microscopic organisms that secreted protective shells made of calcium carbonate (Section 5.2.2). Other limestones are formed from the calcium carbonate shells of larger organisms, as you found with the sample of limestone containing crinoid fossils in the Practical Kit. Similarly, modern coral reefs are built of communities of organisms, which also form calcium carbonate structures for physical support and protection. Some of these coral reefs are large enough to be seen from space (Figure 10.4).

Another way in which the organisms in the biosphere affect the rock cycle is through weathering (Figure 10.5). Rocks are partly broken down by the physical action of wind, rain, ice, and extremes in temperature, but these processes are greatly accelerated by the effects of plant roots, microbes, and other living organisms in the soil. These actions are partly physical – think of grass growing through a pavement, or saplings wedged in the cracks of a boulder – but the most important processes are chemical.

One of the chemical processes works like this. All living things respire and, through respiration, most release carbon dioxide. Plants release some carbon dioxide directly into the soil water through their roots. Carbon dioxide, as you should recall (Book 1, Section 7.3.4), dissolves readily in water, and the dissolved carbon dioxide makes the soil water slightly acidic. The acid is quite weak; in fact, it has about the same acidity as many fizzy drinks. However, prolonged contact with this slightly acid soil water slowly breaks down the

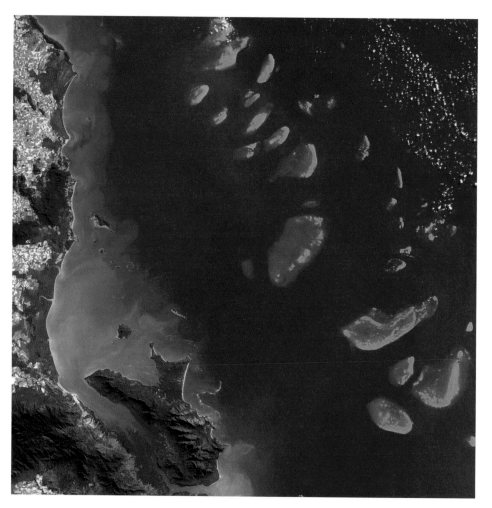

Figure 10.4   Part of the 2000 km long Great Barrier Reef from space. The reef lies off the northeast coast of Australia, seen on the left of the picture, at distances of between 15 and 50 km. This picture, taken from the Space Shuttle 230 km above the Earth, shows several coral islands and reefs; the largest is about 20 km long.

minerals in rocks – they weather faster. Many plants also release other acids that hasten the process and they gain nutrients from the decomposing rocks, for example a lichen slowly crumbling a stone wall is doing so through chemical weathering, and is forming soil for other plants to follow and continue the process (Figure 10.5b).

The contribution to weathering by organisms results in soil formation (soil is a mixture of weathered rock and organic material) and increases the amount of sedimentary material in the rock cycle. We can thus safely say that a significant amount of the Earth's sediments and sedimentary rocks (especially those derived from carbonate sediments formed by organisms and those derived from sediments due to plant-enhanced weathering of rock), and all of its soil, are products of biological processes.

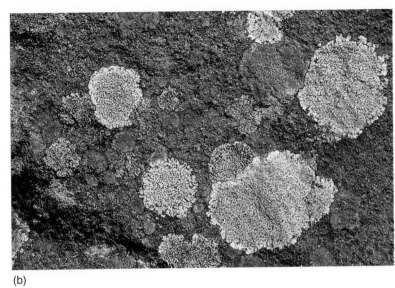

(b)

(a)

Figure 10.5   Physical and chemical weathering of rocks can be greatly enhanced by vegetation. (a) Vegetation breaking apart pavement, showing physical weathering. (b) Patches of lichen a few centimetres across break down the rock they grow on to obtain nutrients.

10.2.3   Life and plate tectonics

The slow grind of plate tectonics influences life, and not just by causing hazardous volcanic eruptions and earthquakes. Continental drift can slowly carry the native species of a continent to a different climate zone, requiring them to migrate or adapt to the new climatic conditions. New species may evolve as a result, and some of the original species may become extinct. Also, the collision of two continents may bring together plants and animals that had previously been separated. For some species, the introduction of more efficient organisms or new predators may spell extinction, whereas for others, the new habitat may allow them to expand their range.

10.3   The Earth as a system

You have now been studying the science of the Earth for several weeks, including Book 1. How would you describe the Earth? You can say it is a sphere about 12 740 km in diameter and made of metal, rocks, water, and gas arranged in layers (the core, mantle and crust, hydrosphere and atmosphere). The depths of these layers, and indeed their chemical compositions are known, even in the case of the deep interior that can't be observed by going there. The mass, volume and density of the Earth are also known. But these basic descriptions neglect the most interesting aspects of the Earth: the Earth is not an inert body in space but a continuously operating 'machine' that harbours life.

The Earth's rocky surface experiences earthquakes and volcanic eruptions that are caused because the strong outer layer of the Earth, the lithosphere, can move slowly around over the hot interior. Plate tectonics creates, destroys and modifies the continents and ocean basins, and controls how they are distributed on the Earth. The ocean basins are made of dense basalt rock that eventually sinks back into the mantle by the process of subduction, whereas the continents are less dense and remain floating at the surface; oceanic lithosphere is generated from the mantle by sea-floor spreading and is cycled back into the mantle by subduction. Plate tectonics accounts for the shape of the Earth's surface and many of the geological processes on the Earth. Because of its ability to explain so much, plate tectonics is one of the central theories or 'big ideas' in science.

At the same time, life and other processes in the atmosphere and oceans create, destroy and modify the rocks, water and gas of the Earth. This means that many aspects of the Earth (such as the greenhouse effect) can only be understood fully by thinking about the Earth as a whole system of interacting components. In the case of the Earth, this system includes its rocks, hydrosphere, atmosphere and biosphere, and extends beyond the Earth to include the Sun – the source of the energy that makes the Earth a planet fit for life.

10.4   Summary of Chapter 10

Rocks are formed by geological processes acting on pre-existing rocks, so that new rocks are produced from materials that come from older rocks. The result is that sedimentary, metamorphic and igneous rocks are produced within a cycle – the rock cycle – which is the path taken by Earth materials in response to chemical, biological and physical processes acting upon rocks.

Those parts of the rock cycle that produce many new sedimentary rocks involve the weathering and erosion of pre-existing rocks, followed by transport and deposition of eroded mineral grains and rock fragments. Other new sedimentary rocks such as limestones and coal deposits are formed by biological processes. Life also affects the rock cycle through enhanced rock weathering and soil formation. All of these processes occur on the surface of the Earth.

Most igneous and metamorphic rocks are produced near the boundaries between lithospheric plates, so these parts of the rock cycle are 'activated' by plate tectonics and take place well beneath the Earth's surface.

The connections between the biosphere, hydrosphere, atmosphere and lithosphere form continuous and intertwined cycles within cycles, with the result that life, plate tectonics, and the rock, carbon and water cycles are connected in various ways.

In studying this chapter, you have used diagrammatic representations of the rock cycle to help understand the way in which the rock cycle is organised and its relationships with other parts of the Earth system.

Chapter 11
The planetary neighbourhood

In the next few chapters, you will explore the Earth's place in the Universe, by making a journey from the Earth to the most distant parts of the Universe. In this chapter, you will start your journey by exploring the Earth's near neighbourhood. The Earth goes around the Sun, as do the other planets and other miscellaneous objects that you will meet later. A few of these objects are worlds in their own right, with geological processes not unlike some of those on the Earth. The system of objects circling the Sun is called the **Solar System**. Our Solar System is not isolated; the Sun is one of hundreds of billions of stars circling a common centre. This vast collection of stars is called a **galaxy**. Our galaxy, named the **Milky Way**, is in the shape of a disc. In later chapters, you will continue your journey outwards and explore farther into the distant Universe, zooming far beyond the Sun's neighbourhood to a vantage point from where the layout of the part of the Universe in which we live is revealed. The distances involved are vast, so much so that this has to be an imaginary journey. You will not travel towards the centre of the Milky Way, but in a direction such that the Milky Way encircles your direction of travel as you leave the Earth, as indicated in Figure 11.1.

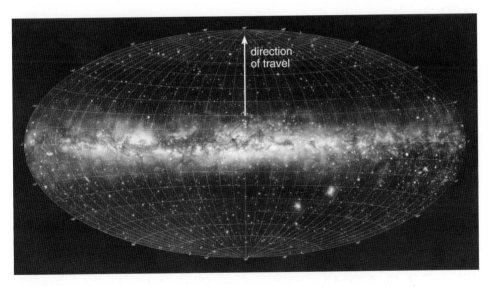

Figure 11.1   The journey into space starts from the Earth in a direction encircled by the Milky Way. (The faint grid and boundary have been used in this image to frame the Milky Way and put coordinates on it. They are not needed for the present purposes.)

11.1   The Solar System

Imagine that you accelerate away from the Earth, and soon reach your cruising speed. The distance from the Earth now increases rapidly, until, at the huge distance of 10^{13} m (nearly 70 times the distance of the Earth from the Sun), you have a good view of the Solar System, with the planets and other smaller objects going around the Sun. If the paths of the planets around the Sun were somehow marked, then from your vantage point you would see them as in Figure 11.2. These paths are called **orbits**, a general term for the path of any celestial body around another.

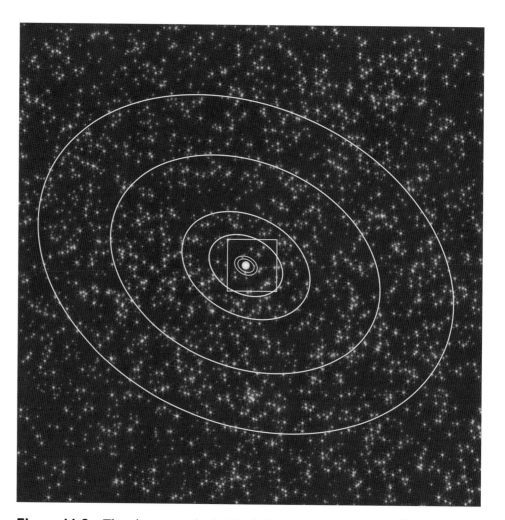

Figure 11.2   The view towards the Earth from a vantage point 10^{13} m along the direction of travel in Figure 11.1. The central box is 10^{12} m $\times$ 10^{12} m. The central disc is the Sun (not to scale), and the lines are orbits of the Earth and planets further from the Sun.

Because of the direction of travel in Figure 11.1, you are seeing the orbits obliquely in Figure 11.2. If you were to view each orbit face-on, i.e. from a direction perpendicular to the plane of the orbit, you would see that each one is not very different from a circle. From a direction perpendicular to the Earth's orbit (i.e. above the Earth), the view of the planetary orbits would be as shown in Figure 11.3a. The orbits of the four inner planets (Mercury, Venus, Earth and Mars) have also been drawn to a larger scale. Even at this larger scale, the Sun is a little too small, and the planets are much too small, to be shown to scale. The Moon is in orbit around the Earth, but its orbit is also just a bit too small to show at this scale.

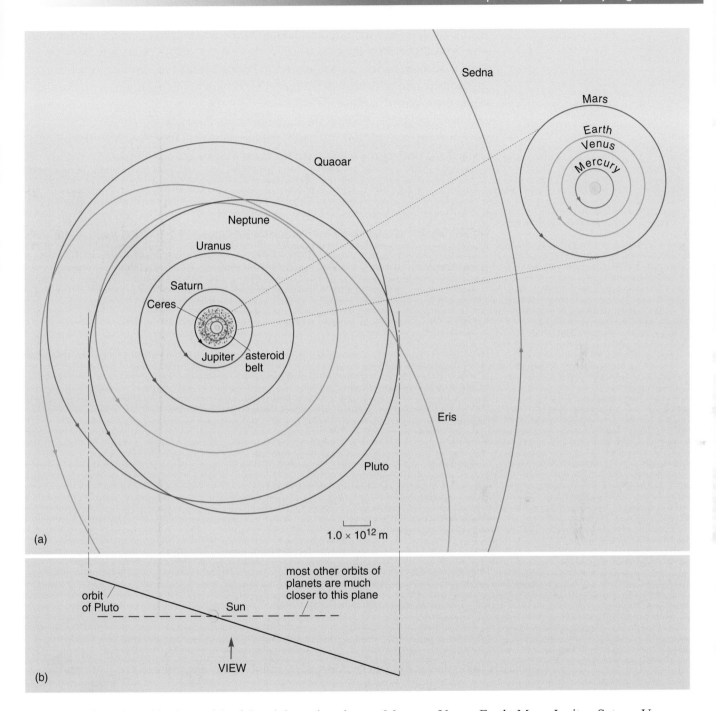

Figure 11.3   The orbits (to scale) of the eight major planets, Mercury, Venus, Earth, Mars, Jupiter, Saturn, Uranus and Neptune; the three dwarf planets, Pluto, Ceres and Eris (Ceres is an asteroid and Pluto and Eris are Kuiper Belt objects); and two other large Kuiper Belt objects (Sedna and Quaoar). See text for explanation. Also shown is the asteroid belt lying between Mars and Jupiter. (a) From a viewpoint perpendicular to the Earth's orbit; (b) from edgewise to the Earth's orbit. The average distance of the Earth from the Sun is 1.50×10^{11} m (150 million kilometres). The yellow disc representing the Sun is not to scale.

From a direction edgewise to the Earth's orbit, the view would be as shown in Figure 11.3b. You can see that the orbits of the planets lie almost on an imaginary flat surface, i.e. in the same plane. However, Pluto has an orbit that is slightly inclined (i.e. tilted) with respect to this plane.

All the objects shown in Figure 11.3a go around their orbits in the same direction. The **orbital period** is the time it takes one celestial body to complete an orbit around another, and so a planetary orbital period is the time it takes the planet to complete one orbit around the Sun. This orbital period increases with the size of the orbit, partly because the larger the orbit the further the planet has to travel around it, and partly because the larger the orbit the more slowly the planet moves along its orbit. For the Earth, the orbital period is one year, by definition. Objects that are more distant from the Sun have longer orbital periods, while objects closer to the Sun than the Earth have orbital periods of less than one year.

It is worth asking at this point, 'What exactly is a planet?' Many objects orbit the Sun, including tiny grains of rock (called dust). Not all are big enough to be considered as planets. How small can a planet be? For many years there was no clear definition of what a planet was. In 2006, however, the International Astronomical Union (essentially the governing body of astronomy) announced a definition of the term **planet** after a heated debate. Broadly, a planet must (a) be big enough for the force of its own gravity (which you will meet in Chapter 14) to make it roughly spherical, (b) orbit the Sun, (c) have swept out a clear path on its orbit round the Sun (i.e. cleared other smaller objects from its path), and (d) not be a **satellite** of another body (i.e. a planet must orbit the Sun rather than another body that is also going round the Sun). This new definition excluded the object Pluto as Pluto has not swept out a clear region of space, but is actually orbiting the Sun with many other similar (albeit mostly smaller) objects. Pluto was demoted to a newly defined category of body: a **dwarf planet**.

So there are now eight planets in our Solar System, and (at the time of writing) three dwarf planets (Pluto, Ceres and Eris). At the time of writing, this is still controversial, and it may be that future meetings of the International Astronomical Union will change or refine their categories. Scientific conventions and terminology do occasionally change with time to reflect changes in scientific thinking. In the meantime, Figure 11.3 shows these major classes of known objects orbiting the Sun. Pluto is at the inner edge of a belt of objects called the **Kuiper Belt** (or sometimes called the Edgeworth–Kuiper Belt; 'Kuiper' rhymes with 'piper' and 'wiper'), which also contains the (currently known) largest dwarf planet, Eris and large Kuiper Belt objects Quaoar and Sedna. As astronomers map this distant region of the Solar System new objects are being discovered regularly. In time, some of the largest objects will no doubt also be classified as dwarf planets. This is probably the fate of the objects Sedna and Quaoar, shown in Figure 11.3a. (There are also several other candidate dwarf planets not shown here.) Already we know that Pluto is not the largest known member of the Kuiper Belt; this is currently Eris. In time, astronomers may discover even bigger objects in the distant Kuiper Belt. Like Pluto, many of the objects in the Kuiper Belt have inclined (tilted) orbits (Figure 11.3b). Furthermore, their orbits can be elongated so they are no longer approximately circular (e.g. Eris in Figure 11.3a). Some obits take the object far from the Sun and, even at their closest point to the Sun, they are still far beyond Pluto (e.g. Sedna in Figure 11.3a).

The planets that are made largely of rock show many of the same geological processes that can be seen on the Earth (which is also a rocky planet). The Earth

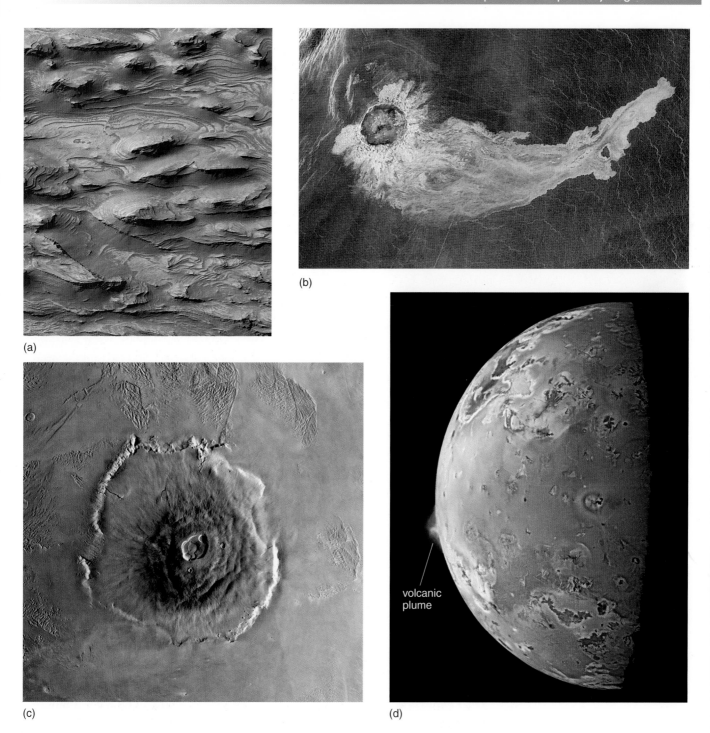

(a)

(b)

(c)

(d)

volcanic
plume

Figure 11.4   Extraterrestrial geology: (a) sedimentary deposits on Mars (height of image is about 2 km);
(b) the 90 km diameter Addams impact crater on the planet Venus, together with a resulting outflow 600 km long;
(c) the Olympus Mons volcano on Mars, which is about 600 km across; (d) a volcanic plume on Io, a 3630 km
diameter satellite of Jupiter.

seems so far to be unique in having lithospheric plates, but as you can see in
Figure 11.4, other planets and satellites have evidence of sediments, volcanism
and cratering. (You saw how cratering affected the Earth in Section 6.3.)

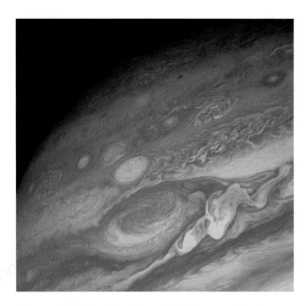

Figure 11.5   The Great Red Spot on Jupiter, taken by the NASA *Voyager* spacecraft. The Great Red Spot is a storm about the size of the Earth.

■   Why are there fewer impact craters on the Earth than on other planets?

☐   Resurfacing on the Earth (e.g. from volcanic eruptions, weathering and erosion) removes impact craters. Also, many small objects (comet or asteroid fragments less than about 50 m across) often burn up in the atmosphere before reaching the Earth's surface.

Most planets have atmospheres, some with circulation patterns more elaborate and violent than the Earth's. Figure 11.5 shows an image taken by the *Voyager* spacecraft of the Great Red Spot on Jupiter, which is a storm big enough to engulf the Earth.

As well as the Sun and the planets in the Solar System, there are also **natural satellites** in orbit around most of the planets (such as the Moon around the Earth). Planetary satellites can also show geological processes, as shown in Figure 11.4d. There is also a belt of **asteroids** (lumps of mainly rock and metal) orbiting the Sun and lying mainly between Mars and Jupiter (i.e. the asteroid belt), the Kuiper Belt (mentioned above) lying beyond the orbit of Neptune, the occasional comet (more of which below), and a very sparse amount of interplanetary dust and gas. (Outer space is not a perfect vacuum.) The asteroids and comets are sometimes called *minor* planets. Be sure not to confuse this with *dwarf* planets.

You will now resume your imaginary journey from the point you left it in Figure 11.2, and travel on in the same direction along which you started (Figure 11.1). You pause again when you have travelled 1000 times further, and have reached 10^{16} m from the Earth. Had you travelled towards the nearest star (Proxima Centauri), you would now only be a quarter of the way there. From this range (Figure 11.6), the Sun is like the other stars in the sky in that no disc is discernible to the unaided eye, although it is still the brightest star.

The distance of 10^{16} m from the Sun is significant because, although you are far from the planets, you have only just left the Solar System. Its boundary is marked by the orbits of its outermost members. These are the **comets**, small bodies, a few kilometres across, that range far and wide across the Solar System, although most of them spend most of their time near the Solar System's extremities. Although there are about 10^{11}–10^{12} comets, they are so tiny and so faint that none is visible in Figure 11.6. The cloud of comets around our Solar System is known as the **Oort cloud**, after its discoverer. Comets can also be found in the Kuiper Belt, and indeed some travel into the inner Solar System too, where we might observe them.

The orbits of the comets, the planets, and all the other bodies in the Solar System, raise the question of what prevents these bodies from shooting off into space. What enables the Sun to hold onto its family? The answer is the gravitational attraction of the Sun, as you will see in Chapter 14. Gravitational attraction is a universal phenomenon, by which any object attracts any other object. An everyday example of gravitational attraction is that of the Earth on you, which stops you floating off into space. The boundary of the Solar System is an

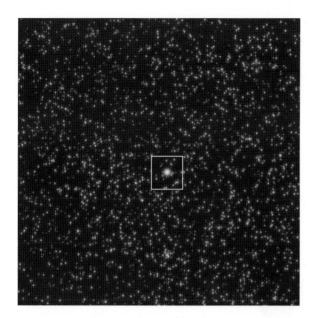

Figure 11.6   A view looking towards the Sun, from a distance of 10^{16} m, from a vantage point along the direction of travel in Figure 11.1. The planetary orbits are too small on this scale to show. The central square box is $10^{15} \times 10^{15}$ m.

imaginary surface centred on the Sun, within which the gravitational attraction of the Sun is greater than that of any other star. In Figure 11.6 you are viewing from a position just outside this surface, and have entered interstellar space.

In the rest of this chapter you will study the objects that orbit the Sun, and in the next chapter you will resume your journey into deeper space.

11.2   The planets and their satellites

The planets are much smaller and much less massive (i.e. of lower mass) than the Sun (Figure 11.7) and their surface temperatures are far lower, ranging from below –200 °C to no more than a few hundred °C. They are too cold for their light to be caused by a glow of heat. Instead, they 'shine' in visible light simply by reflecting the Sun's light.

A more fundamental distinction between a planet and the Sun is that a planet's interior is always too cool for nuclear fusion, (the Sun's power source) to operate. (You will return to nuclear fusion in Book 7.) Indeed, this is why their surface temperatures are far lower. Planets do have internal energy sources, including radioactivity (which you will also meet in Books 6 and 7), but nuclear fusion is ruled out because their interiors never get hot enough. This is a consequence of the lower masses of the planets.

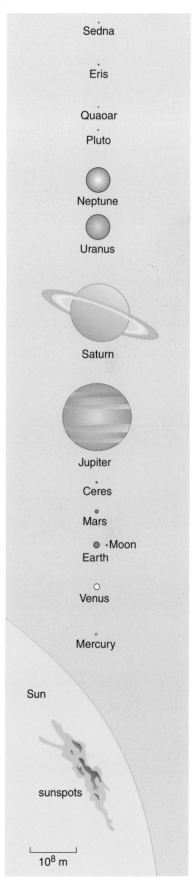

Figure 11.7   The relative sizes of the Sun, the planets and some smaller bodies. The mean radius of Jupiter is 69 910 km (6.991×10^7 m). The planets are shown in order of increasing distance from the Sun, but the distances between the various bodies are not to scale; they are separated by far larger distances than are shown. The smallest objects are only specks in this figure, but are compared against each other and with our Moon in Figure 11.8.

After the Sun, the Moon is the most obvious object in the sky. The Moon looks about the same size as the Sun, but in fact the Moon's radius is about 400 times smaller (a comparison of the Moon to some similar-sized bodies is shown in Figure 11.8). The two bodies appear to be the same size because the Moon is about 400 times closer than the Sun, just as a coin held at arm's length appears to be the same size as a much larger disc further off. Like the planets, the Moon shines by reflecting the light of the Sun, and not by emitting its own visible radiation. If you have a telescope or a pair of binoculars, try looking at the Moon through them. You may be able to see shadows cast by mountains and craters. (*Never look directly at the Sun with the naked eye, and do not even glance at it through telescopes or binoculars, as this may cause very rapid and permanent eye damage.*)

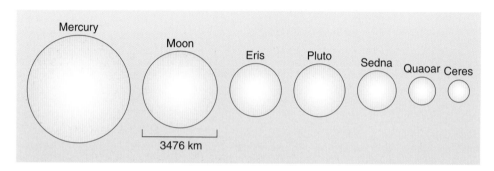

Figure 11.8   The relative size of our Moon compared to Mercury, the dwarf planets (Eris, Pluto and Ceres) and large Kuiper Belt objects Sedna and Quaoar (which may in time be classified as dwarf planets).

There are many other objects in the sky that also shine by reflecting the light of the Sun. The most obvious of these are the planets Venus, Mars, Jupiter, and Saturn, and all except Saturn can seem brighter than the brightest stars. With powerful binoculars, these four planets are visible as tiny discs, although even the largest, Jupiter, has an actual radius of only about one-tenth of the Sun's radius.

You will now have a brief look at the variety of planets in the Solar System. This will also help to place the Earth in a broader context.

11.2.1   Diameter, density and composition

On the basis of radius, Figure 11.7 suggests a broad division into two types of planet-sized object.

■   Divide the eight planets into two groups on the basis of radius.

☐   There is a group of four relatively small planets: Mercury, Venus, Earth and Mars. There is also a group of four large planets: Jupiter, Saturn, Uranus and Neptune.

Unsurprisingly, the four large planets are called giant planets. The four small planets are called terrestrial planets, meaning Earth-like planets. In Figure 11.3 you can see that the terrestrial planets occupy the inner Solar System and the giant planets occupy the outer Solar System. The dwarf planet Pluto appears more akin in size to the terrestrial planets, but it is in the outer Solar System. It thus looks somewhat unusual. It also has an unusual density compared with the planets. Density is a useful quantity in this context as it can hint at the composition of a body, because different substances have different densities.

You should recall that the density of any object is its mass divided by its volume. (You met density in Chapter 6, and in Book 1, Section 4.5.1.) The word equation is:

$$\text{density} = \frac{\text{mass}}{\text{volume}}$$

To write this in symbols, we conventionally replace density with the Greek letter ρ (rho, pronounced 'row' to rhyme with 'go'), mass with m, and volume with V, and obtain:

$$\rho = \frac{m}{V} \tag{11.1}$$

(Be careful not to confuse the Greek letter ρ with the letter p.) When a symbol is used to represent a quantity, it clearly saves space. This is particularly useful when rearranging equations (you'll do this in Book 3), or when there are a lot of equations to consider. The use of symbols, however, carries the penalty that you have to remember what each symbol stands for. In this respect, it clearly helps if the symbol is reminiscent of the full name, such as m for mass. It would not be very helpful to write Equation 11.1 as $i = \frac{Q}{t}$. The symbols used in Equation 11.1 are fairly standard, although variants do exist. Note that in printed text it is usual to italicise symbols, but this italicisation does not extend to symbols for units, such as m for metres. This restriction helps you distinguish between a symbol that represents a quantity and one that represents a specific unit. Note also that it is usual to omit multiplication signs when using symbols, so (for example) $F = ma$ means the same as $F = m \times a$.

The problem with symbols is that we run out of them, even when we use capitals, lower case, and the Greek alphabet, and so the same symbol can stand for several different words or phrases. For example, d can stand for distance, and it can also stand for diameter. (This is partly why ρ is conventionally used to symbolise density, rather than d.) It is therefore always very important to state what a symbol stands for when it is first introduced.

The volume of a planet can be calculated from its radius, which can be obtained directly from astronomical observations, as can the mass. Table 11.1 lists the radius, mass and density of the planets and dwarf planets. There are two gaps, which you should now fill in by doing Activity 11.1.

Table 11.1 Properties of the eight major planets, and three dwarf planets. Zeros at the end of a value can be assumed not to be significant (e.g. 1140 is to 3 significant figures; 5 685 000 is to 4 significant figures).

Planetary body	Radius/km[a]	Mass/10^{20} kg	Density/kg m^{-3}
Mercury	2 440	3 302	5 430
Venus	6 052	48 690	5 240
Earth	6 371	59 740	
Mars	3 389	6 419	3 910
Jupiter	69 910	18 990 000	1 240
Saturn	58 230	5 685 000	620
Uranus	25 360	866 200	1 240
Neptune	24 620	1 028 000	1 610
Ceres	470	9.5	2 200
Eris	1 200	150	2 100
Pluto	1 140	130	

[a] The radius given here is the mean radius, as some planets (particularly Jupiter and Saturn) have greater diameters at their equators than at their poles.

Activity 11.1   Calculating the density of Pluto and the Earth

We expect this activity will take you approximately 30 minutes.

This activity will give you practice in putting numbers into symbolic equations. The volume of a sphere is given by the equation:

$$\text{volume} = \frac{4}{3} \times \pi \times (\text{radius})^3$$

or, in symbols:

$$V = \frac{4}{3}\pi r^3$$

where V is the volume, r is the radius of the sphere, and π is 3.14159 to 6 significant figures. (You may remember that the Greek letter π, or pi, pronounced 'pie', is also the circumference of a circle divided by its diameter.) The radius is the distance from the centre of the sphere to the edge, or (equivalently) half of the sphere's diameter.

Calculate the volumes of Pluto and then the Earth. You can do each planet in four stages. Start with the radius r. Firstly, calculate r^3 (i.e. 'r cubed'), which is the same as $r \times r \times r$. Secondly, multiply your answer by 4. Thirdly, multiply your answer by π. Finally, divide your answer by 3. Note that the radius is cubed first. If, instead, the cubing was left until last, you would get a different (and wrong) answer. This is because $\frac{4}{3}\pi r^3$ means $\frac{4}{3}\pi$ times r^3, whereas $\left(\frac{4}{3}\pi r\right)^3$ means $\left(\frac{4}{3}\pi r\right)$ all cubed.

Calculate the densities of Pluto and the Earth, using Equation 11.1. You should find Pluto's density to be somewhere between 2000 kg m^{-3} and 2500 kg m^{-3}, and the Earth's density to be somewhere between 5000 kg m^{-3} and 6000 kg m^{-3}.

Insert your values for the density into Table 11.1, and then check with the answer given in the comments on this activity at the end of this book.

The completed Table 11.1 (see comments on Activity 11.1) shows that Pluto has a substantially lower density than the terrestrial planets, indicating a different composition, and this is another reason for excluding it from the group of terrestrial planets.

The inference of the composition of a planet from its density is possible because of the great differences in density of substances that are serious candidates for making up an appreciable proportion of the mass of a planet. In the broadest terms, there are just three categories of substance. First, there are the substances that dominate the Sun, the two lightest elements hydrogen and helium. Second, there are **rocky materials**. As their name suggests, these comprise the sorts of materials that make up rocks (and this includes metals, notably iron). Finally there are **icy materials**, such as water. The term 'icy materials' can be misleading because 'icy' suggests cold solids. However, it is the name astronomers use for a group of chemical substances, and though they do occur frozen in some planetary interiors, they also occur as hot liquids. Likewise rocky materials can be solid or liquid.

Hydrogen and helium have low densities, even when compressed into liquids in planetary interiors. Icy materials have intermediate densities, and rocky materials high densities. Under conditions at the Earth's surface, liquid or solid water has a density of about 1000 kg m^{-3}, and rocky materials have densities in the approximate range 3000 to 8000 kg m^{-3}.

■ In which of the groups of planets (terrestrial or giant) are rocky materials likely to dominate? What is the evidence? (Use Table 11.1.)

☐ In the terrestrial planets; these have densities in the range quoted above for rocky materials.

Figure 11.9 shows plausible models of the interiors of the planets in terms of the three categories of material and ignoring many details of internal structure. Each planet is shown in cross-section, although only as a segment in each case. The giants are distinguished by having massive cores of icy and rocky materials overlain by hydrogen and helium as major or dominant components. You might wonder why the densities of Jupiter and Uranus are so similar (Table 11.1), even though Jupiter has a higher proportion of hydrogen and helium. The reason is the much greater pressures in Jupiter than in Uranus. The greater the pressure, the greater the compression of a given substance to higher densities. The greater pressures in Jupiter are a consequence of Jupiter's greater mass.

Figure 11.9 Plausible models of the interiors of the planets, plus Pluto, in terms of three categories of material. The radii of the planets are all drawn to the same scale. Pluto is too small to show at this scale. Note that all the composition boundaries in the giants are probably 'fuzzy', and not as sharp as shown here.

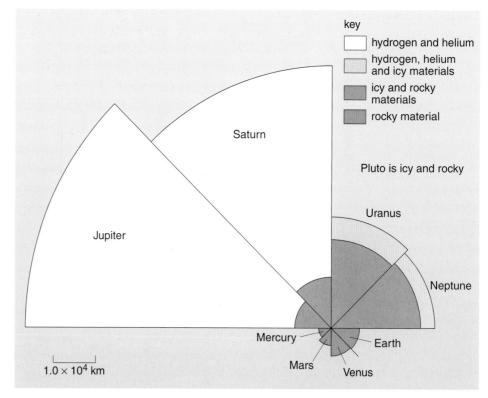

The terrestrial planets consist almost entirely of rocky materials. In Figure 11.9, no internal layering is shown at all, although all of the terrestrial planets are intricately layered, and the layering of the Earth is known in considerable detail, as you saw in Chapter 6. Pluto is odd in that icy materials account for a greater fraction of its mass than is the case for any major planet. However, Pluto has companions in some of the large satellites that are of comparable size and are comparably icy. It could even be that some of these satellites were once dwarf planets in their own right, subsequently captured by neighbouring planets in some cataclysm. By contrast, other large satellites (including the Moon) are rocky in composition. The smaller satellites are variously rocky, or icy and rocky mixtures.

Question 11.1

On the basis of Figure 11.9, justify the creation of a subdivision of the giant planets, called subgiants, and comprising Uranus and Neptune.

11.2.2   Surfaces and atmospheres

The surfaces and atmospheres of the planets are as varied as their interiors. The atmospheres of Neptune and Uranus are broadly similar, so Neptune will be taken to represent the subgiants. An image of Neptune is shown in Figure 11.10. The view is dominated by a deep haze, with a few cloud features buried in the haze. The planet can be regarded as having a deep atmosphere of hydrogen and helium (plus traces of other substances) with a surface beneath consisting of a planet-wide ocean of rocky and icy materials, notably water. These surface materials extend to the centre (Figure 11.9).

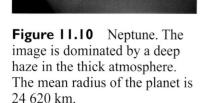

Figure 11.10 Neptune. The image is dominated by a deep haze in the thick atmosphere. The mean radius of the planet is 24 620 km.

Figure 11.11 shows Jupiter, where what you are seeing is the top of the uppermost of several layers of cloud. The uppermost layer consists of small crystals of ammonia, richly coloured by traces of other substances. The cloud patterns are the result of atmospheric winds. There is really no distinction between atmosphere and interior: the atmosphere has much the same composition as the interior (except near the centre – see Figure 11.9), and with increasing depth, the atmosphere gets hotter and denser until it is a hot ocean of hydrogen and helium, with no solid surface. Saturn's atmosphere is broadly similar to that of Jupiter, and it lacks a surface for the same reason. A well-known distinction between the two planets is that Saturn is surrounded by an extensive system of rings. These are made up of small bodies, typically a few centimetres to a few metres across, which have an icy–rocky composition, and which are travelling in circular orbits around the planet. (In fact, the other giant planets also have very minor ring systems, but not as spectacular as Saturn's.)

The terrestrial planets have well-defined surfaces, and they are rocky. The surface of Mercury (Figure 11.12), like that of the Moon, is heavily cratered by the impacts of small rocky bodies from space, accumulated throughout Solar System history. That there are so many craters shows that the surface of Mercury has not, for a long time, been subjected to geological processes that erase craters (such as volcanic activity). Mercury has virtually no atmosphere.

By contrast, the surface of Venus is overlain by an atmosphere about 100 times as massive as that of the Earth and consisting mainly of carbon dioxide. Although

Figure 11.11 Jupiter. The rich patterns are created by the winds in the upper cloud layer that consists of ammonia crystals coloured by traces of other substances. The mean radius of the planet is 69 910 km.

Figure 11.12 The surface of Mercury, heavily cratered by impacts. The mean radius of the planet is 2440 km.

it has by far the most massive atmosphere of the terrestrial planets, the atmosphere of Venus is still just a thin veneer, accounting for a negligible fraction of the planet's mass. High in the atmosphere is a planet-wide layer of cloud, consisting largely of sulfuric acid droplets, and this hides the surface from direct visual scrutiny. The surface is everywhere very hot, with a global mean surface temperature (GMST) of about 460 °C, whereas the GMST of Mercury is about 170 °C.

■   Why is the surface temperature of Venus higher than that of the surface of Mercury, even though Venus is further from the Sun?

☐   The high surface temperature is a consequence of the powerful greenhouse effect sustained by the massive atmosphere consisting largely of the greenhouse gas carbon dioxide (Book 1).

Although the surface of Venus is shrouded in cloud, radar has been used to obtain images of its surface. Volcanoes and other evidence of volcanic activity seem to be widespread. This explains the scarcity of impact craters: they have been covered by the products of volcanic eruptions.

Mars also has an atmosphere consisting mainly of carbon dioxide, but a square metre of surface on Mars has about 60 times *less* mass of atmosphere above it than a square metre on the Earth. It is also a very dry atmosphere. The greenhouse effect is therefore weak; with Mars being 1.5 times further than the Earth from the Sun, the GMST is about −60 °C. There are polar caps consisting largely of permanent deposits of water ice overlain by a layer of carbon dioxide frost, which for the northern cap is present only in the winter. Spacecraft orbiting Mars have also found water ice elsewhere (Figure 11.13). Clouds are common, although they are not so widespread as on the Earth, and as well as water ice crystals they also contain carbon dioxide crystals. In one hemisphere, ancient impact craters still survive in abundance, but in the other hemisphere, they have been largely obscured by volcanic activity. In the cratered hemisphere there appear to be dry river valley systems (Figure 11.14) – evidence that long ago Mars was a wetter, warmer place than it is today. Robotic missions to Mars from the American and European space agencies (NASA and ESA respectively) have found evidence that geological activity has occurred relatively recently, within the last 30 Ma or so. Whether life became established during that distant time is an area of intensive investigation, as you will discover in Book 8.

And so we come to the Earth, which you have studied earlier in this book. In the context of the other planets, the Earth's surface and atmosphere are remarkable in four ways. First, the atmosphere contains a significant amount of oxygen. Second, most of the rocky surface is covered by oceans of liquid water, with the atmosphere also holding large amounts of water in the form of vapour or clouds. Third, although the rocky surfaces of all the terrestrial planets have been shaped by a variety of geological processes, some of those that are shaping the Earth's surface appear to be unique in the Solar System, such as lithospheric plates. The fourth distinctive feature of the Earth's surface is that it harbours life (i.e. the biosphere).

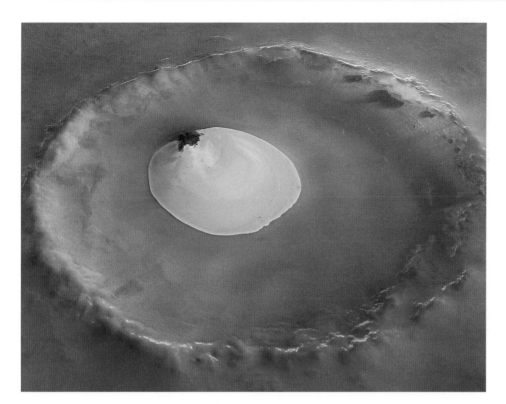

Figure 11.13   Water ice in the Vastitas Borealis Crater on Mars. The crater is 35 km wide.

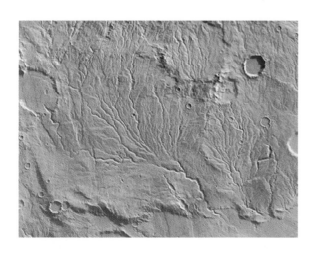

Figure 11.14   Dry river valleys on the older hemisphere of Mars, indicating that warmer, wetter conditions once prevailed. The width of the region shown is about 200 km.

Question 11.2

State two ways in which the Earth (a) resembles and (b) differs from the other terrestrial planets.

11.3   The small bodies in the Solar System

Figure 11.15   The tails of comet Hale–Bopp during its spectacular passage through the inner Solar System in 1997. This comet was discovered in 1995 by two American amateur astronomers, Alan Hale and Thomas Bopp. The blue tail consists largely of hot gas, and the other tail largely of dust. The scalebar is ten times the apparent diameter of the Sun in the sky. This image was obtained on 1 April 1997, when the comet was at its closest to the Sun (1.4×10^{11} m) and when it was about 2×10^{11} m from the Earth. The solid comet is at the heart of the fuzzy head, far too small to be visible, and in any case obscured by the head.

The comet Hale–Bopp passed through the inner Solar System in 1997 and put on a fine show (Figure 11.15). Comets are small, irregularly shaped solid bodies comprised of a mixture of (mainly) water ice and rocky fragments (dust), and are rarely more than a few tens of kilometres across. They are transformed in the inner Solar System by solar radiation. The radiation causes sublimation (where solid material turns to gas; Book 1, Section 4.5.2) of the ice from the surface of the comet, such that the resulting gas flows out from the surface into space, carrying entrained dust particles with it. The gas and dust particles go to form the huge tail of the comet, which is large enough to be observed from Earth. In fact, the tail is often seen as having two separate components: a dust tail produced by light reflecting and scattering off dust grains, and a gas tail produced by heated gas giving off light (as in a fluorescent light bulb). Figure 11.15 shows the tails of Hale–Bopp. In the outer Solar System, cometary tails are not present, and the solid comets are so small that they cannot normally be detected much beyond the orbit of Saturn even with the largest of telescopes. The composition of comets is inferred from the composition of their tails, which reveals the comets to be loose aggregates of icy and rocky materials. As you saw at the start of this chapter, most comets lie in the outer Solar System, in regions called the Oort cloud and the Kuiper Belt. Only when a comet happens to pass into the inner Solar System does it develop the dramatic tails.

■ What are the Oort cloud and Kuiper Belt?

□ The Oort cloud is the cloud of comets surrounding the Sun at the extremity of our Solar System. The Kuiper Belt comprises the objects, including Pluto, that are further from the Sun than the planet Neptune. It is not yet clear whether or not the Kuiper Belt joins continuously onto the Oort cloud.

Another main class of small body (or minor planet) in the Solar System are the asteroids. These are rocky bodies, and the largest, Ceres (pronounced 'series'), has a mean diameter of 940 km and has been designated a dwarf planet. There are about 10^5 asteroids that are larger than 100 m. The smaller ones are irregularly shaped, and so it is more appropriate to refer to a typical distance across the body as 'size' rather than to their diameters. The smaller the size the greater the number of bodies, and there are so many rocky bodies smaller than 100 m, and they have sufficiently varied orbits, that every day some of the very smallest (mm to cm in size) enter the Earth's atmosphere, where they are seen as meteors (informally known as 'shooting stars', although this term is quite erroneous as they are totally unrelated to stars). Before entering the atmosphere, they are known as meteoroids. A further population of meteoroids comes from comet fragments, and a small number are pieces of the surfaces of Mars and the Moon, blasted off those bodies by the impacts of bodies from space. If a meteoroid escapes complete vaporisation in our atmosphere, and survives to reach the Earth's surface, it is called a meteorite. A great number of meteorites have been found, providing scientists with important samples of extraterrestrial Solar System materials.

11.4   The origin of the Solar System

The striking differences between the various bodies in the Solar System, and the layout of the Solar System, can be explained by a widely accepted theory of its origin. In this theory, the Solar System formed from a rotating disc of gas composed mainly of hydrogen and helium, plus smaller proportions of other materials. The centre of the disc was the site of the Sun's formation, as illustrated in Figure 11.16, and the Sun's chemical composition was the same as that of the disc.

Figure 11.16   Artist's impression of the formation of the Solar System. The circular disc of gas (plus a trace of dust) is viewed obliquely here.

■   How does this theory account for the chemical composition of the Sun?

□   The disc was mainly hydrogen and helium. Therefore, so too is the Sun.

The planets formed from the remainder of the disc, which probably had a mass of about 10% of that of the Sun and was prevented by its rotation from contracting into a single object. In the inner part of the disc, grains of dust formed which had a mainly rocky composition. This is because it was too hot for icy materials to form solid ices. The rocky dust then gathered together to form larger bodies, which also combined to eventually form the terrestrial planets.

■ Is this account in accord with the composition of the terrestrial planets?

☐ Yes, the terrestrial planets have a rocky composition.

The later stages of formation of the terrestrial planets took the form of the gathering up of small solid bodies, peppering the planetary surfaces with impact craters.

Further from the Sun the disc was cooler, and so the grains of dust could also contain icy materials, notably water ice. This extra icy component led to the formation of four icy–rocky bodies. These were so massive that the gas in the disc was gravitationally captured by them, and thus the giant planets were formed. The capture of the remaining gas was brought to an end by radiation from the newly active Sun, which drove the remaining gas in the disc out into interstellar space.

The formation of the Solar System was largely completed by about 4600 Ma ago; the time it took the Solar System to form was several hundred million years.

The comets and asteroids are left-over fragments that escaped incorporation into a major planet. Most of the comets now orbit the Sun far beyond Neptune, although there are a number closer in. Objects in the Kuiper Belt (including Pluto) are the largest examples of these icy–rocky leftovers. Not all the asteroids are original. Most of the original bodies aggregated into larger bodies, many of which were later smashed by collisions among themselves, to yield today's asteroid population. The gravitational effect of Jupiter has been responsible for preventing a large planet from forming in the asteroid region. The subsequent impact of some of these bodies onto the surfaces of planets (and their satellites) has added to the initial endowment of impact craters, or has replaced craters lost through geological activity.

There is a great deal of evidence in support of this theory for the origin of the Solar System, not only from within the Solar System, but in recent years from the discovery of discs of gas and dust around very young stars, and of giant planets in orbits around other stars. Whether there are any Earth-like planets around other stars, and whether these support life, are questions that might be answered within a few decades.

11.5   Summary of Chapter 11

The Earth orbits the Sun, as do many other objects, some of which are tiny (e.g. dust grains), and some of which are large enough to be considered worlds in their own right, with geological and atmospheric processes similar to those on the Earth (although not identical). Collectively, this system circling the Sun, plus the Sun itself, is called the Solar System. There are eight planets in our Solar System (using the definition of 'planet' at the time of writing) and several dwarf planets including Pluto (which until recently was described as the ninth planet). The orbits of the planets in the Solar System are roughly circular and lie in nearly the same plane. All the planets go around their orbits in the same direction.

Between the planets Mars and Jupiter are rocky bodies called asteroids, and at the edge of the Solar System is the Kuiper Belt consisting of icy–rocky bodies, and the Oort cloud of comets. The comets have a great variety of orbits, and most of them spend most of their time near the outer edge of the Solar System in the Oort cloud.

Many satellites orbit planets in our own Solar System, such as our own Moon. Satellites also show geological processes. The densities and radii of planets, satellites and other objects give clues as to their composition.

The planets can be grouped into the terrestrial planets (Mercury, Venus, Earth and Mars), which are rocky in composition and occupy the inner Solar System, and the giant planets (Jupiter, Saturn, Uranus and Neptune), which occupy the outer Solar System.

Planetary bodies are much smaller than the Sun, and shine at visible wavelengths by reflecting sunlight.

In studying this chapter, you have replaced word equations with symbols. You have practised calculations that substitute numbers into symbolic equations, and compared and classified planets on the basis of their densities and other characteristics.

Chapter 12
Our Sun and the stars

You will shortly resume your journey from the Earth, out of the Solar System, and into the wider Galaxy, to the point where the Sun looks like any other star in the sky. On a clear, dark and moonless night the sky is brilliant with stars, whereas during the day it is the Sun that dominates. What is the relationship between the Sun and the stars? Are they fundamentally different sorts of body? At what distances do stars lie from the Earth? These are the sorts of question that are answered in this chapter. But to understand other stars, you first need to understand the nearest star to the Earth, our Sun.

12.1   The Sun

In the last chapter, you met the Solar System. At its centre is the Sun, which is by far the largest single object in the Solar System.

In Book 1, you saw that solar radiation sustains the Earth's surface temperature, and the Sun is therefore essential for the existence of life on this planet. Were the Sun suddenly 'switched off', the Earth's surface temperature would plunge to 0 °C within a few weeks, on its way to far lower temperatures. Eventually the oceans would freeze, and then the atmosphere would condense and freeze too.

The Sun is a copious source of radiation because its surface is very hot. This radiation energy output per second is called the solar **luminosity** (Book 1, Section 4.3), which is another name for its total output power (recall from Book 1, Section 4.1 that power is the energy output per second). At 5500 °C, the Sun's surface is at a much higher temperature than the surface of the Earth, which averages only about 15 °C. As temperatures become higher, the light emitted is concentrated over shorter and shorter wavelengths. In Book 1, Section 4.3, you saw that the colour of light is related to its wavelength. Solar radiation is concentrated mainly at visible wavelengths, but there is also some radiation at adjacent ultraviolet and infrared wavelengths (Book 1, Figure 4.6).

■ How does the wavelength range of solar radiation compare with that of the radiation emitted by the Earth's surface? (You may need to refer back to Book 1, Figure 4.6 and Section 4.5.3.)

☐ Radiation emitted by the Earth's surface is concentrated at infrared wavelengths, which have a longer wavelength than visible light.

■ How would the luminosity (power) of the Sun's surface compare with that emitted by the Earth's surface, *if the two bodies had the same surface area*?

☐ Because its temperature is much higher, the power emitted by the Sun would be much greater than that emitted by the Earth's surface.

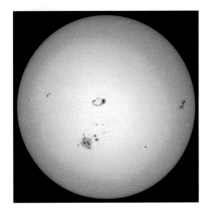

Figure 12.1   An image of the Sun. The dark spots, called sunspots, are regions where the temperatures are lower than the 5500 °C of the rest of the surface, ranging down to about 4000 °C.

This question raises the issue of the comparative sizes of the Earth and the Sun. As well as being hotter than the Earth, the Sun is also much bigger (Figure 11.7). This makes it an even more copious source of radiation than if it were merely hotter but the same size as the Earth. In other words, the high luminosity of the Sun is a result of both its large size *and* its high surface temperature.

The Earth and the Sun are spheres (i.e. ball-shaped) and indeed if they were shrunk to the size of a snooker ball, they would each be almost as smooth. The spherical shape of the Earth is not immediately apparent, because we are so close to its surface. In the case of the Sun, a typical image through a telescope (Figure 12.1) looks like a disc, although this is no more than the illusion you get when, for example, you view a uniformly illuminated ball at arm's length. (*Note that you can easily damage your eyes by looking at the Sun even with the unaided eye, so please avoid looking at the Sun, and don't even glance at it through binoculars or a telescope, or you may suffer severe and irreversible eye damage.*)

The size of a sphere is specified by its radius or by its diameter. Measurements made from the surface of the Earth have shown that the average radius of the Earth is 6.371×10^6 m and that the Sun's radius (the solar radius) is about 109 times greater.

Figure 12.2 shows the Earth and part of the Sun drawn to the same scale. A pair of everyday objects with approximately the same ratio of radii is a soccer ball (for the Sun) and the head of a pin a bit more than 1 mm radius (for the Earth). The Sun is therefore very much bigger than the Earth. It looks small in the sky only because of its huge distance from us, about 24 000 times the Earth's radius.

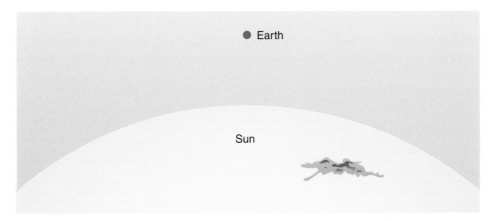

Figure 12.2   The Earth and part of the Sun drawn to scale. The Earth's radius is 6.371×10^6 m, and the Sun's radius is 6.96×10^8 m. Note that the distance between the Sun and the Earth is not drawn to scale; it would be 24 m if drawn to the same scale as the Earth and the Sun. The average distance between the Earth and the Sun is 1.50×10^{11} m.

Question 12.1

What would happen to the Sun's total power output (luminosity) if (a) its surface temperature fell, or (b) its radius increased? (Assume all other factors remain constant.)

12.2   What is inside the Sun?

You have already seen that the Sun is a luminous body with a high surface temperature of about 5500 °C. The luminous surface of the Sun is called the **photosphere**. This is a 'fuzzy' surface, with radiation from the photosphere reaching us from a range of depths, and so it is rather like looking into a bank of cloud, with whatever lies beyond always hidden from our direct view. The photosphere is about 500 km thick, just 0.07% of the 696 000 km from the photosphere to its centre. The Sun gradually gets hotter and denser with increasing depth, the density ranging from about 1 kg m^{-3} in the photosphere to about 1.5×10^5 kg m^{-3} at the centre. To get a feel for these values, note that the density around the photosphere is about the same as that of the Earth's atmosphere at sea level, and that the density at the centre is about 150 times greater than the density of tap water (which is about 10^3 kg m^{-3}).

The material at the centre of the Sun has a density corresponding to about the mass of an adult human crammed into a pint glass! (A pint is about half a litre.) You might expect such a dense substance to be solid, but it is not. This is because the temperature at the centre of the Sun is a mighty 1.5×10^7 °C or so. Under these extreme conditions the material is fluid, and can be regarded as a very dense, very hot gas.

Elsewhere in the Solar System, the centre of Jupiter comes closest to the densities and temperatures in the solar interior, but even at 2×10^4 °C and with a density about 20 times that of tap water, it is not nearly as extreme as the centre of the Sun.

Question 12.2

Explain why there is a depth in the Sun at which the density is the same as that of tap water, but no depth at which the temperature is 10^8 °C.

The sustained high temperature of the solar interior maintains the Sun's high luminosity. Were the interior to cool, then the solar surface would cool and the Earth, which is heated by the Sun, would freeze over. To sustain the interior temperature there must be a source of energy, just as to keep the water in an electric kettle on the boil, the kettle must be kept connected to the mains electricity supply. The Sun's source of energy is a process called nuclear fusion, which was mentioned briefly in the last chapter. You will meet this again in Book 3 and in Book 7.

As you turn the pages of this book, the energy you use to turn the pages has come from food you've eaten. Vegetables grow by turning carbon dioxide into oxygen (released into the air) and carbon (which becomes part of the vegetable), using energy from the Sun (i.e. photosynthesis – Book 1, Section 7.3.1). If you ate meat, the animal would still have grown by eating vegetation, which still grew using sunlight. Almost all life on Earth depends entirely on energy from the Sun. Almost all human activity also depends on energy from the Sun; coal and oil are fossilised remains of prehistoric plants and animals, and only a small proportion of our energy comes from 'artificial' nuclear power. So, how does the Sun generate this energy?

In fact, as you saw in Book 1, energy cannot be generated or destroyed. The Sun is using nuclear fusion to change some of the energy stored in atoms into light energy. Nuclear fusion is a different type of process from chemical reactions. In chemical reactions, the outer parts of atoms interact with each other (you will be finding out about this in Book 4), whereas in nuclear reactions it is the centre of the atom – the nucleus (plural nuclei) – that interacts with another nucleus.

There are over 100 chemical elements, each defined by the type of atom that comprises it. Different atoms have different mass. The hydrogen atom has the smallest mass. In order of increasing atomic mass, the next element is helium. It is familiar in gaseous form in its use to fill small balloons and airships. The atoms of the remaining elements are more massive still. For any particular element, the atoms need not all have exactly the same mass, but broadly speaking we can say that helium is a more massive element than hydrogen, that carbon is yet more massive, and so on. In this context, it is usual to use the terms 'heavier' and 'lighter' rather than 'more massive' and 'less massive'. For example, we say that helium is a lighter element than carbon, and that hydrogen is the lightest element of all. All the other elements are heavier than hydrogen. About 73% of the Sun's mass is hydrogen, and nearly all the rest is helium. This is a very different chemical composition from that of the Earth.

In chemical reactions, atoms are joined to or separated from different atoms. In nuclear fusion, lighter chemical elements are converted to heavier chemical elements, by joining (fusing) the atoms' nuclei, which releases some energy. In the case of the Sun, nuclear fusion converts hydrogen to helium (this process actually involves several fusion reactions). Although hydrogen is abundant throughout the solar interior, the fusion of hydrogen is concentrated only in the Sun's core. This is because the rate at which fusion occurs increases as temperature increases, and temperature increases with increasing depth into the Sun. It is only below a certain depth that the solar temperatures are high enough for the fusion of hydrogen to occur at a significant rate. The threshold temperature is about 10^7 °C.

In the central core of the Sun, the temperatures first exceeded 10^7 °C about 4600 Ma ago, at the birth of the Sun. These high core temperatures were the result of the contraction of the Sun from a cloud of interstellar gas – this process will be discussed in Book 7. The fusion of hydrogen gives out energy, and as soon as the fusion of hydrogen started, this generated sufficient internal pressures to halt the contraction. The temperature was then maintained without further contraction. The Sun thus became self-sustaining, and has remained so ever since. It is this nuclear fusion that sustains the Sun's luminosity.

The fusion of helium to form yet heavier elements also gives out energy. However, the temperatures required for the fusion of helium are even higher than those required for the fusion of hydrogen, and the core of the Sun is not hot enough for helium fusion to be very important. Fusion involving the elements that make up the remaining 2% of the Sun's mass is insignificant. Hydrogen in the core of the Sun is thus the Sun's sole significant nuclear fuel.

The Sun's core contains so much hydrogen, and the energy yield from the fusion of hydrogen to helium, per kilogram of hydrogen, is so enormous, that the Sun will sustain its luminosity for an extremely long time before it runs out of fuel. Nevertheless, the hydrogen in the core is being relentlessly used up, and consequently the amount of helium in the core is building up. Eventually the hydrogen fuel will be gone and the Sun will then undergo enormous changes. One consequence will be the destruction of life on Earth. Fortunately, the Sun will not run out of hydrogen until about 5000 Ma from now, and so it is only about halfway through the hydrogen-fuelled phase of its life.

Question 12.3

Why is the fusion of hydrogen an insignificant source of energy in (a) the interior of Jupiter, and (b) the Sun's photosphere?

12.3   The stars

When you look up on a clear, moonless night from a dark site, you may see about 1000 stars, and with binoculars you can see a lot more. You cannot immediately tell how far away the different stars are. Measurements show that the stars lie at a great range of distances beyond the Solar System. The nearest star beyond the Sun, called Proxima Centauri, is 266 000 times further away from the Earth than the Earth is from the Sun, and the most distant stars visible with the unaided eye are about 2000 times further than Proxima Centauri! It's a pity we can't perceive with our eyes this great cosmic perspective.

Question 12.4

In measuring the distances to the stars, will there be a significant difference if they are measured from the Sun rather than from the Earth?

We turn now to the physical nature of the stars. What do astronomers know about them? A variety of measurements show that the stars are nearly spherical and have radii ranging from about 1% of the solar radius (i.e. the radius of the Sun) to about 1000 times the solar radius.

■ Why then, to the unaided eye, do the stars look like points in the sky, rather than like discs?

☐ This is because of their great distances from the Earth.

Only for a few particularly large and relatively close stars have astronomers obtained images of the discs, and even then, only with the most powerful telescopes.

The stars appear to shine for the same reason that the Sun shines – they have hot surfaces, with surface temperatures of different stars ranging from about 2000 °C to about 40 000 °C. Therefore, some stars are hotter than the Sun, and some are cooler. All stars are believed to convert nuclear energy to light energy, or to have previously done so. The more massive stars have cores hot enough for nuclear fusion with helium, unlike the Sun's core. Hot, large stars are far more luminous than the Sun, and appear to be fainter only because they are so much further away. This is just the same effect as a candle flame seeming a lot brighter when it is a metre from you than a bonfire a kilometre away.

The range of stellar surface temperatures is apparent to the unaided eye through the colour tints of the stars – the higher the temperature, the shorter the wavelength, and the bluer the colour. Cooler stars look reddish.

Activity 12.1   Seeing the temperature differences of stars

We expect this activity will take you approximately 15 minutes.

The colour of a star depends almost entirely on its temperature. If you have a clear sky one night and not too much light pollution, you may be able to discern their different colours. You might need to allow your eyes time to become adapted to the darkness; it can help to close your eyes and count to 100. Figure 12.3 shows a constellation visible from most places on the Earth during (northern) hemisphere winter, with the colours of the stars indicated, which may help you find the constellation in the sky. Can you make out the redder colour of the star in the upper left, Betelgeuse? This star is cooler than the other stars in this constellation. The bluer stars are hotter (this is the opposite way round to the labels on hot and cold water taps). You should alternatively be able to make out the subtly different colours of stars in other constellations, at all times of the year. Some have an orange tint, some have a yellowish tint, and some have a bluish tint. Using a pair of binoculars you can enhance the effect, particularly if you defocus them slightly. Incidentally, Betelgeuse is sometimes pronounced as 'beetle juice', and sometimes pronounced to rhyme (with an accent from some parts of England that suppresses the 'r') with 'kettle furs', with a hard 'g' as in 'go'.

Figure 12.3   The constellation Orion (visible in winter). Betelgeuse is the upper-left bright star (shown as a red disc in the diagram).

There are no comments on this activity.

Question 12.5

If two stars are at the same distance from the Earth, and they have the same surface temperature, what stellar property can make one star appear brighter than the other? Will the two stars have the same colour tint?

You have now accumulated some intriguing information about the stars that allows you to compare them with the Sun:

- Like the Sun, stars are nearly spherical, and the range of stellar radii includes the Sun's radius.

- Like the Sun, they shine because they have hot surfaces, and the range of stellar temperatures includes the Sun's surface temperature.

■ What does this information suggest about the Sun?

☐ It suggests that the Sun is a star of rather modest size and temperature.

Why is there such a variety of stars? There are two main reasons. First, stars have life cycles. They are born, they live, they grow old, they die. Some of the variety in the stars is because we are seeing stars at different times in their lives. Second, stars are born with different masses, and with slightly different compositions.

Our Sun is a modest, middle-aged star, among hundreds of billions of other stars orbiting a common centre in our galaxy, the Milky Way. In the next chapter, you will continue your tour of the Universe, and look at the Sun's position in our galaxy, and our galaxy's position in the wider Universe.

12.4   Summary of Chapter 12

The Sun is much larger than the Earth and has a far hotter surface. Consequently, it emits far more radiation than the Earth, and much of this radiation is at visible wavelengths. The Sun is a star, and compared with other stars it has a modest surface temperature and radius.

The stars are very much further away from the Earth than is the Sun and the other planets.

Stars emit their own radiation. The energy source for this radiation is nuclear fusion in the core of the star, where the matter is very hot and very dense.

The hotter the star, the bluer its colour; the cooler the star, the redder its colour.

In this chapter, you have predicted how the luminosity of the Sun would change if its surface area or temperature changed, and have reasoned about the interiors of the Sun and Jupiter. You have also discerned the temperature differences of stars by seeing their different colours.

Chapter 13
To the edge of the observable Universe

If you can look up on a clear, moonless night from a dark site you may not only see 1000 or so stars, but also, during much of the year, what looks like a ragged white cloud arching across the sky from one horizon to another, as in Figure 13.1a. To many people of ancient civilisations, it looked like a stain of milk on the black backdrop of the heavens; even today, we call it the Milky Way (Figure 11.1). Unfortunately, there is now so much light pollution at night that from many places this magnificent spectacle is obscured. But from a dark site its true nature is revealed, even with modest binoculars; the Milky Way consists of a great number of stars. This is also apparent in Figure 13.1b. Seen without binoculars, the individual stars are so faint and so packed together in the sky that they appear to merge into a faint band of light.

Within the Milky Way, clusters of a few hundred stars are common. Elsewhere, in the huge spaces between the stars – interstellar space – there are glowing clouds of gas, and what appear to be star-free voids, which turn out to be dark dust clouds obscuring the stars beyond them. This interstellar matter is very sparse – interstellar space is almost a perfect vacuum – but it is extensive enough in some places to show up easily.

The Milky Way appears to encircle the Earth, but how does this faint band of stars, star clusters and interstellar matter relate to the stars, star clusters and interstellar matter that are all over the rest of the sky? The time has come for you to resume your journey into deep space.

13.1 The Galaxy

At 10^{18} m from the Earth, the Sun is lost among millions of stars, many of them shining far brighter than the Sun. You travel on, and reach 10^{21} m. Around you, the stars are far more thinly dispersed than they were at the start of your journey. Looking back towards the Earth (Figure 13.2a), the stars seem to have blended together to give you a view quite different from any you have had before.

The distance of 10^{21} m may sound only three more than 10^{18} m, but it is of course 1000 times farther. To get to grips with enormous sizes in astronomy, powers of ten have to be used. You should be familiar with powers of ten; Book 1, Box 3.2 offered a reminder of using powers of ten and entering them into your calculator. Box 13.1 now revisits the topic and offers further revision of manipulating powers of ten within calculations.

Figure 13.1 (a) A fish-eye lens view of the Milky Way, stretching from one horizon to the other. The circular edge is the Earth's horizon in this very wide-angle photograph. (b) A photograph of part of the Milky Way. Note the numerous stars, the glowing patches of gas in the space between the stars, and dark clouds obscuring the stars beyond them. The brightest stars are overexposed, which makes them look like large blobs, however it does make their colours more obvious.

(a)

(b)

(a)

(b)

Figure 13.2 Two schematic views of the Galaxy. (a) A view looking towards the Sun, from a distance of 10^{21} m, from a vantage point along the direction of travel in Figure 11.1. The location of the Sun (and the Earth) is marked as point **S**. (b) The edge-on view of the structure in (a). The direction of travel is shown as a white arrow. The disc (with spiral arms) is about 1.2×10^{21} m diameter.

Box 13.1 Using powers of ten

One thousand is $10 \times 10 \times 10$, or 10^3 (spoken as 'ten to the power of three', 'ten to the three', or 'ten cubed'). Ten thousand is $10 \times 10 \times 10 \times 10$, or 10^4 (ten to the power of four). The power tells you how many tens appear in the string of multiplication. So, ten to the power of 18 is $10^{18} =$ $10 \times 10 \times 10 \times 10 \times 10 \times 10 \times 10 \times 10 \times 10 \times 10 \times$ $10 \times 10 \times 10 \times 10 \times 10 \times 10 \times 10 \times 10$.

If 10^{18} is multiplied by 10^3 (i.e. a thousand), three more tens are added to the string of 18 tens, and so the result has $18 + 3 = 21$ tens. So, $10^{18} \times 10^3 = 10^{21}$. So, multiplying the numbers together has the effect of *adding* the powers (provided that you're dealing with powers of the same thing, 10 in this case, and not mixing in powers of other numbers).

■ Can you see why $10^0 = 1$?

☐ 10 to the power of 0 must equal 1, because (for example) $18 + 0 = 18$, so $10^{18} \times 10^0 = 10^{18}$, and the only number that doesn't change things when you multiply by it is the number one.

What about division? Here is a clue: $\frac{10^{21}}{10^3} = 10^{18}$.

Dividing by 1000 (which is 10^3) has the effect of removing three tens from the string of 21 tens. Now, $21 - 3 = 18$. So, dividing the numbers has the effect of *subtracting* the powers.

This suggests another way of writing it: $10^{21} \times 10^{-3} = 10^{18}$. In other words, dividing by 10^3 is the same as multiplying by 10^{-3} (spoken as 'ten to the power of minus three' or 'ten to the minus three'). But what does 10^{-3} mean?

If 10^{-3} is taken to mean 'the number that, when you multiply something by it, it has the same effect as dividing that something by 1000', then $10^{-3} = 0.001$. The sequence can be continued: $10^{-2} = 0.01$, $10^{-1} = 0.1$, $10^0 = 1$, $10^1 = 10$, $10^2 = 100$, $10^2 = 100$, $10^3 = 1000$ (see Table 13.1). So the negative powers are just the continuation of the sequence of positive powers. In science, we deal with the tiniest sub-atomic particles to the biggest cosmic galaxy superclusters. It can be helpful to know which power of ten the size of an object is closest to. An atom has a size of about 10^{-10} m, while a galaxy supercluster can be about 10^{18} m across. The nearest whole power of ten is called the **order of magnitude** of a quantity. For example, the nearest order of magnitude of 8×10^2 is 10^3.

Table 13.1 Powers of ten.

$10^4 =$	10 000
$10^3 =$	1000
$10^2 =$	100
$10^1 =$	10
$10^0 =$	1
$10^{-1} =$	0.1
$10^{-2} =$	0.01
$10^{-3} =$	0.001
$10^{-4} =$	0.0001

If dividing by 10^3 is the same as multiplying by 10^{-3}, then what about dividing by 10^{-3}? For everything to work consistently, dividing by 10^{-3} must be the same as multiplying by 10^3.

Similarly, $\frac{1}{10^{-1}} = 10$ (i.e. one divided by 10^{-1} is one times 10^1, which is one times 10, which is ten).

One last point is worth making about powers. What is the number that, when multiplied by *itself*, gives ten? Suppose that number is a. Then $a \times a = a^2 = 10$. The number a is known as the square root of 10, sometimes written as $\sqrt{10}$. So, if $a^2 = 10$, then $a = \sqrt{10}$. But $10 = 10^1$, and $\frac{1}{2} + \frac{1}{2} = 1$. So why not say $a = 10^{\frac{1}{2}}$, so that $10^{\frac{1}{2}} \times 10^{\frac{1}{2}} = 10^1$? If we can live with negative powers, why not fractional ones? This is, in fact, standard practice in science and mathematics. This doesn't tell us how to calculate the square root of 10 though; it's just been given a different name. The square root of 10 is a bit more than three and is not a whole number, but $3 \times 3 = 9$, so $\sqrt{9} = 3$ exactly.

If you refer back to this box, you may find the following examples helpful:

$$10^0 = 1$$

$$10^1 = 10$$

$$10^3 = 10 \times 10 \times 10$$

$$10^{-3} = \frac{1}{10 \times 10 \times 10}$$

$$10^{-3} = \frac{1}{10^3}$$

$$10^{-1} = \frac{1}{10}$$

$$\frac{1}{10^{-1}} = 10$$

$$\frac{1}{10^{-3}} = 10^3$$

$$10^{18} \times 10^3 = 10^{(18+3)} = 10^{21}$$

$$10^{18} \div 10^3 = 10^{(18-3)} = 10^{15}$$

$$10^{\frac{1}{2}} = \sqrt{10}$$

$$10^{\frac{1}{2}} \times 10^{\frac{1}{2}} = 10^{\frac{1}{2}+\frac{1}{2}} = 10^1 = 10$$

$$9^{\frac{1}{2}} = \sqrt{9} = 3$$

Question 13.1

(a) How many times bigger is the distance to the Sun from the viewpoint in Figure 13.2a, compared with the distance to the Sun from the viewpoint in Figure 11.6? Express your answer in powers of ten notation.

(b) Comment on the statement: 'If you had continued your journey from 10^{21} m to 10^{22} m, you would not have gone much further, because 22 is not much bigger than 21.'

13.1.1 The layout of the Galaxy

Figure 13.2 shows a huge assemblage of about 10^{11} stars, plus interstellar matter. This assemblage is called the **Galaxy**. (The capital G distinguishes it from other galaxies of which our Sun is not a member.) You can see that most of the stars are concentrated into a thin disc, and this is the case for the interstellar gas and dust too. This Galactic disc (as it is called) is about 1.2×10^{21} m in diameter, and about 2×10^{19} m thick, a ratio of diameter to thickness of about 60 : 1. For comparison, for a DVD the corresponding ratio is about 100 : 1. Therefore, a rough physical model of the galaxy would be obtained by placing two DVDs together, though it must be stressed that, unlike those of a DVD, the surfaces of the Galactic disc are very 'fuzzy', the average distance between the stars increasing gradually as you travel out of the disc. The thickness of the disc is therefore a somewhat arbitrary value.

Figure 13.2 also shows the location of the Sun, and you can see that it is within the Galactic disc. What we call the Milky Way can now be explained: it is the view we have from the Earth of the more distant parts of the Galactic disc. We see the disc as a great band of stars and interstellar matter encircling the Earth. The stars are so numerous and so distant that, to the unaided eye, they seem to blend together. The stars and interstellar matter that appear to lie outside the Milky Way are actually mostly within the disc too – they happen to be close to us and so can appear in all directions, as illustrated in Figure 13.3.

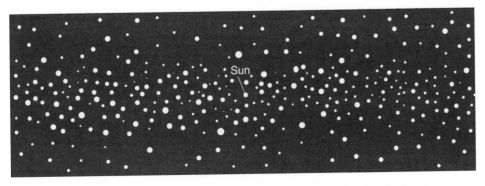

Figure 13.3 A schematic edge-on view of the Galactic disc in the Sun's neighbourhood. Nearby stars in the Galactic disc can lie in any direction. The more distant stars are concentrated in directions that lie along the Galactic disc.

Figure 13.1a shows that the Milky Way is thicker in some directions than in others. This is our view of the extremities of the bulge at the centre of the Galactic disc, apparent in Figure 13.2, and called the nuclear bulge. ('Nuclear' here has nothing to do with nuclear energy but arises from the bulge being at the heart, or nucleus, of the Galaxy.) As well as being thicker than the disc, the concentration of stars and interstellar matter is generally greater in the nuclear bulge than elsewhere, and at its centre there is something pouring out copious amounts of energy. Astronomers have tracked the motions of stars around this central object, and it is so dense that it is almost certainly a giant black hole, several million times more massive than our Sun. (A black hole is an object so dense that nothing can escape from its boundary. Even light cannot escape, which is why it is called black.) Matter and light disappear into this black hole, giving out energy before they cross its threshold. Our view of the Galactic centre is blocked at visible wavelengths by interstellar dust, and so it is to other wavelengths that we look to explore this mysterious region, including infrared and radio waves (which is light with a very long wavelength).

Outside the nuclear bulge, the most obvious feature in the view in Figure 13.2a is the spiral pattern called, unsurprisingly, the spiral arms of the Galaxy. This might seem to indicate a strong clustering of stars into these arms, but this is not so! Stars and interstellar matter in general are not much more concentrated in the arms than elsewhere in the disc. Instead, the arms contain a greater abundance of *bright* stars and a larger proportion of interstellar gas that is glowing brightly.

■ Where is the Sun located with respect to a spiral arm?

☐ From Figure 13.2a, you can see that the Sun is near the edge of a spiral arm, about half of the way from the Galactic centre to the edge of the disc.

From the Earth, it is not easy to pick out the spiral arms, but detailed mapping of the stars and interstellar matter reveals their existence.

The Galactic disc is enclosed by a volume with a poorly known radius, but certainly exceeding the radius of the disc. This is called the Galactic halo, and it is illustrated in Figure 13.4. It contains far fewer stars that the disc, and its interstellar gas and dust are more thinly dispersed. However, its huge volume means that it contains a significant proportion of the total mass of the Galaxy. A large fraction of the stars in the halo are contained in globe-like clusters, called globular clusters (Figure 13.5), each containing up to about a million stars, though even in the relatively packed centres of globular clusters the stars are still separated by *huge* distances compared to their diameters. The clusters in the Galactic disc are much less densely packed and are more irregular in shape – these are called open clusters.

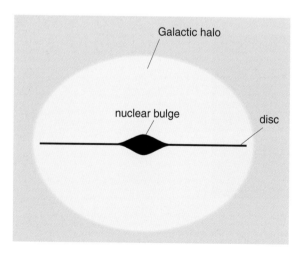

Figure 13.4 The halo that encloses the disc of the Galaxy. Its diameter is poorly known.

In addition to stars and sparse interstellar gas and dust, the halo also contains a lot of other matter. Evidence for its existence is outlined in Section 13.2.

That completes our account of the layout of the Galaxy. Table 13.2 summarises some sizes and distances in the Galaxy, and Activity 13.1 should enable you to get a better feel for these.

Table 13.2 Sizes and distances in the Galaxy.

Size or distance	Length/m
Radius of the Earth	6.37×10^6
Radius of the Sun	6.96×10^8
Average distance of the Earth from the Sun	1.50×10^{11}
Distance from the Sun to the nearest star (Proxima Centauri)	3.99×10^{16}
Thickness of the disc of the Galaxy (approximate, outside the bulge)	2×10^{19}
Diameter of the disc of the Galaxy (approximate)	1.2×10^{21}

Figure 13.5   A globular cluster called M13. This is about 10^{18} m in diameter, which is about 10^3 times smaller than the diameter of the Galactic disc.

Activity 13.1   A scale model of the Galaxy

We expect this activity will take you approximately 15 minutes.

Scale models are useful for helping us to visualise the very large and the very small. By choosing appropriate scales, huge objects like the Galaxy and microscopic objects like an atom can be represented by models that fit on a table top. Of course, scale models generally only represent some specific features of the real object. So a scale model of the Galaxy cannot represent the millions of individual stars, nor their relative motion, but it can convey the relative dimensions of the Galaxy more directly than numbers involving large powers of ten. In this activity, you will plan scale models of the Galaxy.

In a scale model, the sizes of all the individual parts are reduced (or magnified) by the same amount, and this amount is often known as the scale factor (or simply the scale) of the model. To take an example, if an architect produces a scale model of a new housing development in which a house that is 7.0 m high is represented by a model that is 3.5 cm (0.035 m) high, then:

0.035 m in the model corresponds to 7.0 m in the real world

and dividing these model and real world sizes by 0.035, you can see that:

$\dfrac{0.035\,\text{m}}{0.035}$, i.e. 1 m in the model corresponds to $\dfrac{7.0\,\text{m}}{0.035}$, i.e. 200 m in the real world.

The ratio 1 : 200 is the scale of the model, and this simply means that any model distance is 200 times smaller than the corresponding real world distance. So to find the model height for a person who is 1.6 m tall, you simply divide their height by the scale factor:

1.6 m in the real world corresponds to $\dfrac{1.6\,\text{m}}{200}$, i.e. 8.0×10^{-3} m, or 8.0 mm, in the model.

This is exactly the same as the scale of a map. On a map that has a scale of 1 : 50 000, a distance of 5 cm corresponds to 5 cm × 50 000, i.e. 250 000 cm, which is 2500 m, or 2.5 km.

The task of this activity is to fill in the missing values in Tables 13.3 and 13.4.

(a) In the first scale model, the radius of the Earth will be represented by 0.100 mm, or 1.00×10^{-4} m, so the Earth in the model will be a tiny sphere 0.200 mm in diameter. The actual radius of the Earth is 6.37×10^6 m, so 1.00×10^{-4} m in the model corresponds to 6.37×10^6 m in the Galaxy.

(i) Use this relationship to determine the scale factor of this model.

(ii) Use the scale factor you have worked out to calculate the values required to complete the third and fourth columns of Table 13.3. Use scientific notation for the values in metres, but don't use powers of ten notation when you write down the scale values in the fourth column, as it will be easier to compare the numbers if they are written in full.

(b) In the second scale model, you should use 0.100 mm to represent the distance from the Sun to the nearest star. Complete Table 13.4 by first calculating the scale factor for this model, and then calculating the scale model values, in metres and millimetres, for the three other sizes. Do not use powers of ten notation in the scale model values in the final column.

Table 13.3 A scale model of the Galaxy, in which the Earth's radius is 0.100 mm.

Size or distance	Actual value/m	Scale model value/m	Scale model value/mm
Radius of the Earth	6.37×10^6	1.00×10^{-4}	0.100
Radius of the Sun	6.96×10^8		
Average distance of the Earth from the Sun	1.50×10^{11}		
Distance from the Sun to the nearest star	3.99×10^{16}		

Table 13.4 A scale model of the Galaxy, in which the distance from the Sun to the nearest star is 0.100 mm.

Size or distance	Actual value/m	Scale model value/m	Scale model value/mm
Distance from the Sun to the nearest star	3.99×10^{16}	1.00×10^{-4}	0.100
Diameter of the globular cluster M13	1×10^{18}		
Thickness of the disc of the Galaxy	2×10^{19}		
Diameter of the disc of the Galaxy	1.2×10^{21}		

Check your method and answers with those given in the comments on this activity at the end of this book, then study the scale model values in these two tables to get an impression of the relative sizes and distances in the Galaxy. You could try drawing some of the scale model values as lines on a piece of paper to help visualise their relative sizes.

13.1.2   Motion in the Galaxy

The stars and interstellar matter in the Galaxy are not stationary but are in motion. In the disc of the Galaxy the predominant motion is a circular swirl around the Galactic centre. This motion is in the plane of the disc, as shown (approximately) in Figure 13.6. Thus most of the stars and interstellar matter are in approximately circular orbits around the Galactic centre. From Figure 13.6 you can see that the further a body is from the Galactic centre, the smaller the fraction of its orbit that it covers in a given time. After 60 Ma, the Sun (B) has moved a quarter of the way around its orbit, but a star at the edge of the disc (A) has moved around much less than a quarter of its orbit.

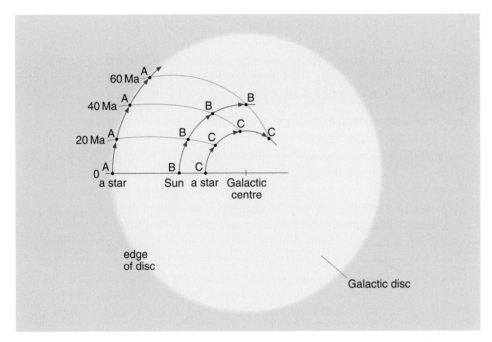

Figure 13.6   Motion in the plane of the Galactic disc. A, B and C denote stars at different distances from the Galactic centre, at four times in their orbits. The time interval between successive depictions is 20 Ma.

■ What is the orbital period of the Sun around the Galactic centre?

☐ It moves a quarter of the way around its orbit in 60 Ma, and therefore the orbital period is 240 Ma.

As well as the Sun, nearly all the matter in the disc at the same distance as the Sun from the Galactic centre takes about 240 Ma to complete one orbit. Closer to the centre the orbital period is less, and further from the centre it is greater.

■ If the Galaxy rotated like a rigid disc (such as a wheel or a DVD), then how would the orbital period vary with distance from the centre?

☐ The orbital period would be the same at all distances: the time taken to rotate once around the centre is the same for a point near the centre of a wheel (or a DVD) as for a point near the periphery.

Question 13.2

Use Figure 13.6 to make *rough* estimates of the orbital periods around the Galactic centre of:

(a) a star (like C) at about two-thirds of the distance of the Sun from the Galactic centre

(b) a star (like A) at the outer edge of the Galactic disc.

You can assume that the orbits are circular and that the stars go around their orbits at constant speed.

The stars travel in circular orbits around the Galactic centre because of the universal phenomenon of gravitational attraction. Therefore, in the Galaxy any star or piece of interstellar matter is attracted to all the other stars and interstellar matter. Quite how this explains the circular orbits around the Galactic centre will become apparent in Section 14.5. For now, the important point is that gravity does explain motion in the Galaxy.

Gravity explains motions outside the disc as well as within it. Outside the Galactic disc the motion is less orderly. The individual stars and globular clusters orbit the Galactic centre, but they swarm around in all directions, those in inclined orbits plunging through the disc as they do so. They also retreat to the farthest-flung parts of the halo, and when stellar motions in those distant regions are examined something very curious emerges. The amount of matter far out in the halo can be inferred from the effect its gravitational attraction has on the motion of these distant objects. It turns out that there is more matter out there than can be seen as stars and interstellar gas and dust. The matter detected *only* by its gravitational effect is called dark matter and there could be at least ten times as much dark matter in the Galaxy as non-dark matter, much of it in the halo. The nature of this dark matter is unknown and (at the time of writing) it is a hot area of research.

The spiral arms are not fixed features; they are more like traffic jams on a motorway. Stars pass into the spiral arms and out of them. This also applies to interstellar gas. When the gas enters an arm, it becomes slightly compressed by its surroundings. The cooler, denser regions of the gas were on the verge of contracting, and this slight compression triggers the contraction. The contracting gas forms open clusters of stars. Left-over gas in the vicinity of star formation is bathed in radiation from the new stars, particularly from the most luminous of these stars, and this causes the gas to glow, as in Figure 13.7. A few million years later, when the new stars and interstellar matter emerge from the leading edge of the spiral arm, the gas around many young stars has dissipated, and the most luminous of the young stars are so short-lived that they have vanished. Thus the spiral arms are lit up rather in the manner of a set of flash bulbs that go off inside the arms. It is this that delineates the arms, and not the slightly greater concentration there of stars and interstellar matter. Stars do form outside spiral arms, but less frequently.

Figure 13.7   A young cluster of stars, with glowing interstellar gas and dark dust. The distance across this image is about 1.6×10^{17} m.

Outside the arms the less luminous stars live on, and the open clusters in which they were born gradually break up to yield isolated stars, or stars in small clusters of two or three. Later, these stars will enter a spiral arm again, as the Sun has done many times.

13.2   The journey time

To calculate how long the imaginary journey in Section 13.1 would have taken you, you must assume a speed of travel. Speed is the distance travelled divided by the time interval taken. Recall that the word equation for this is:

$$\text{speed} = \frac{\text{distance travelled}}{\text{time interval}}$$

which in symbolic notation is:

$$s = \frac{d}{t} \qquad\qquad (13.1)$$

where the speed is denoted by s, the distance travelled by d, and the time interval by t.

To calculate the time taken to travel a certain distance at a given speed, this equation must be rearranged so that it has the form 'time interval = …'. If you are not familiar with rearranging equations, you will learn how to do this in Book 3. In the meantime, the answer is:

$$\text{time interval} = \frac{\text{distance travelled}}{\text{speed}}$$

(This is the same as Equation 8.2.) In symbolic notation this is:

$$t = \frac{d}{s} \qquad\qquad (13.2)$$

where the symbols have the same meaning as in Equation 13.1.

If distance is measured in the SI unit metres, and time in the SI unit seconds, then the speed is in the SI unit metres per second, or m s^{-1}. The greatest speed at which spacecraft can presently leave the Earth is about 3×10^4 m s^{-1} (30 km per second). A feasible goal for the 22nd century might be for a spacecraft to be able to travel 1000 times faster than this, at 3×10^7 m s^{-1}. At this speed, a spacecraft would circumnavigate the Earth in 1.3 seconds, and would be able to reach the Sun in 5000 seconds (83 minutes).

Question 13.3

If you had travelled at 3×10^7 m s^{-1}, how many years would it have taken you to reach the end of your journey in Figure 13.2, exactly 10^{21} m from the Earth? (There are 3.16×10^7 seconds in a year.)

The answer to Question 13.3 shows that, even at the huge speed of 3×10^7 m s^{-1}, the view in Figure 13.2a would be attained only after 10^6 years (about 40 000 human generations). It is a journey humans will probably never make, unless, somehow, we can travel at far, far greater speeds. Alas, there seems to be a cosmic speed limit.

The greatest speed possible, according to our present understanding, is the speed at which light travels through a vacuum. (In science fiction, this is often called 'warp factor 1', a rather low speed in science fiction terms.) The **speed of light** is 3.00×10^8 m s^{-1} (to three significant figures).

■ What percentage of the speed of light is your anticipated speed of 3×10^7 m s^{-1}?

□ The percentage is $\left(\dfrac{3 \times 10^7 \text{ m s}^{-1}}{3.00 \times 10^8 \text{ m s}^{-1}} \right) \times 100\%$, which is 10%.

Your anticipated speed is thus a substantial fraction of the cosmic speed limit. But if you can reach 10% of the speed of light, why not 100%? It turns out that the greater the speed, the greater the amount of energy needed to increase the speed by a given amount. A spacecraft speed of 10% of the speed of light is ambitious, so the prospects for travel at much more than 10% of the speed of light in the foreseeable future are poor.

13.3   Galaxies galore!

The Galaxy is clearly a huge, complicated structure. But is it the entire Universe? Is there nothing but a boundless void beyond it, or is the Galaxy itself just one entity among many?

This question was not answered until the 1920s. Up to that time there was a vigorous debate among astronomers about the nature of some of the so-called nebulae (pronounced 'neb-you-lee') that had been observed for generations. A **nebula** is a celestial object that under low magnification looks like a continuous patch of light ('nebula' is the Latin word for 'mist'). By 1920 many such nebulae were known, and the brightest 100 or so had been catalogued much earlier, in the 1780s, by the French astronomer Charles Messier. Messier's objects are numbered M1 to M110 and are often referred to by these numbers even if they are included in other catalogues or have proper names. Figure 13.8 shows some typical examples of his nebulae.

Under high magnification, such as in Figure 13.8, some nebulae were long ago seen to be collections of stars – open and globular clusters of which Figures 13.8a and b are examples. Other nebulae remained mist-like, and analysis of the light from them showed that they consist of hot gas. These hot gas clouds vary considerably from one to another in appearance, and in other properties: Figure 13.8c is just one example. Yet other nebulae could not be seen as separate stars at even the highest magnification available in the 1920s, though analysis of the light they emit showed that they must contain large numbers of stars, plus interstellar gas: Figures 13.8d and 13.8e show two examples of these. They belong to another class of objects that vary considerably in appearance, and also vary in other ways, such as the average properties of the stars that they contain, and the proportion and properties of interstellar matter.

But are the nebulae within the Galaxy or beyond it? The crucial evidence required to answer this question is the distance of the nebulae from us, and the size of the Galaxy. If the nebulae are at distances beyond the boundary of the Galaxy, then they must be external; otherwise, they must be within the Galaxy. The US astronomer Edwin Powell Hubble (1889–1953) made a particularly important contribution to the distance measurements, and we will describe how he did this in Book 7. The crucial measurements were made in the 1920s, and they showed that though some nebulae lie within the Galaxy, some are external to it. The Galaxy was thus shown *not* to comprise the whole Universe.

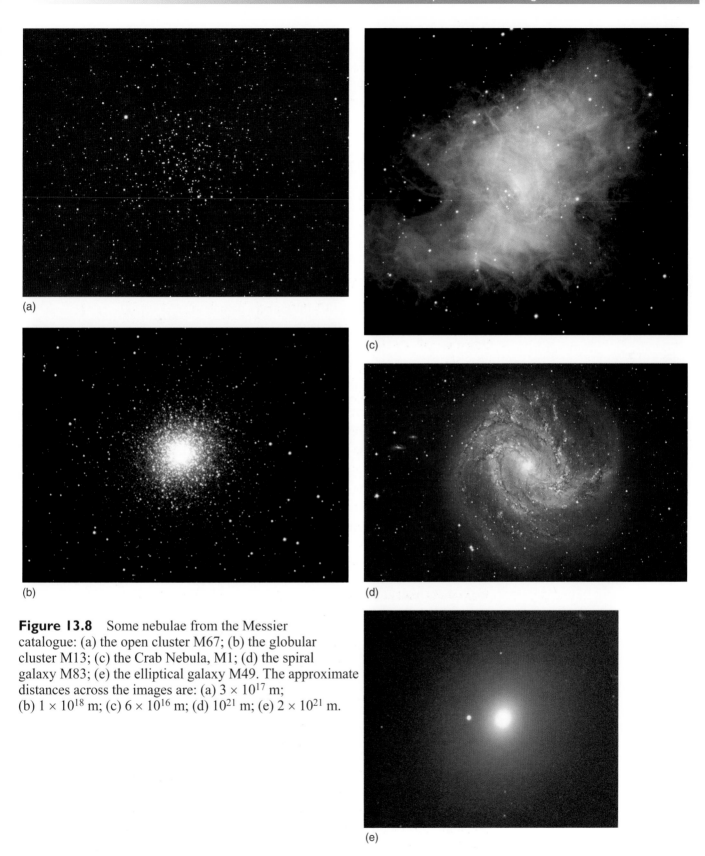

Figure 13.8   Some nebulae from the Messier catalogue: (a) the open cluster M67; (b) the globular cluster M13; (c) the Crab Nebula, M1; (d) the spiral galaxy M83; (e) the elliptical galaxy M49. The approximate distances across the images are: (a) 3×10^{17} m; (b) 1×10^{18} m; (c) 6×10^{16} m; (d) 10^{21} m; (e) 2×10^{21} m.

Of the different types of object in Figure 13.8, star clusters and gas clouds (Figure 13.8a–c) are found within the Galaxy. The types of nebulae found to lie external to the Galaxy are those of which Figures 13.8d and 13.8e are examples, i.e. those that consist of large numbers of stars, plus interstellar matter. These external structures are themselves now called **galaxies**, not nebulae. Note the use of the lower case 'g' to distinguish these other galaxies from our own galaxy, the Galaxy. This convention extends to 'galactic' versus 'Galactic', for example as in 'a galactic centre' and 'the Galactic centre'. Figure 13.8d shows an example of a spiral galaxy, so called because of its spiral arms. Figure 13.8e shows an example of an elliptical galaxy, a different class of galaxy that is devoid of spiral arms but has a regular shape. Some elliptical galaxies are roughly spherical; some are tangerine-shaped; some are rather like rugby balls. Within these different shaped boundaries there are stars everywhere, although with some concentration towards the centre. The other major class of galaxy is the irregular galaxy, which, as its name suggests, is characterised by a ragged shape.

■   What class of galaxy does the Galaxy belong to?

☐   It has spiral arms (Figure 13.2a), so it is a spiral galaxy.

The realisation that the Galaxy is a spiral galaxy has enabled astronomers to use observations of other spiral galaxies to help understand the nature of ours.

Activity 13.2   Observing the Milky Way and other galaxies

We expect this activity will take you approximately 15 minutes.

If you have a clear night sky and not too much light pollution, it may be possible for you to see the Milky Way. As with Activity 12.1, you might need to allow your eyes time to become adapted to the darkness; it can help to close your eyes and count to 100. The Milky Way passes next to the constellation Orion (see Figure 12.3) but is visible all year round. In the autumn of the Northern Hemisphere, if you are lucky enough to have a dark enough site, it is also possible to see light from another galaxy, the Andromeda Galaxy (through binoculars or even with the naked eye). This galaxy is so distant that it takes light over 2 Ma to reach the Earth; it looks like a faint smudge. Figure 13.9 shows you

Figure 13.9   Star chart for finding the Andromeda Galaxy. This is visible from the Northern Hemisphere and is most easily viewed in autumn.

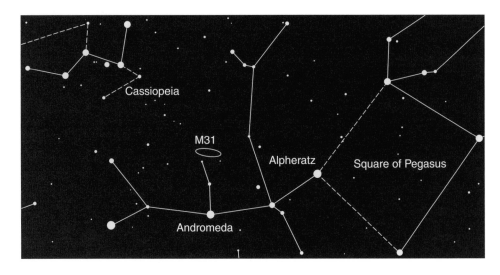

how to find it. This is the most distant object that can be seen with the naked eye. In the Southern Hemisphere, you can see two nearby dwarf galaxies, called the Large Magellanic Cloud and the Small Magellanic Cloud, that may be falling into our galaxy. Figure 13.10 shows an image of them; they look like pieces broken off the Milky Way. These are the most clearly visible galaxies seen from the Earth (apart from our Milky Way).

Figure 13.10 The Large Magellanic Cloud (upper-right galaxy) and the Small Magellanic Cloud (lower-left galaxy). These can be seen to the south from the Southern Hemisphere, at most times during the year.

There are no comments on this activity.

Question 13.4

Suppose that the Solar System were relocated near to the centre of an elliptical galaxy that was nearly spherical.

(a) In two or three sentences, describe the main differences between the appearance of the night sky in this new location and the night sky from our present location.

(b) Noting that an elliptical galaxy has no spiral arms, state, with a brief justification, whether there will be any open clusters in the sky. (You can assume that star formation has the same requirements in all types of galaxies.)

Billions of galaxies are now known, some much less massive and smaller than our own galaxy, others more massive and larger. In Activity 13.2, you may already have seen another galaxy with your naked eye. There are several galaxies within 10^{22} m of the Galactic centre, which is a distance only ten times larger than the 10^{21} m diameter of the Galactic disc.

Galaxies, like stars, are grouped in clusters. The galaxies are in motion within the clusters, and the clusters move as a whole with respect to each other. An example of a galaxy cluster is shown in Figure 13.11. This cluster is close enough on a cosmic scale to be called 'nearby', even though it is about 5×10^{23} m away! At these distances, astronomers tend to speak in terms of **light-years**, where one light-year is the distance light travels in one year, i.e. about 9.5×10^{15} m. Note that a light-year is a measure of *distance*, not time.

Figure 13.11   The Virgo Cluster of galaxies.

These galaxy clusters themselves clump together. As astronomers surveyed larger and larger distances, they have found bigger and bigger clumps, but on the very largest scales, the Universe appears to smooth out. Figure 13.12 shows the galaxies found by one very intensive survey of galaxies, which searched for galaxies in two strips of the sky. After measuring the distance to each galaxy, the astronomers plotted their positions along each strip and found giant filaments of galaxies, and equally enormous voids where galaxies are rare. The image tapers off at the largest distances because the galaxies become too faint to see.

To see the structure of the Universe on even larger scales, one needs to use more luminous objects. A type of very luminous astronomical object that would do is the **quasar**. At the centre of our galaxy is a black hole, and matter falling into it emits light before passing inside it. Other galaxies have much bigger black holes, and quasars are believed to be very massive black holes with matter falling

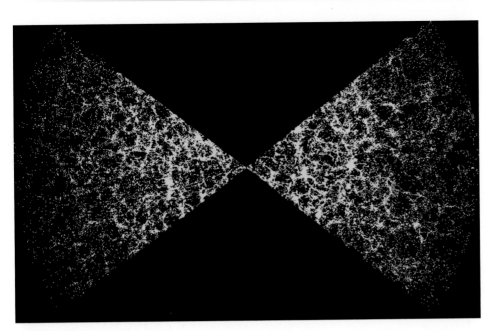

Figure 13.12   The galaxies found by the Two-Degree Field Galaxy Redshift Survey. The size of this map is 6 billion light-years, or 5×10^{25} m. The survey covered two strips of sky, which means they cover two cone-like volumes, each the shape of a rectangular-based pyramid, with the Earth at the apex. This map shows the two cones, as seen from above.

in, at the centres of the galaxies. They can be much more luminous than even an entire galaxy, so they can be seen to far greater distances than typical galaxies. Figure 13.13 shows another picture of the large-scale structure of the Universe, this time from a major quasar survey. The Universe appears much more smooth in this image. Again, the survey peters out at the highest distances because the quasars become too faint to see, but also at short distances because objects that were obviously nearby were deliberately omitted.

This large-scale architecture of the Universe, and its large-scale motions, will be explored in Book 7. These structures and motions are believed to be caused by galaxies being pulled towards each other by the force of gravity. This is the same force that we see acting in our Solar System, and can even measure in laboratories. Gravity therefore acts in the same way on things at least as small as everyday size scales right up to 10^{26} metres and beyond! The next chapter will introduce you to this astonishingly universal law that underlies so much of the structure of our Universe. But this chapter will conclude with one final image, to end your tour out to the edge of the observable Universe. The most distant galaxies found so far are so distant that it has taken most of the history of the Universe for the light to reach us. We therefore see these galaxies as they were in the distant past. These most distant galaxies do not look like our nearby galactic neighbours. Figure 13.14 shows part of the Ultra Deep Field made by the Hubble Space Telescope. Many of the galaxies in Figure 13.14 are primordial objects in the very early Universe and are unlike nearby spiral or elliptical galaxies; rather,

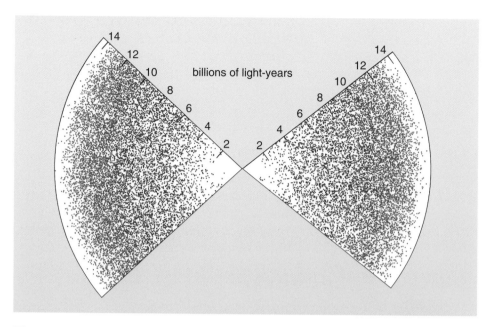

Figure 13.13   The quasars found by the Two-Degree Field Quasar Redshift Survey. The more distant quasars have been given a redder colour in this plot. The size of this map is 28 billion light-years, or 2.5×10^{26} m.

Figure 13.14   Distant galaxies found by the Hubble Space Telescope in its Ultra Deep Field. The light from many of the galaxies in this image has taken most of the history of the Universe to reach us.

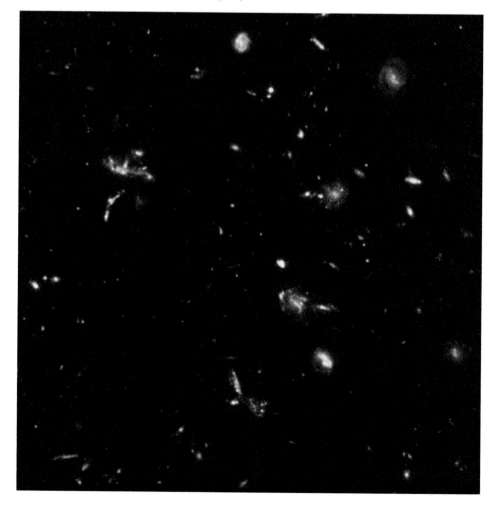

they have complicated structures that suggest the galaxies are still in the process of formation. By seeing how galaxies change with distance from us, we are watching the very birth and growth of the first things in the Universe.

13.4   Summary of Chapter 13

The Milky Way is our view of the more distant parts of the Galactic disc seen from our location within the disc. The disc contains most of the 10^{11} stars and most of the visible interstellar matter that constitutes the Galaxy. The disc displays spiral arms that rotate as a rigid pattern, in contrast to the orbits of the stars and other matter around the Galactic centre, which have orbital periods that generally increase with distance from the centre. The disc is about 100 times thinner than it is wide (to the nearest order of magnitude). The arms are delineated by a larger number of bright young stars, and by a higher proportion of glowing interstellar gas than in the disc between the arms. Gas entering the arms is compressed and contracts to form star clusters.

In the central region of the disc is the nuclear bulge, at the centre of which there appears to be a massive black hole.

The disc is surrounded by a halo where visible interstellar matter is more thinly dispersed than in the disc, and where there are fewer stars, many of them in globular clusters. There is, however, a huge mass of dark matter in the halo.

Beyond the Galaxy, there is a huge number of various sorts of other galaxies. Some of them are spiral galaxies like our Galaxy, but others have no spiral arms. Galaxies cluster together, but in the very largest-scale maps, the Universe seems fairly smooth. The light from the most distant galaxies found so far has taken most of the history of the Universe to reach us, so we see them as they were when the Universe was young.

In this chapter, you have revised the powers of ten notation, and how adding or subtracting powers of ten changes a quantity, and how that relates to multiplying or dividing by powers of ten. You met square roots and the order of magnitude of a quantity. You have used some of these skills to compare cosmological distances, and in constructing scale models to help appreciate relative sizes. You have made rough estimates of numerical quantities from a diagram. You have practised replacing words with symbols in equations, and have substituted numbers into symbolic equations. Finally, you might have tried to observe the Milky Way and another galaxy, and speculated about how the night sky would look if we lived in an elliptical galaxy rather than a spiral galaxy.

Chapter 14
Motion and gravity

Why does the Moon stay in the sky? Why doesn't it fall to the ground? After all, everything on Earth falls unless it is supported somehow. The ancient Greeks explained this by supposing the celestial Universe somehow worked differently from the terrestrial world. Galileo's spectacular telescopic discoveries in the early 1600s of the moons orbiting Jupiter, the mountains, valleys and craters on the Moon, and stars in the Milky Way too faint to be seen by the naked eye except as a haze, paved the way for a radically different understanding of the celestial Universe.

Isaac Newton (Figure 14.1) was born on 25 December 1642 at Woolsthorpe Manor in Lincolnshire. He was educated at Grantham Grammar School and then at Trinity College, Cambridge, from where he graduated in 1664. He stayed on at Cambridge, but in 1665 and 1666 England was ravaged by the Great Plague. Consequently, many people spent as much time as they could in the country, where the chance of catching the deadly infection was lower. Thus it was that when the University was closed, Newton returned to rural Lincolnshire.

During these years, Newton made a magnificent discovery: it is possible to describe the motions in the Solar System, and the falling of objects on the Earth, with the *same* rules. There is no need to separate the celestial Universe from the Earth-bound; instead there is, he conjectured, a single law of gravity that applies in the same way to our bodies as it applies to the planets. This idea of a physical law or rule which applies everywhere in the Universe was a new and bold step forwards, and Newton's laws successfully explained so many disparate observations and experiments that the poet Alexander Pope wrote 'Nature and nature's laws lay hid in night; God said "Let Newton be" and all was light.'

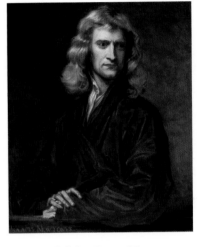

Figure 14.1   Isaac Newton (1642–1727), painted a few years after he published his theory of gravity.

It is possible that his deliberations were provoked in part by his observation of the fall of an apple in the garden of Woolsthorpe Manor, hence the famous (but probably fictitious) tale that Newton formulated his theory of gravity after being hit on the head by a falling apple. In this chapter, you will learn about Newton's universal law of gravity, and his three universal laws of motion. But remember at all times that these laws are *theories*, not facts. They are enormously successful and explain a great deal, but we know, for example, that there are small effects that Newton's law of gravity cannot explain, and which are only explained by Einstein's theory, derived much later in 1915. Is Einstein's theory therefore the 'correct' one? No, because there are still situations where Einstein's equations break down. You may be shocked to discover that there is *no* known theory that explains all experiments and observations. The current state-of-the-art in physics is not even self-consistent! physicists are still searching for the most fundamental underlying laws that explain every experiment, perhaps inspired by Newton's spectacular successes. Perhaps, in time, you will contribute yourself to the quest for these laws. In the meantime, Newton's laws are so nearly correct in so many situations that they are still used, and there is much to be learned from them about the underlying workings of our Universe.

14.1   Newton's first law of motion

What do you think is the 'natural' state of motion of an object? In other words, how does it move (if at all) when there is no external influence on it? You might well have answered that the object stays where it is – it remains at rest. All around us, we seem to have examples of the need to disturb something to make it move. For example, a glass on a table just sits there unless it is disturbed in some way, perhaps by being pushed, or lifted. If you push the glass, it comes to rest soon after you stop pushing it. If you throw a ball, it ultimately comes to rest. It would seem that being at rest is the undisturbed state of motion, and indeed this was the view of many of the philosophers of antiquity, notably the Greek philosopher Aristotle (384–322 BC). It might therefore come as a surprise to learn that this is *not* the viewpoint that underlies Newton's laws of motion.

To come to the Newtonian viewpoint, suppose you now place the glass on a very smooth table. You could then give it a push, and after you had finished pushing it, it would continue moving, only gradually slowing down, and possibly falling off the end of the table with unfortunate consequences.

■ Would the glass move across the table in a straight line, or along a curved path?

☐ The glass would move in a straight line.

A puck on an ice rink behaves in a similar way – it slides along in a straight line and only slowly comes to rest. Astronauts floating in space have a similar experience: once they have pushed off from somewhere, they continue moving in a straight line until they encounter another object. The difference between the ice rink, the floating astronaut, or the very smooth table and an ordinary table is that with the ordinary table there is considerable friction between the surface and the glass. Friction opposes sliding motion. Try continuously pushing a glass across a rough table and then across a smooth table and you can feel the greater opposition to motion in the former case.

You are now going to do a thought experiment and imagine a super-smooth horizontal surface that has no friction at all. In this case, once you set the glass moving, it will not slow down but will continue moving at constant speed in a straight line. The only way to slow it down, or speed it up, or change its direction of motion while it is on this surface, is to disturb it, by pushing it again, in front, or from behind, or to one side. Thus the undisturbed motion in this case is constant speed in a straight line. The floating astronaut experiences almost no disturbance at all, so continues serenely in an almost uninterrupted straight line. Friction is a disturbance, which is why objects moving on real surfaces eventually come to rest unless there is something pushing them along. Note that when friction eventually brings the glass to rest, the frictional disturbance then vanishes. The glass is again undisturbed, so being at rest is merely a special case of undisturbed motion, and not the only case as was believed by Aristotle.

In all situations, it can be concluded that undisturbed motion is either being at rest, or moving in a straight line at a constant speed. The proper scientific name for the sort of disturbances being considered here is **force**: a push is a force, friction is a force, and there are many other kinds, some of which will be considered later in this chapter. A disturbance that destroys the undisturbed state of motion of an object is an **unbalanced force**.

This is **Newton's first law of motion**:

> An object remains at rest or moves in a straight line at constant speed unless it is acted on by an unbalanced force.

This first law will now be explored, to clarify what is meant by motion 'in a straight line at constant speed', and to explain what 'an unbalanced force' means.

14.1.1   Exploring the first law of motion

Motion in a straight line at constant speed

The simplest and clearest example of motion in a straight line at a constant speed is the astronaut floating in space. There is no detectable force of gravity acting in this case. Now, it is perhaps just possible that you are in the lucky position of reading this book from within a space station, in which case you can try throwing the book and you will see it carry on in a perfectly straight line until it hits something (we hope nothing important). The rest of us, however, have to make do with real-world examples that involve gravity.

(There is a subtlety here: astronauts are affected by gravity as if they are in orbit around the Earth, because it's the Earth's gravity that keeps them in orbit. However, the astronauts and their space station are affected by gravity in exactly the same way. Because of this, astronauts stay floating relative to the space station. Therefore, it seems exactly as if there were no gravity within the space station. Why does gravity affect the space station and the astronauts in exactly the same way? This was answered by Einstein in his General Theory of Relativity, which you may meet in Level 3 Open University courses.)

Imagine going for a drive, during which, at different times, you travel over the four stretches of road shown in Figure 14.2.

■   Which of these pieces of road are straight, in that they curve neither left or right, nor up or down?

☐   The roads in Figures 14.2a and 14.2b.

In Figure 14.2a the road is not only straight but also horizontal – there is no gradient down or up. The road in Figure 14.2b is also straight, but now there is a steady gradient – a hill of uniform slope to climb or descend. The road in Figure 14.2c is clearly not straight but follows a bend, whereas the one in Figure 14.2d curves up and then down as it crosses the bridge.

Consider now the meaning of 'constant speed'. You have already met the word equation for speed:

$$\text{speed} = \frac{\text{distance travelled}}{\text{time taken}}$$

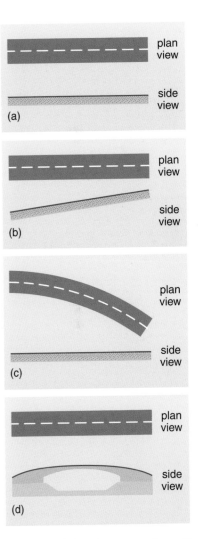

Figure 14.2   Four stretches of road: (a) straight and horizontal; (b) straight but climbing a uniform hill; (c) a horizontal curve; (d) a curve over a bridge.

This was written in symbolic form (Equation 13.1) as:

$$s = \frac{d}{t}$$

where the speed is denoted by s, the distance travelled by d, and the time interval by t. For the speed to be constant, the distance travelled in a fixed time interval must be constant. For example, if the time interval is 10 seconds, the distance travelled must be the same during every interval of 10 seconds. Moreover, the distance travelled must be the same during every interval, regardless of how short that time interval is; otherwise, you could travel during one interval of, say, 6 seconds at the same speed at every instant, and in the next six seconds you could travel very slowly for the first three seconds and then make up for this by travelling very quickly for the remaining three. Figure 14.3 shows snapshots of a car moving at a constant speed along the straight roads in Figures 14.2a and 14.2b. These snapshots are taken at intervals of 2 seconds, and you can see that the distances covered are the same during each interval.

■   What is the speed of the car in each case?

☐   In Figure 14.3a, the car covers 28 metres in 2 seconds, so, from Equation 13.1: speed = 14 m s^{-1}.

In Figure 14.3b, the car covers 20 metres in 2 seconds, so, from Equation 13.1: speed = 10 m s^{-1}.

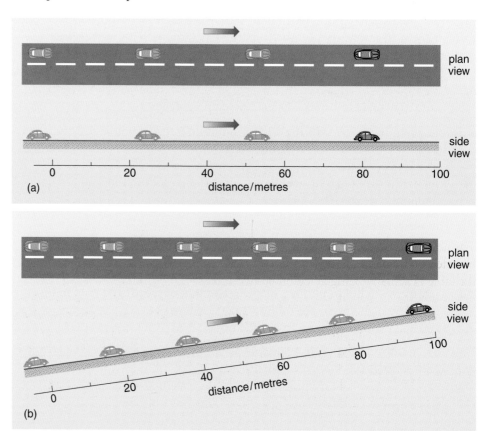

Figure 14.3   Snapshots every 2 seconds of a car moving at constant speed: (a) along a straight, horizontal road; (b) up a straight, uniform hill.

Now consider the car moving along the straight roads that were shown in Figures 14.2a and 14.2b, but with snapshots, as in Figure 14.4. Clearly, the distances travelled change from one 2-second interval to another, and so the speed is varying: in these cases, the motion is in a straight line, but it is *not* at constant speed. Thus, from Newton's first law of motion it can be deduced that an unbalanced force must be acting on the car: if an object is *not* at rest and *not* moving in a straight line at constant speed, then it is being acted on by an unbalanced force.

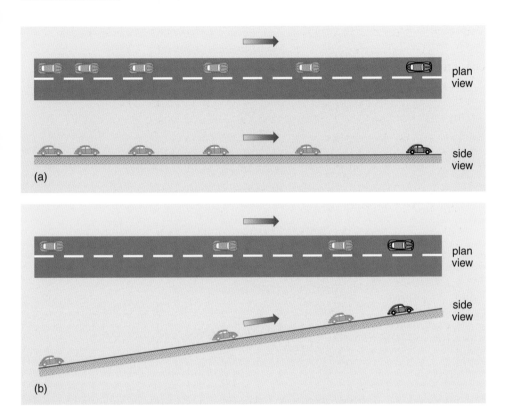

Figure 14.4   Snapshots every 2 seconds of a car moving at a varying speed: (a) along a straight and horizontal road; (b) up a straight hill of uniform slope.

Balanced and unbalanced forces

The notion of an unbalanced force arises from the possibility that an object can be acted on by more than one force at a time. In Figure 14.5a, the glass at rest on the table is actually being acted on by two forces. One is the downward force of gravity due to the gravitational attraction of the Earth on the glass, and the other is the upward push of the table surface on the glass. The upward push arises from the slight compression of the surface of the table when the glass is placed on it. The downward pull of gravity on the glass forces it against the table surface, and as a result the atoms in the surface layers of the table are pushed slightly closer together. This is rather like compressing a spring, and like a spring the atoms push back, and there is an upward push force on the glass.

Figure 14.5   A glass on a table: (a) at rest; (b) moving with constant speed in a straight line along a frictionless table; (c) being pushed in a straight line at constant speed along a table with friction.

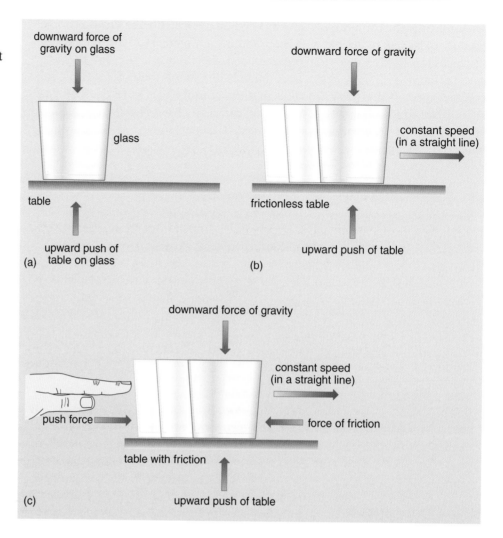

The forces on the glass are, however, balanced. The downward force from gravity is as equally strong as the upward force from the table, and so they balance each other out and the glass remains at rest. Now imagine that the surface of the table is perfectly frictionless. The glass is given a quick nudge to set it moving. When the nudging has finished, the only forces on the glass are again the downward force of gravity and the upward push of the table. These are still balanced and so the glass moves in a straight line at constant speed (Figure 14.5b), just like the astronaut floating in a straight line at a constant speed on a space station.

Now suppose that the table is *not* frictionless. This time, the glass will need to be pushed continuously to keep it moving at constant speed in a straight line. In this case, there are four forces acting on the glass, as in Figure 14.5c, but again they are balanced; the downward force of gravity and the upward push of the table still balance, and so now do the push force and the force of friction. Of course, to get the glass going, the push force had to exceed the force of friction initially. If the push force is removed, the force of friction will bring the glass to rest.

If the push force is increased in Figure 14.5c, then the force in the direction of motion is no longer balanced; there is 'too much push' and so the glass gains speed.

■   What happens if the push force is reduced?

□   The glass will lose speed.

The glass will also lose speed if the frictional force increases.

Cars work in a similar way. The car driver's right-hand pedal does not control the speed, but rather the push force from the engine. If the car is on a flat, straight road, and the driver only wants to continue in the same direction at a constant speed, then he or she only has to supply enough push force from the engine to balance the friction (including air resistance). If the road is slightly downhill, gravity may be enough to balance friction and the driver may not need to use the right-hand pedal at all. To slow down or stop the car, the driver increases friction by applying the brake. However, cars are a complicated example to use, because the push force from the engine works by turning the wheels (rather than summoning a giant external finger to push the car from behind), and there are lots of forces to consider in this process, including friction between the tyres and the road which gives the tyres their grip and helps to propel the car forward. (Describing all of this now would mean going too far off the present topic.)

Another example of balanced forces is shown in Figure 14.6a. The gravitational attraction of the Earth on the apple tries to pull it downwards, but the apple remains at rest because the upwards pull of the twig on the stem is equal to the gravitational force. However, if the stem breaks from the twig, then the only force acting on the apple is gravity, and there is no force to balance it. Consequently, the apple increases its speed towards the centre of the Earth (Figure 14.6b). It hits the surface of the Earth, and comes to rest (after bouncing and rolling a bit) when the upward push force of the surface of the Earth balances the downward force of gravity (Figure 14.6c).

Note that in Figures 14.6a and 14.6b, the force of gravity is shown below the apple, whereas in Figure 14.5 it is above the glass, and in Figure 14.6c it is above the apple. There is no significance to this. It is just a matter of convenience in fitting all the arrows on the diagram. The important point is that the direction and size of each force acting on each object are represented clearly.

Question 14.1

An oil tanker is moving through the sea in a straight line at a constant speed. There is no wind and there are no ocean currents.

(a) What forces are acting on the tanker, and how does Newton's first law of motion indicate that they are balanced?

(b) A head wind springs up. Why does the tanker slow down? How can the original speed be restored?

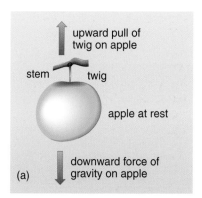

(a)

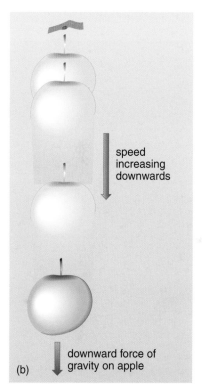

(b)

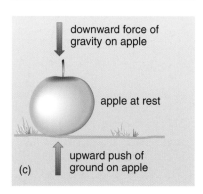

(c)

Figure 14.6   An apple: (a) at rest under balanced forces; (b) increasing its speed due to the unbalanced force of gravity; (c) again at rest under balanced forces.

Question 14.2

Imagine a tug-of-war contest between red and blue teams.

(a) Early on in the proceedings, the two teams are equally matched and so there is no movement of the rope at all.

(b) Having been more moderate over lunch, the blue team begins to pull the red team along at an increasing speed in a straight line.

(c) The red team steady themselves but only to the point where they are being pulled at constant speed in a straight line.

Describe each of the stages (a)–(c) in this contest in terms of the forces exerted by the teams on the rope, and whether or not the forces are balanced.

In Section 9.3, you looked at the factors that influence plate motion: frictional drag, slab pull and ridge slide. These are all forces, so obey Newton's laws of motion. The force of frictional drag acts to slow or stop plate motion, unless the motion is maintained by the forces of slab pull and ridge slide.

14.1.2   Speed and velocity

From Newton's first law of motion, you have seen that if an object is *not* at rest and *not* moving in a straight line at constant speed, then it is being acted on by an unbalanced force. So far, you have examined cases where there is evidence of an unbalanced force because, although the object was moving in a straight line, it was *not* doing so at constant speed. Thus, the glass, car, apple, tanker and tug-of-war rope all increased or decreased their speed in a straight line when there was an unbalanced force.

What about the case when a car is moving at constant speed but *not* in a straight line? Figure 14.7 shows a set of snapshots at 2-second intervals.

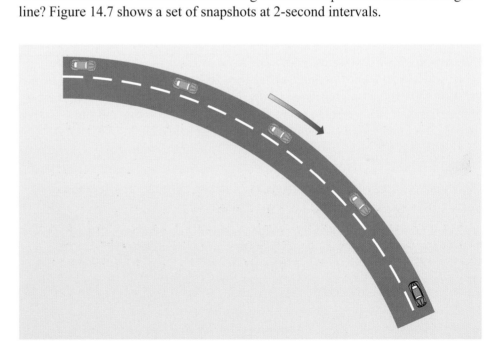

Figure 14.7   A car going around a bend at constant speed. The snapshots are at 2-second intervals.

■ Is the car in Figure 14.7 taking the bend at constant speed?

☐ Yes – the distance covered is the same for each 2-second interval.

So the car is moving at constant speed, but *not* in a straight line. Therefore, according to Newton's first law of motion, there must be an unbalanced force acting on the car. To see what this force is, imagine that you are with a friend who is pushing a loaded supermarket trolley along at constant speed in a straight line. You come to a corner, and because you both know the difficulty of steering a supermarket trolley from behind, your friend makes no attempt to steer it, but continues to push it at constant speed. It is you who steers it around the corner, and, as you may readily discover, you have to push the trolley sideways as shown in Figure 14.8. You can feel the force you have to exert on the trolley, so it can easily be a part of everyday experience that an unbalanced force causes a change of direction, even at constant speed.

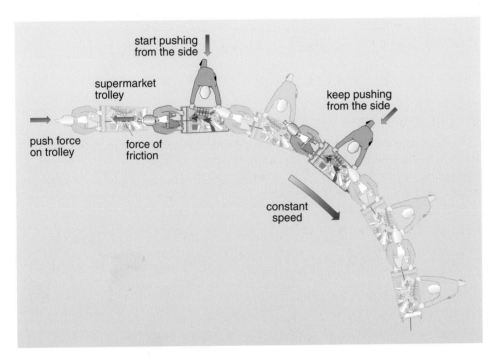

Figure 14.8 A sideways force causes a change in direction of a supermarket trolley.

Another example is that of someone running around a bend in a road. In order to change their direction, they have to push sideways on the road. The road surface becomes slightly distorted, and as a result it pushes sideways back on their shoes. Runners can feel the sideways push they have to exert on the road, and the road responds by pushing sideways back on them. On ice (with normal shoes) the necessary sideways force cannot be set up, and consequently they cannot take a bend.

A further example of an unbalanced force causing a change of direction is when you swing an object around on the end of a piece of string, as in Figure 14.9. In this case, you can feel the force you are exerting on the object through the string, as a result of which the object moves around in a circular path.

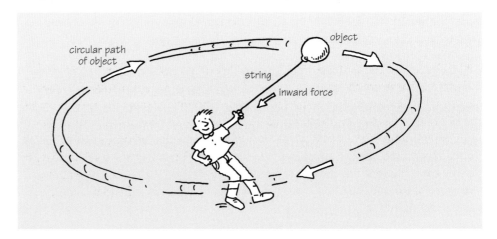

Figure 14.9   An object being whirled around in a circular path.

■   What would happen if you let the string go?

☐   The object would continue in a straight line in whichever direction it was moving when you let go of the string (Figure 14.10).

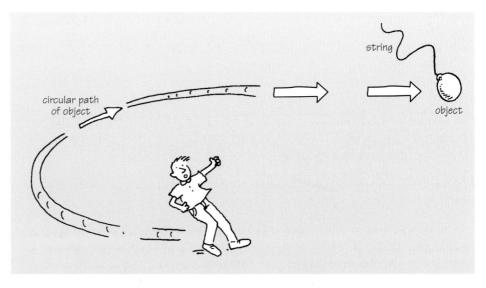

Figure 14.10   Letting go of an object that has been whirling around in a circular path.

Were it not for the Earth's gravity that makes the object fall to Earth, and the friction of the atmosphere, the object, once released, would travel in a straight line at constant speed. You will return to an object being swung around in Section 14.4, where it is used as an analogy for a planet orbiting the Sun, or a star orbiting the Galactic centre.

You can see, then, that there is indeed an unbalanced force acting when there is a change in direction at constant speed. You had already seen that an unbalanced force is acting when there is a change in speed with no change in direction. It follows that there is also an unbalanced force acting on an object when it changes its direction *and* changes its speed. One example is a car going around a bend at increasing or decreasing speed.

Velocity

It has become clear that the motion of an object has two attributes: speed and direction. These are the two attributes of what is called the **velocity** of a body. In everyday speech, velocity and speed are used interchangeably. In science, speed is just one of the two attributes of velocity, namely its magnitude. This is the numerical value of the velocity. The other attribute of velocity is its direction. Thus it is correct to say that the speed of a car is 22 m s^{-1}, and that the velocity of the car is 22 m s^{-1} in the northwest direction. It is incorrect to say that the velocity of the car is 22 m s^{-1}, or that the speed of the car is 22 m s^{-1} in the northwest direction.

■ Does force have two comparable attributes?

☐ Yes. Force has a strength – a magnitude – and a direction.

Now that velocity has been introduced, Newton's first law of motion can be restated in a more compact form:

> An object moves with constant velocity unless it is acted on by an unbalanced force.

The case of an object at rest is covered in this restatement, because such an object has zero velocity, which is a constant velocity.

Question 14.3

The oil tanker in Question 14.1 is again moving through the sea at a constant speed in a straight line. A side wind springs up that does not reduce the speed. Why does this wind cause a change in velocity?

14.1.3 Towards the second law of motion

An unbalanced force will cause a change in velocity, i.e. a change in speed, or a change in direction, or a change in both. But what is the precise relationship between an unbalanced force and the corresponding changes in speed and direction? Newton's first law only tells us that there will be changes but not what these changes will be. It is Newton's second law of motion that tells us what they will be, but before the second law is given, it is useful to restate the first law in terms of acceleration.

Acceleration in a straight line

Figure 14.3a is reproduced in Figure 14.11a along with a graph which will be discussed shortly. In Section 14.1.1, you saw that the speed of the car in

Figure 14.3a is constant, with a value of 14 m s^{-1}. In Figure 14.11b, the speed is clearly not constant, but is increasing. The car is said to be accelerating. To examine the acceleration more closely, the motion in each case is shown as a graph of speed at various times. For the case of constant speed, the graph is the horizontal line in Figure 14.11a. At every time shown, the value of the speed is 14 m s^{-1}. For the case of acceleration, the graph is again a straight line but it is no longer horizontal (Figure 14.11b): it shows that the speed is steadily increasing.

■ What is the speed at 2 seconds, and at 6 seconds?

☐ Reading from the graph in Figure 14.11b (using the guide lines), the speed at 2 seconds is 14 m s^{-1}, and at 6 seconds it is 22 m s^{-1}.

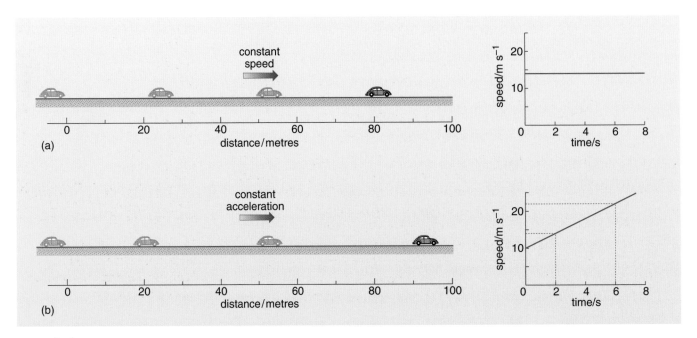

Figure 14.11   Snapshots at 2-second intervals, and graphs of speed versus time: (a) a car moving in a straight line at constant speed; (b) a car moving in a straight line at constant acceleration, where the speed increases by equal amounts in equal time intervals.

Recall from Equation 13.1 that speed is given by:

$$\text{speed} = \frac{\text{distance travelled}}{\text{time taken}}$$

Equivalently, this could be regarded as:

$$\text{speed} = \frac{\text{change in position}}{\text{time taken}}$$

Likewise, the acceleration in Figure 14.11b is given by:

$$\text{magnitude of acceleration} = \frac{\text{change in speed}}{\text{time taken}} \tag{14.1}$$

(The use of 'magnitude' implies that acceleration also has direction, a point returned to shortly.) The magnitude can be obtained by choosing any time interval along the time axis in Figure 14.11b and reading off the corresponding change in speed.

■ Calculate the magnitude of the acceleration in Figure 14.11b by determining the change in speed for the time interval between 2 s and 6 s.

☐ The speed at 2 s is 14 m s⁻¹, and at 6 s it is 22 m s⁻¹. Thus, from Equation 14.1:

$$\text{magnitude of acceleration} = \frac{22 \text{ m s}^{-1} - 14 \text{ m s}^{-1}}{6 \text{ s} - 2 \text{ s}}$$

$$= \frac{8 \text{ m s}^{-1}}{4 \text{ s}}$$

$$= 2 \text{ m s}^{-1} \text{ s}^{-1}$$

$$= 2 \text{ m s}^{-2}$$

(Remember that $s^{-1} \times s^{-1} = s^{-1-1} = s^{-2}$, just as $10^{-1} \times 10^{-1} = 10^{-1-1} = 10^{-2}$, as you saw in Box 13.1.) In words, this is two metres per second per second, where 'metres per second per second' or metres per second squared (m s⁻²) is the SI unit of acceleration. For a small family car, 2 m s⁻² is good acceleration.

For the graph in Figure 14.11b, you can show that, regardless of where the time interval is placed, and regardless of how large it is, the magnitude of the acceleration is always 2 m s⁻², and so in every second the car's speed increases by 2 m s⁻¹. This is called constant acceleration (in a straight line in this case). In the case of Figure 14.11a, the change in speed is zero, and so the acceleration is zero. Had the car been losing speed, it would have been decelerating. Figure 14.12 shows constant deceleration. In every second the speed decreases by 2 m s⁻¹, as you can see by reading off the graph. The magnitude of the deceleration is thus 2 m s⁻¹. Scientists call this an acceleration of −2 m s⁻² ('minus two metres per second squared', or sometimes 'minus two metres per second per second').

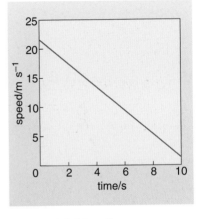

Figure 14.12   Constant deceleration: the speed decreases by equal amounts in equal time intervals.

Acceleration in circular motion

Consider again the case of an object going around in a circle at constant speed at the end of a piece of string, as in Figure 14.13. If it is travelling at constant speed, then you might think that it is not accelerating. This is not so! The proper definition of **acceleration** is that it is the rate of change in velocity. Recall that velocity has a speed attribute and a direction attribute. Therefore, any departure from motion at constant speed in a straight line is an acceleration. You have already met the case of a change in speed with no change in direction, but there are two further cases: a change in speed with a change in direction, and (as in the example of the object on the string) a change in direction with no change of speed. If there were no change in direction of the object on the string, then the object would move along the straight line shown in Figure 14.13 at the same speed at which it is following its circular path. To follow the circular path, the direction of motion has to continuously change. So the object is continuously accelerating.

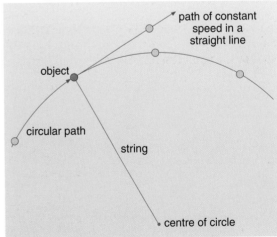

Figure 14.13   An object moving around a circle at constant speed: the distances between successive positions are equal, and are traversed in equal times. There is nevertheless an acceleration (towards the centre of the circle).

207

Thus, an acceleration occurs whenever there is a change in speed, or a change in direction, or a change in both. More compactly, as said earlier, an acceleration is a rate of change in velocity. Like velocity, acceleration has a magnitude, and a direction. For example, 'The car accelerated at 2 m s^{-2} in a southerly direction.'

A restatement of Newton's first law of motion

Newton's first law of motion was stated earlier in the form 'an object remains at rest or moves in a straight line at constant speed unless it is acted on by an unbalanced force'. In terms of acceleration, this law can be restated as follows:

An object does not accelerate unless it is acted on by an unbalanced force. Equivalently: if an object is acted on by an unbalanced force it will accelerate.

This makes a very useful link with Newton's second law of motion, which will tell us by how much the object accelerates, and in what direction, when an unbalanced force acts on it.

Question 14.4

Which of the following are changes in velocity? Which of them are accelerations? In which cases is an unbalanced force acting? Justify your answers.

(a) A train on a straight track slows down.

(b) A car goes around a bend at constant speed.

(c) A shark turns to chase its unfortunate prey and increases its speed as it does so.

(d) A plane descends along a straight flight path at constant speed.

14.2   Newton's second law of motion

Newton's second law of motion states that the magnitude of the unbalanced force on an object equals the mass of that object multiplied by the magnitude of its acceleration (the acceleration being in the same direction as the unbalanced force). In symbolic notation this is:

$$F = m \times a$$

where F is the magnitude of the unbalanced force, m is the mass of the object, and a is its acceleration. This equation is equivalent to:

$$F = ma \tag{14.2}$$

The first thing to note about the second law is that it gives precise meaning to mass. Mass is a measure of the 'quantity of substance' in an object and it is measured in kilograms (in SI units). Equation 14.2 shows that **mass** is also a link between an unbalanced force acting on an object and the resulting acceleration. For an unbalanced force of given magnitude, the greater the mass of an object the smaller the acceleration. Conversely, the smaller the mass of an object the greater the acceleration.

■ Look at Figure 14.4, which shows one glass accelerating along a surface (Figure 14.14a) and then two glasses accelerating along the surface (Figure 14.14b). If the mass is doubled, as in Figure 14.14b, while the unbalanced force is kept the same, then by what factor does the magnitude of the acceleration change?

□ If the mass doubles, then the acceleration must halve, so that the product of the mass times the acceleration stays the same.

This means that mass is a property of an object that expresses its 'reluctance' to accelerate: the greater the mass, the smaller the acceleration for a given unbalanced force. This is in accord with everyday experience of the forces required to accelerate objects of different mass. The scientific name for this 'reluctance' to accelerate is **inertia**. So mass is a measure of inertia.

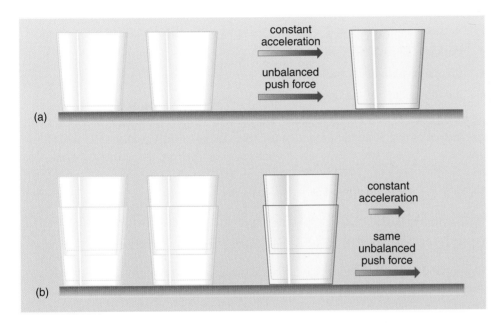

Figure 14.14   Snapshots at equal time intervals of (a) one glass, and (b) two stacked identical glasses being accelerated along a surface by an unbalanced force.

The second thing to note about Newton's second law is that it defines the unit of force: the unit of force is the unit of mass multiplied by the unit of acceleration. If SI units are used for mass (kg) and acceleration (m s^{-2}), then the SI unit of force is kg m s^{-2}. In words, this is kilograms metres per second per second. This mouthful cries out for a special name, and it's got one!

The SI unit for force is also called the **newton**, symbol N (named after Isaac Newton). Thus, a force with a value of 1 kg m s^{-2} is the same as a force with a value of 1 newton, or 1 N.

You will meet this again in Book 3. In the meantime, an example will give you an idea of the size of this unit.

■ In the motoring example in Figure 14.11b, while the car accelerates at 2 m s^{-2}. If the mass of the car and its occupants is 900 kg, calculate the magnitude of the unbalanced force.

□ The magnitude of the unbalanced force is given by Equation 14.2:

$F = ma$

$= 900 \text{ kg} \times 2 \text{ m s}^{-2}$

$= 1800 \text{ kg m s}^{-2}$

$= 1800 \text{ N}$

$= 2 \times 10^3 \text{ N}$ to one significant figure.

14.2.1   Using the second law of motion

The second law of motion (Equation 14.2) can be used to calculate any one of:

- the mass of an object, m
- the magnitude of its acceleration, a
- the magnitude of the unbalanced force acting on it, F

provided that the other two quantities are known. This requires Equation 14.2 to be rearranged to make the required quantity the subject of the equation. We will show you how to do this in Book 3, but in the meantime here are the rearrangements:

$$m = \frac{F}{a} \tag{14.3}$$

$$a = \frac{F}{m} \tag{14.4}$$

The second law also gives one other vital piece of information. It tells us the direction of the acceleration: this is the same as the direction of the unbalanced force.

Question 14.5

A family car plus two occupants has a total mass of 1100 kg (to three significant figures). It accelerates at a constant rate in a straight line along a level road from 0 to 26.8 m s^{-1} in 10.0 s. What are the magnitude and the direction of the unbalanced force acting on the car?

Question 14.6

The oil tanker in Question 14.1 meets a following wind during a particular voyage that exerts an unbalanced force of magnitude 4.0×10^5 N. The oil tanker has a mass of 2.0×10^8 kg (200 000 tonnes). Calculate the magnitude of the acceleration of the tanker, and state the direction of the acceleration.

In Question 14.5, and in Question 14.6, the acceleration involved an increase in speed along a straight line, and the unbalanced force, which must be in the same direction as the acceleration, was in the direction of motion. The unbalanced force caused no change in direction: to do so, it would have had to have been at an angle to the direction of motion.

What about those cases discussed in Section 14.1.2 of an unbalanced force causing a change in direction at constant speed – the supermarket trolley, the runner taking a bend, the object on a string? What is the second law telling us now? It is telling us that there is still an acceleration and that it is still in the direction of the unbalanced force. In each of these cases, the unbalanced force is directed across the direction of motion, as shown in Figures 14.8 and 14.9. It follows that the acceleration is also directed across the direction of motion. In the case of the object on the string (Figures 14.9 and 14.13), the unbalanced force is along the string, which is towards the centre of the circular path, and so this is also the direction of the acceleration. Note that this force, directed towards the centre, is always perpendicular to the circular path, i.e. it makes an angle of 90 degrees to the path. Consequently the force causes no change in the speed around the path, only a change in direction.

■ What is the necessary condition for an unbalanced force to change a speed?

☐ It must *not* be perpendicular to the direction of motion.

An unbalanced force that is neither perpendicular to the direction of motion nor along the direction of motion will cause both a change in speed *and* a change in direction.

How can acceleration due to a change in direction be quantified? The details are beyond the scope of this book, but the more strongly curved the path and the faster the object is following the curved path, the greater the acceleration. From Newton's second law of motion, this means that the more strongly curved the path and the faster the object is following the curved path, the greater the sideways force must be. This is reasonable: if a car takes a certain curve at ever-increasing speeds then the sideways force must get bigger and bigger if the car is going to stay on the road. Also, going around a tight bend at 30 m s^{-1} requires a bigger sideways force than going around a gentle bend at the same speed.

14.3 Newton's third law of motion

There is just one further Newtonian law of motion, called, unsurprisingly, Newton's third law of motion. In several places, you have met the notion that if one object exerts a force on another object, then the second object will exert a force back on the first object. For example, when runners take a bend they push on the road, and the road pushes back on them. Newton's third law is about the relationship between these two forces. It states that if one object pushes on a second object with a certain force, then the second object pushes back on the first object with a force of the same magnitude, but in the opposite direction.

This is how rockets get launched: the rocket exerts a force on the fuel, which is accelerated out of the bottom of the rocket, and the fuel exerts an equal force in the opposite direction on the rocket, which is therefore accelerated upwards into space. This is also why firing a rifle forces the bullet out of the muzzle, but also forces the butt of the rifle into the person's shoulder.

Newton's third law of motion will not be explored any further in this book, principally because, unlike his first and second laws of motion, it is not needed in order to understand the motion of planets in the Solar System, and stars in the Galaxy. However, there is another of Newton's laws that needs to be explored – his law of gravity.

14.4   Newton's law of gravity

Gravity is a force that attracts one object (with mass) to another – any object to any other object. You are pulled towards the surface of the Earth by the gravitational attraction that the Earth's mass exerts on your mass and, because of this gravitational attraction, even the best athletes can jump not much more than about a couple of metres or so away from the surface of the Earth. If you climb stairs, you lift yourself against the Earth's gravitational attraction and it takes a lot more effort than walking along a horizontal surface. Were it not for the considerable assistance that technology gives us, in the form of aircraft, rockets, etc., we would be trapped close to the Earth's surface.

If you are standing on the solid Earth, or on a rigid structure resting on the Earth, you are being pulled by gravity towards the Earth's centre. But (neglecting the rotation of the Earth) you will not accelerate towards or away from the centre. This means that there is no unbalanced force in the vertical direction.

■ Why is this?

☐ Gravity is not the only force acting on you. Just as, in Section 14.1, there was an upward push of the table on the glass, and an upward push of the road on the car, so there is an upward push of the surface beneath your feet on you.

Newton's law of gravity states that the gravitational force between two objects increases when either of their masses increases or when they are brought closer together. We'll argue that these are intuitively reasonable features. Consider distance first. For spherical bodies like the Earth and the Sun, the distance is measured from their centres. If you are at sea level, you are about 6370 km from the centre of the Earth. If you boarded a spacecraft and travelled to the outer reaches of the Solar System, you would expect the gravitational attraction of the Earth on you to decrease, and indeed it would. Considering the mass of two objects, if you now journeyed to a point halfway between the Earth and the Sun so that you were the same distance from each, you would expect the gravitational attraction of the massive Sun on you to exceed that of the far less massive Earth, and again it would. The exact relationship between the gravitational force that one object exerts on another, the masses of the objects, and their distance apart, was described by Newton, who also realised that gravity is a universal force, not just confined to the attraction of objects to the Earth. The direction of the force on one object is towards the other object.

Question 14.7

Imagine that some aliens (with rather advanced technology) came and removed much of the interior of the Earth. Why would the gravitational force of the Earth on you decrease?

You will meet Newton's law of gravity again in Book 7.

14.5   Orbital motions in the Solar System and in the Galaxy

Because any object is gravitationally attracted by any other object, the Earth is gravitationally attracted by the Sun. This force of gravity on the Earth is not balanced by any other force, so what stops the gravitational force of the Sun on the Earth from pulling the two bodies into a collision? The answer is the 'sideways' motion of the Earth around the Sun. The Earth is in a roughly circular orbit around the Sun and, for the present purposes, it is a good enough approximation to assume that the orbit is a perfect circle with the Sun at the centre and with the Earth moving around the orbit at a constant speed (Figure 14.15a). You are now going to do a thought experiment, in which the gravitational force of the Sun on the Earth is suddenly switched off. To answer the question 'What happens next?' you apply Newton's first law of motion. If the gravitational force becomes zero, then the acceleration becomes zero, meaning that there is no change in speed or direction (i.e. no change in velocity). The Earth must head off along the straight line in Figure 14.15b at the same constant speed as it had in its orbit. Thus the effect of gravity is to turn the Earth's path towards the Sun: the Earth is always falling towards the Sun but its sideways motion means that it always misses. Indeed it stays at very nearly the same distance from the Sun throughout its orbit.

There are strong parallels here with the object on the string in Section 14.1.3. The Earth is accelerating towards the Sun in just the same way as the object on the string was accelerating towards the centre of its circular path. In the case of the object on the string, there was a force on the object exerted by the string. In the case of the Earth, there is the force of gravity exerted on the Earth by the Sun.

Further insight into the orbital motion of the Earth can be obtained by means of another thought experiment, in which the Earth's orbital speed is suddenly reduced to zero, as in Figure 14.15c. The Earth momentarily has zero speed. The Earth would still be acted on by the same gravitational force of the Sun as before, and therefore it would continue to accelerate towards the Sun at the same rate as before. But now, without the benefit of sideways motion, it would move directly towards the Sun, and collide with it (some 58 days later).

So far you have seen how the force of gravity explains the circular orbit in Figure 14.15a. None of the planets has an orbit quite like this: the orbits are slightly non-circular, and the Sun is not quite at the centre. An extreme case is the orbits of comets, and Figure 14.16 shows the orbit of comet Hale–Bopp. In non-circular orbits it is still the case that, at all points in the orbit, the Sun's gravitational force on the object is directed towards the Sun, and therefore the acceleration is also directed towards the Sun. However, at most points in the orbit the force is *not* perpendicular to the direction of motion. Therefore the speed of the comet in the orbit changes as well as the direction, and so the overall acceleration is partly due to the change of direction, and partly due to the change of speed.

■ For the orbit in Figure 14.16, what is the condition for the comet's acceleration to be due only to a change of direction, and not a change in speed?

☐ This is when the gravitational force of the Sun on Hale–Bopp is in a direction perpendicular to the comet's direction of motion.

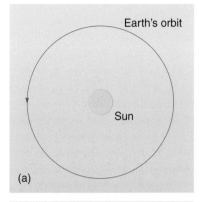

(a)

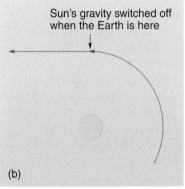

(b)

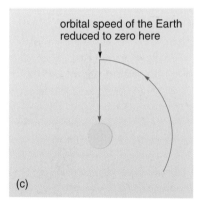

(c)

Figure 14.15   (a) The Earth's orbit around the Sun. (b) The effect of 'switching off' gravity. (c) The effect of suddenly reducing the orbital speed to zero.

213

In Figure 14.16b you can see that this happens only when the comet is at its closest to the Sun. The comet increases in speed to this point, and decreases in speed thereafter. The gravitational force of the Sun on the comet is again in a direction perpendicular to the orbit when it is furthest from the Sun, but this is much too far off to be shown in Figure 14.16.

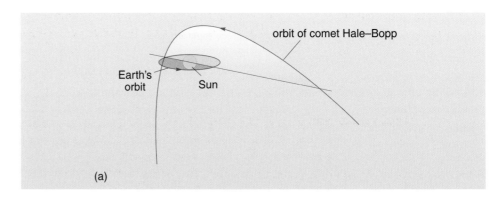

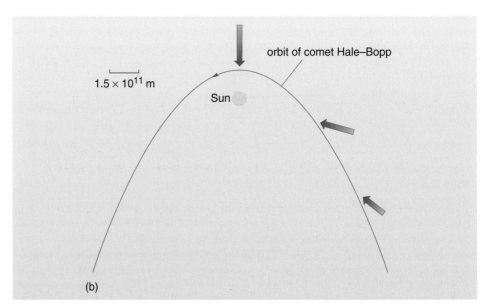

Figure 14.16 (a) The orbit of comet Hale–Bopp with respect to the orbit of the Earth. Hale–Bopp passed through the inner Solar System in 1997 (Figure 11.15). Its orbital period is about 2500 years and it will recede to a maximum distance from the Sun equal to 370 times the average distance of the Earth from the Sun. (b) A face-on view of the orbit of comet Hale–Bopp. The large arrows denote the direction of the gravitational force of the Sun on the comet at various points in the comet's orbit.

Newton's laws of motion and his law of gravity provide an excellent explanation of motions in the Solar System. The laws allow astronomers to calculate very accurately the orbits of the planets, comets, spacecraft, and other bodies.

Newton's laws explain motions beyond the Solar System too. Consider the orbit of the Sun around the Galactic centre (Section 13.1.2). It turns out that the gravitational forces on the Sun of all the matter in the Galaxy further from the Galactic centre than the Sun approximately balance: the pull on the Sun in one direction (very nearly) equals the pull in the opposite direction. The unbalanced gravitational force due to this more distant matter is therefore zero. For the matter in the Galaxy nearer the Galactic centre than the Sun, it turns out that the net gravitational force on the Sun is much as if all of the mass were concentrated at the Galactic centre. The orbital motion of the Sun can therefore be explained. It is orbiting the centre of the Galaxy in much the same way as the Earth is orbiting the Sun.

14.6   Summary of Chapter 14

Newton's first and second laws of motion are as follows:

First law

An object remains at rest or moves in a straight line at constant speed unless it is acted on by an unbalanced force.

Second law

The magnitude of the unbalanced force on an object equals the mass of the object multiplied by the magnitude of the acceleration of the object, the acceleration being in the same direction as the unbalanced force.

In symbolic form, the second law is $F = ma$, the acceleration being in the same direction as the unbalanced force.

Acceleration is the rate of change of velocity. An object will be accelerating if its speed is changing, or if its direction of motion is changing, or if both are changing.

Force, velocity and acceleration all have both a magnitude and a direction associated with them.

The SI unit of force is the newton, N, and $1\ \text{N} = 1\ \text{kg m s}^{-2}$.

Gravity is a universal force, acting between all objects with mass. According to Newton's law of gravity, the gravitational force increases with increasing mass of the objects and decreasing distance between them. The direction of the force on one object is towards the other object.

Objects in the Solar System orbit the Sun because of the gravitational force of attraction that the Sun exerts on the objects. The stars and interstellar matter are in orbit around the Galactic centre because of the gravitational attraction of the matter inside the orbit.

In this chapter, you have met the concept of physical laws, used Newton's first two laws of motion, and met his third law. In these contexts, you again practised substituting numbers into symbolic equations. You also met Newton's law of gravity, and used it to determine how the Earth's interior affects objects on the Earth's surface.

Chapter 15
Summary of Book 2

This book has covered a lot of ground, as you'd expect from a book titled *Earth and Space*. Key scientific concepts that have been covered in this book include the circulation pattern of water in the ocean; the nature of earthquakes and volcanic eruptions and the processes by which rocks are made; the structure of the Earth's interior; plate tectonics; the rock cycle; the make-up and layout of the Solar System, galaxies and the Universe; and Newton's laws of motion and gravity. Your study of these topics has involved you in using graphs, maps and other diagrams that show information, or illustrate ideas or processes. Plotting your own graphs, drawing best-fit lines through data, and measuring gradients on graphs have given you more experience of handling quantitative data. For instance, graphs of distance against time cropped up in several situations, relating to the speed of seismic waves, the speed of sea-floor spreading, and the idea of acceleration. You've also done some practical science by making qualitative observations of rock samples and of the stars in the night sky, and you've found out how these observations can be interpreted in terms of geological processes and the hidden properties of stars, respectively. Parts of this book have required you to think about earthquakes, volcanic eruptions and distances in space that vary in size by many powers of ten; this is where using powers of ten scales (such as Richter magnitude) and scientific notation become very useful.

This short final chapter now draws together the main themes of the book, with the aims of highlighting connections between what can appear to be very different topics, and looking ahead to the next book in your exploration of science. You may feel that your head is bursting with all the information that you've met, and worry that you can't remember it all. We're not expecting you to remember it all, but we are expecting that you've made sense of most of what you've read and are continuing to develop the skills of studying and doing science through the various questions, activities and assessments. In other words, we expect you to be making progress in achieving the learning outcomes for the course. The following activity gives you the opportunity to reflect on your progress. As well as using this book, websites and multimedia activities in your study, the assessment material should also be helping you in your learning, both by helping you to pace your study and through the feedback from your tutor.

Activity 15.1   Your progress towards the course learning outcomes

We expect this activity will take you approximately 30 minutes.

Now think a bit more about the knowledge and understanding and skills you've learned and practised while studying this book. Look at the learning outcomes for the course and write a list of the ones you think that you have got to grips with in the context of your study of this book.

You may like to compare your list with one prepared by a tutor. If so, go to Activity 15.1 on the course website where you will find a list compiled by a tutor.

There are no comments on this activity.

Now, to take stock, recall that you had learnt in Book 1 how energy from the Sun provides energy to the Earth's atmosphere, keeping the surface at a temperature suitable for life. This energy also fuels photosynthesis, weather, ocean currents, and the recycling of the Earth's surface materials by sedimentary processes. Continuing with the temperature theme, Book 2 showed evidence that the interior of the Earth is hot, with molten rock (magma) erupting at volcanoes, and molten iron forming the Earth's outer core. So the Earth can now be thought of as a hot planetary body cooling into space. Parts of the cool surface layer (oceanic lithosphere) slowly sink (subduct) into the mantle, driving plate tectonics. Plumes of hot mantle slowly rise from the deep mantle to the surface, where hot-spot volcanoes like Hawaii erupt. These currents of relatively hot and cold material are a form of convection, which you met in Book 1 in the context of heat energy transfer throughout the atmosphere. Plate tectonics is the surface expression of slow convection currents moving in the Earth's mantle transferring heat energy to the surface. Living on the Earth's surface, we are sandwiched between energy streaming in from the Sun and energy flowing up from beneath. That's why life, plate tectonics and the rock cycle (not to mention the carbon and water cycles) come face-to-face at the Earth's surface, giving us both the comforts and the natural hazards (climate change, extreme weather, sea-level rise, earthquakes and volcanoes) of our home planet. Planets with a different type of atmosphere or interior, or with different amounts of solar or internal heating, won't be the same as Earth.

A common feature of the phenomena that you've studied in Book 2 is that they involve movement – ocean currents, drifting continents, sand grains on a beach, planets orbiting the Sun, rotating galaxies, and so on. All of these things, and all living things, are sustained by the energy they possess or exchange with their surroundings. This means that a scientific understanding of energy can be a great help in understanding how the Earth and the Universe work, and you'll be finding out about this in Book 3 *Energy and Light*. You are already part-way along this path of understanding. For example, the computer models of the Earth's climate system that were mentioned in Book 1 are based on descriptions of how energy is added to, moves between, or leaves different parts of the atmosphere–ocean system. It's time to explore energy further.

Answers to questions

Comments on the answers are given in square brackets [...].

Question 2.1

(a) According to Figure 2.1, the temperature at the surface is about 20 °C, whereas at 2 km depth it is about 2 °C.

(b) Near the surface, the temperature does not change much down to a depth of 100–200 m (i.e. 0.1–0.2 km), and below about 500 m the temperature decreases only gradually. Between these two zones is a zone within which the temperature decreases much more dramatically with increasing depth (i.e. the rate of change of temperature is very high). In Figure 2.1, the most rapid change occurs between about 250 m and 500 m.

Question 2.2

As you leave the southern British Isles, you cross the continental shelf (pale blue). The water then deepens over a small distance. Continuing westwards, the depth remains fairly constant (uniform shade of deep blue) before becoming irregular (several shades giving a speckled appearance) and shallower (pale blue) about half-way across the North Atlantic. Further westward, the depth to the ocean floor increases irregularly before reaching moderately constant depth again, and then decreasing over a small distance onto the continental shelf of the North American continent.

Question 2.3

(a) The ridge is about 3.5 cm wide in Figure 2.5, and since 1 cm is equivalent to 500 km, the actual width is 3.5 × 500 km, or about 1750 km.

(b) The ridge crest is about 7 mm below the ocean surface, equivalent to a depth of 3.5 km, and the abyssal plain is about 11 mm below the surface, equivalent to a depth of 5.5 km.

(c) The height of the ridge can be measured on Figure 2.5 or calculated from the answers to part (b): it is about 5.5 km − 3.5 km = about 2 km high.

Question 2.4

Following the Mid-Atlantic Ridge south, it splits into two branches. The shorter, westward branch (not labelled in Figure 2.6 but called the South American–Antarctic Ridge) is less distinct than the eastern branch, which is the Southwest Indian Ridge. The latter ridge extends to the northeast before it splits into the Central Indian Ridge, which connects with the Carlsberg Ridge (which then intersects Arabia), and the Southeast Indian Ridge. The Southeast Indian Ridge can be followed between Australia and Antarctica, before its name changes and becoming the Pacific–Antarctic Ridge. This in turn branches into the East Pacific Rise and the Chile Rise. Figures 2.3 and 2.6 show that the Juan de Fuca Ridge, off the western coast of North America, is not connected with the rest of the mid-ocean ridge system.

Question 3.1

(a) The fault has displaced streams and small valleys. The stream (Wallace Creek) in the lower-middle part of the image flows from the top right but has been displaced (by about 130 m) to the left where it crosses the fault.

(b) The block in the foreground has moved to the left, which is to the northwest. The block on the other side of the fault has therefore moved to the southeast.

Question 3.2

This is an increase of $8.1 - 6.1 = 2$ units on the Richter scale, which is an increase of:

(a) $10^2 = 10 \times 10 = 100$ times in terms of ground motion

(b) about $40^2 = 40 \times 40 = 1600$ times in terms of energy released.

Question 6.1

See Figure 6.17. Remember that body waves travel faster than surface waves, so arrive earlier. Of the surface waves, Love waves usually travel faster than Rayleigh waves. Surface waves produce more ground motion than body waves, with Rayleigh waves producing more ground motion than Love waves. By analogy with Figure 6.2, the Love wave arrival is where a wave with a different shape arrives – the beginning of the larger ground motion and more time between peaks and troughs.

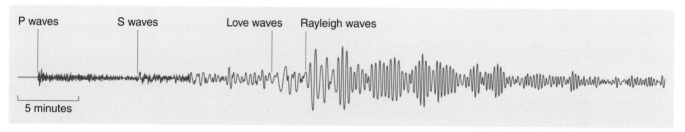

Figure 6.17   Answer to Question 6.1.

Question 6.2

(a) Seismic. This boundary was identified and located using seismic data alone. You might have considered Figure 6.14 and included density in your answer (the boundary is very clear on the density–depth curve), but the position of the boundary was deduced first from seismic data, then the density–depth curve was worked out to fit in with this.

(b) Seismic and magnetic. S waves do not travel through the outer core, which supports the interpretation that it is liquid. The Earth's magnetism is probably produced by a metallic liquid layer.

Question 7.1

The climate-sensitive sediments fall more or less into their correct climate zones on the pre-drift reconstruction. The sandstones and the coal deposits appear to be more or less restricted to the latitude ranges for the desert and tropical climates of today. Similarly, the glacial till deposits also fall much closer to their appropriate climate zone near the South Pole. [This reconstruction is evidence in support of continental drift. The distribution of climate-sensitive sediments only fits their expected latitudinal range if the continents are rearranged in such a way as to bring together many land masses that are separated today.]

Question 7.2

(a) The number of switches from black to white and white to black is 11. There have therefore been 11 polarity reversals in the last 4 Ma.

(b) Normal, reversed, and reversed.

(c) The most recent change from normal (black) to reversed (white) took place 0.99 Ma ago.

(d) It could have formed any time between 1.95 and 1.79 Ma ago, or between 1.07 and 0.99 Ma ago, or between 0.78 Ma ago and the present day.

(e) 0.78 Ma.

Question 7.3

19 mm y^{-1}. This is because 19 km = 19 × 10^3 m = (19 × 10^3) × 10^3 mm and 1 Ma = 10^6 y. So :

$$\frac{19 \text{ km}}{1 \text{ Ma}} = \frac{1.9 \times 10^7 \text{ mm}}{1 \times 10^6 \text{ y}} = 1.9 \times 10^1 \text{ mm y}^{-1} = 19 \text{ mm y}^{-1}.$$

[A shortcut is simply to remember that the value of the speed in km Ma^{-1} is the same as the value in mm y^{-1}, as shown earlier in Section 7.3.1.]

Question 8.1

Lithosphere: stronger, rigid, lower temperature, crust and top of the mantle, earthquakes occur.

Asthenosphere: weaker, more easily deformed, higher temperature, within the mantle, no earthquakes occur.

Question 8.2

See Figure 8.18. The western boundary will be a divergent plate boundary, as plate A is moving away from plate B here. Both the eastern boundaries are convergent, although obliquely. Figure 8.18 shows plate A descending beneath plate B, but you could instead have shown plate B descending beneath plate A, if you drew the barbs on plate A instead of plate B.

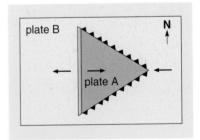

Figure 8.18   Answer to Question 8.2.

Question 8.3

See Figure 8.19. The Cocos Plate is shown moving away from the other plate at the western and southern divergent boundaries and towards the convergent northeastern boundary, so the relative movement must be in the direction of the arrow (you could have drawn this equally validly at a slightly different angle to that shown here). Remember, however, that this simplified situation of just two plates is unreal; the Cocos Plate is actually surrounded by three different plates.

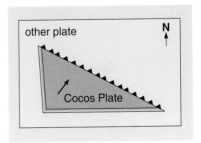

Figure 8.19   Answer to Question 8.3.

221

Question 8.4

(a) The highest relative speeds are where the Pacific and Nazca Plates are moving away from each other at a speed of up to 185 mm y^{-1}. The boundary between them is a divergent plate boundary. This is the East Pacific Rise (see Figure 2.6).

(b) The highest relative speed for a different type of plate boundary is at the west coast of South America, a convergent boundary between the Nazca and South American Plates, with a speed of 106 mm y^{-1}. This boundary is along the Peru–Chile Trench.

(c) The lowest rate of sea-floor spreading (17 mm y^{-1}) is in the northern Indian Ocean, between the African and Indian Plates, on a mid-ocean ridge called the Carlsberg Ridge. [By the way, the ridge *is* named after the brewery, which sponsored the oceanographic expedition that discovered it. If you study a detailed map of ocean-floor features you will find other familiar names.]

Question 8.5

(a) From Equation 8.1, distance travelled = speed × time interval:

$$185 \text{ mm y}^{-1} = 185 \times 10^{-3} \text{ m y}^{-1}$$

So distance travelled = 185×10^{-3} m y^{-1} × 10^6 y

$$= 185 \times 10^3 \text{ m}$$

$$= 185 \times 10^3 \times 10^{-3} \text{ km}$$

$$= 185 \text{ km}$$

(b) From Equation 8.2:

$$\text{time interval} = \frac{\text{distance travelled}}{\text{speed}}$$

London is on the Eurasian Plate and New York is on the North American Plate. In Figure 8.4 these plates are separating at a rate of 25 mm y^{-1}, or 25×10^{-3} m y^{-1}. So, as 1 km = 10^3 m:

$$\text{time interval} = \frac{10^3 \text{ m}}{25 \times 10^{-3} \text{ m y}^{-1}}$$

$$= 4 \times 10^4 \text{ y, or 40 000 years}$$

(Recall that $\dfrac{1}{y^{-1}} = y$)

[However, the plate motion is not parallel to a line between London and New York, so the London–New York separation rate will be lower than 25 mm y^{-1}, and therefore the time will be somewhat more than 40 000 years.]

Question 8.6

Basaltic pillow lavas (2) are produced by volcanic eruptions onto the ocean floor (C).

Sheeted dykes (3) are a series of dykes which transported basalt magma along vertical cracks in the crust (A).

Gabbro (1) is produced by slow crystallisation of basalt magma (B). [Gabbro is a coarse-grained intrusive rock, which indicates it cooled slowly underground.]

Question 8.7

(a) At the Izu–Bonin Trench, the oceanic Pacific Plate is converging with the oceanic Philippine Plate; (b) along the western side of South America, the oceanic Nazca Plate is converging with the continental part of the South American Plate; (c) in the region of the Himalayan mountains, a continental part of the Indian Plate is converging with the continental part of the Eurasian Plate.

Question 8.8

AB is the Aleutian Trench; BC is the Queen Charlotte Fault; CD is the Juan de Fuca Ridge; EF is the San Andreas Fault; FG is the East Pacific Rise.

Question 9.1

(a) Just as on the travel time versus distance graphs for seismic waves (e.g. Figure 6.8), the speed at which sites of volcanic activity move is the inverse of the gradient of the best-fit straight line in Figure 9.2b. To calculate the gradient, and hence the speed, choose two points on the best-fit straight line which are some distance apart and find their coordinates in order to find the 'rise' and 'run'. For example, at a distance of 5500 km the age is 65 Ma, and at a distance of 1000 km the age is 11 Ma. The gradient of the line is:

$$\frac{\text{rise}}{\text{run}} = \frac{65\,\text{Ma} - 11\,\text{Ma}}{5500\,\text{km} - 1000\,\text{km}} = \frac{54\,\text{Ma}}{4500\,\text{km}} = 0.012\,\text{Ma km}^{-1}$$

The speed is therefore:

$$\frac{1}{0.012\,\text{Ma km}^{-1}} = 83\,\text{km Ma}^{-1}$$

This is equivalent to 83 mm y^{-1}. You may have used different points and got a slightly different answer. [A more accurately determined value is 86 mm y^{-1}.]

(b) Towards the southeast overall. [However, it started moving south before changing to moving southeast.]

Question 9.2

The fastest plate is the Pacific Plate. The slowest is the African, although the Eurasian and Antarctic Plates move only slightly faster.

Question 9.3

(a) The fast-moving Pacific Plate has a subducting slab on one side (attribute 2) and a divergent plate boundary on the opposite side (3). The Pacific Plate contains very little continental lithosphere (the South Island of New Zealand).

(b) The slow-moving African Plate is partly bounded by a divergent boundary (3) but also contains a large area of continental lithosphere (1). [Similar attributes are held by the slow-moving Eurasian and Antarctic Plates. None of the slow-moving plates are attached to significant lengths of subducting slabs.]

Question 9.4

The crumpling and convergence of continental lithosphere at BC will eventually cease, because of the resistance of the rock to further crumpling, so the supercontinent will not change in width. This means the ocean will also have to keep the same size, which it could do in two ways. The first is illustrated in Figure 9.11, where the ocean has developed subduction zones at its edges, with the rate of spreading balanced by the rate of subduction. (You may have drawn a diagram with only one subduction zone, which would also be a valid answer.) The second way involves the ocean stopping spreading and not developing subduction zones. This is unlikely, as it would mean that plate-tectonic driving forces had ceased. There are no oceans on the Earth at the moment without spreading ridges or trenches.

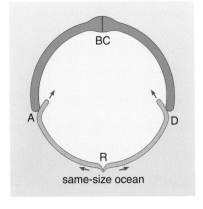

Figure 9.11   Answer to Question 9.4.

Question 9.5

See Figure 9.12. The Atlantic and Indian Oceans are expanding; the Pacific Ocean is contracting.

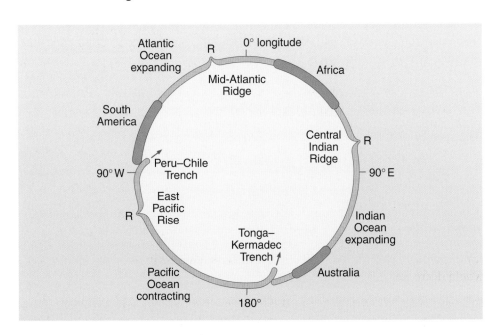

Figure 9.12   Answer to Question 9.5.

Question 9.6

The time can be calculated using Equation 8.2 as follows:

$$\text{time interval} = \frac{\text{distance travelled}}{\text{speed}}$$

The distance is 560 km, and the speed is 20 mm y^{-1} = 20 km Ma^{-1}. (Remember from Section 7.3 that the numerical values of speed are the same whether units of mm y^{-1} or km Ma^{-1} are used.) Therefore:

$$\text{time interval} = \frac{560 \text{ km}}{20 \text{ km Ma}^{-1}} = 28 \text{ Ma}$$

(Recall that $\dfrac{1}{Ma^{-1}} = Ma$)

Question 11.1

From Figure 11.9, you can see that Uranus and Neptune are substantially smaller in size than Jupiter and Saturn. Figure 11.9 also shows that hydrogen and helium are significant components but not as dominant as in Jupiter and Saturn; indeed, Jupiter and Saturn resemble each other, and Uranus and Neptune resemble each other. Thus the creation of a subdivision is justified, and *sub*giant is a good name for a subdivision containing objects that are smaller than the others.

Question 11.2

(a) The Earth resembles the other terrestrial planets in:
- its density and composition; Table 11.1 shows that they have similar densities and Figure 11.9 shows that they all have rocky compositions
- size. [Although the Earth is the biggest and most massive of the terrestrial planets (Table 11.1), it is merely at the upper end of a modest range of mass and diameter rather than in a class of its own.]

(b) It differs from the other terrestrial planets in:
- having an oxygen-rich atmosphere
- having oceans of liquid water
- some apparently unique geological processes (e.g. plate tectonics)
- supporting living organisms.

[You were asked for only two differences.]

Question 12.1

(a) If the Sun's surface temperature fell, then its luminosity (total radiated power) would decrease.

(b) If its radius increased, then its luminosity would increase. [The power radiated by a given area is fixed by the temperature (part (a)), so if the area increases and the temperature stays the same, the total radiated power will increase.]

Question 12.2

The density of the Sun increases gradually from about 1 kg m^{-3} in the photosphere to about 1.5×10^5 kg m^{-3} at the centre. Therefore, at some depth it must have a density of 10^3 kg m^{-3}, the density of tap water. The temperature also increases gradually with depth, but only reaches 1.5×10^7 °C in the centre. This is well short of 10^8 °C, so there is no depth at which the temperature is this high.

Question 12.3

(a) The interior of Jupiter is too cool for the fusion of hydrogen: its internal temperatures do not exceed 2×10^4 °C, far short of the 10^7 °C needed for hydrogen fusion. [There is plenty of hydrogen in the interior of Jupiter – it's the low temperature that's the problem, not the lack of fuel.]

(b) The Sun's photosphere, at about 5500 °C, is far too cool for the fusion of hydrogen.

Question 12.4

No. The distance from the Earth to the Sun is small compared with the vast distances to other stars. The difference between measuring from the Earth or from the Sun is therefore such a small fraction of the total distance involved that it does not matter whether the measurement is made from the Earth or from the Sun.

Question 12.5

If two stars have the same surface temperature, then the power radiated *per unit area of their surface* will be the same. Therefore, if the two stars are at the same distance, the star that appears brighter must be bigger. If they have the same surface temperatures, the stars must have the same colour tint.

Question 13.1

(a) The distance to the Sun from the viewpoint in Figure 13.2a is 10^{21} m, and the distance from the viewpoint in Figure 11.6 is 10^{16} m. Now, 10^{16} times 10^5 is 10^{21} (Box 13.1), because $16 + 5 = 21$. Figure 13.2a is therefore 10^5 times bigger than Figure 11.2. This is the same as saying it is 100 000 times bigger, because $10^5 = 100\ 000$. Another way of saying this is that it is five orders of magnitude bigger.

(b) 10^{22} m is ten times 10^{21} m, so you would have gone ten times further. It is misleading, therefore, to consider 10^{22} m to be not very different from 10^{21} m. A point that is 10^{22} m away lies 9×10^{21} m beyond a point that is 1×10^{21} m away. [This is a common error in comparing large powers of ten: even 10^{1001} is ten times larger than 10^{1000}.]

Question 13.2

(a) In 60 Ma, star C has travelled about a third of the way around its orbit, so its orbital period is about 180 Ma.

(b) In 60 Ma, a star (like A) at the outer edge of the disc has travelled about one-eighth of its way around its orbit, so its orbital period is about 480 Ma.

Question 13.3

To reach the viewpoint in Figure 13.2a, you have travelled a distance of 10^{21} m at 3×10^7 m s^{-1}. To obtain the time interval, Equation 13.2 is used:

$$\text{time interval} = \frac{\text{distance travelled}}{\text{speed}}$$

or, in symbolic notation:

$$t = \frac{d}{s}$$

$$= \frac{10^{21} \text{ m}}{3 \times 10^7 \text{ m s}^{-1}}$$

$$= 3.3333 \times 10^{13} \text{ s}$$

There are 3.16×10^7 seconds in a year. Therefore:

$$t = \frac{3.3333 \times 10^{13}}{3.16 \times 10^7} \text{ years } = 1 \times 10^6 \text{ years to one significant figure.}$$

The speed was quoted to one significant figure, and so the answer should be quoted to this precision. Thus the time interval is 1×10^6 years, to one significant figure, i.e. about a million years.

[Note that even light, which travels at 3.00×10^8 m s^{-1}, would take 100 000 years to travel from the Sun to the end point of your journey. Therefore, from this distant viewpoint, you would see the Sun and its neighbourhood as it was 100 000 years earlier.]

Question 13.4

(a) From near the centre of a nearly spherical elliptical galaxy, the stars will be equally distributed in all directions rather than being concentrated in a broad band across the night sky. There will therefore be no equivalent of the Milky Way. [More careful observations would reveal no nuclear bulge, and no spiral arms.]

(b) Spiral arms seem to be major sites of star formation in the Galaxy, and the stars form in open clusters. Without spiral arms there will be little star formation, and open clusters will be few, or perhaps completely absent.

Question 14.1

(a) Two of the forces are the underwater thrust arising from the propellers, and the friction of air and water. You know that these forces are balanced because the tanker is moving in a straight line at constant speed. There are two other forces: the downward force of gravity, and the upward force of the water. As the tanker is not sinking, nor rising into the air, these forces are also balanced.

(b) If a head wind springs up, the forces are no longer balanced. The tanker will slow down, but the original speed can be restored if the thrust of the propellers is increased.

Question 14.2

(a) If the rope is at rest, then the force on the rope exerted by one team is balanced by that exerted by the other team.

(b) If the speed of the rope is increasing in the direction of the blue team, then the blue team are pulling with a greater force than the red team. The forces on the rope are unbalanced.

(c) The red team have now increased the force of their pull to be equal in value to that of the blue team. This halts the increase of speed, and so the rope moves at a constant speed in a straight line; the forces now being balanced.

Question 14.3

The wind exerts a sideways force that will cause a change of direction. Therefore, whereas the speed remains constant, the velocity of the tanker changes.

Question 14.4

In cases (a), (b) and (c), there is a change in velocity. Therefore, by definition, there is an acceleration. Therefore, by Newton's first law of motion, an unbalanced force is acting.

(a) A train slows down on a straight track: there is no change in direction but there is a change in speed, so there is a change in velocity.

(b) A car goes around a bend at constant speed: there is no change in speed but there is a change in direction, so there is a change in velocity.

(c) A shark turns to chase its unfortunate prey and increases its speed as it does so: there is a change in speed and a change in direction, so there is a change in velocity on both counts.

(d) A plane descends along a straight flight path at constant speed: this is motion in a straight line at constant speed, so there is no change in velocity, and consequently no acceleration and no unbalanced force.

Question 14.5

The acceleration (Equation 14.1) is:

$$\text{magnitude of acceleration} = \frac{\text{change in speed}}{\text{time taken}}$$
$$= \frac{26.8 \text{ m s}^{-1} - 0 \text{ m s}^{-1}}{10.0 \text{ s}}$$
$$= 2.68 \text{ m s}^{-1} \text{ s}^{-1}$$

which is 2.68 m s^{-2}.

Then, from Newton's second law of motion (Equation 13.2):

magnitude of the unbalanced force on the car $= (1100 \text{ kg}) \times (2.68 \text{ m s}^{-2})$

$$= 2948 \text{ kg m s}^{-2}$$

$$= 2950 \text{ N to three significant figures.}$$

(Note that the final answer has been given to three significant figures – the same as in the data.)

The direction of the unbalanced force is the direction of the acceleration along the straight road.

Question 14.6

You need to use a rearranged version of Equation 14.2 for Newton's second law of motion to make the acceleration the subject. The equation to use is:

$$a = \frac{F}{m}$$

The unbalanced force due to the following wind is given in the question as 4.0×10^5 N. Thus:

$$\text{magnitude of acceleration of tanker} = \frac{4.0 \times 10^5 \text{ N}}{2.0 \times 10^8 \text{ kg}}$$

$$= 0.0020 \text{ N kg}^{-1}$$

Remember that the newton (N) is shorthand for kg m s^{-2}, so:

$$\text{magnitude of acceleration of tanker} = 0.0020 \text{ kg m s}^{-2} \text{ kg}^{-1}$$

$$= 0.0020 \text{ m s}^{-2}$$

The direction of the acceleration is the direction of the unbalanced force: the forward direction. [So the tanker gains speed in the direction in which it was travelling before the wind started.]

Question 14.7

The gravitational force would decrease because the mass of the Earth decreased. The distance to the Earth's centre would not change, so this is not a factor.

Comments on activities

Activity 3.1

(a) Earthquakes are not distributed evenly across the Earth's surface, so it does not seem sensible to describe the pattern simply as a variation from west to east across the map. The fact that earthquakes occur in distinct regions of the Earth's surface is reflected in the answer given below:

> Earthquakes are concentrated in specific regions of the Earth, and they often occur in linear or arc-shaped belts. One belt surrounds the Pacific Ocean, including Japan, Alaska and the western coast of North, Central and South America. Another region is from southeastern Europe through the Middle East and the Himalayan Mountains. There are also earthquakes in linear zones in the oceans. There are a few earthquakes that are not in linear zones, such as those in east Africa. (*78 words*)

The decision to structure the answer in this way was made after looking at Figure 3.6. If the question had asked you to look at a different map and describe the variation of something different, such as population, you would probably have ordered your answer in a different way (possibly continent by continent) so as to give the most logical answer.

(b) This investigation involves looking at two very different maps and noting their different scales. (Try to get into the habit of looking for a scale whenever you look at a map or a diagram, and also to put a scale on any diagrams you produce to help other people understand what you are depicting.) Comparing Figure 3.6 with Figures 2.3 and 2.6 leads to the following conclusions about the relationship between shallow- and deep-focus earthquakes and surface features:

(i)   Shallow-focus earthquakes appear to be associated with mid-ocean ridges, with mountain ranges in the interior of the continents of Europe and Asia, and with the mountains and ocean trenches that surround the Pacific Ocean.

(ii) Deep-focus earthquakes appear to be associated with the mountains and ocean trenches that surround the Pacific Ocean (for example, near the coast of South America, or the coast of Japan).

Activity 3.2

(a)

(i)   Mountains and ocean trenches surrounding the Pacific Ocean: magnitude 8.0–8.9.

(ii) Mountain belts in Europe: magnitude 7.0–7.9; mountain belts in Asia: magnitude 8.0–8.9.

(iii) Mid-ocean ridges: magnitude 7.0–7.9. (In fact the maximum magnitude at mid-ocean ridges is 7.5, but this is not shown in Figure 3.6.)

(b) See Table 3.3.

In Chapter 7 you will find out how these observations about the distribution of seismic zones on the Earth can be explained by plate tectonics.

Table 3.3 Completed version of Table 3.1. The depths and sizes of earthquakes at different locations.

| | Mountains and ocean trenches surrounding the Pacific Ocean | Mountain belts | | Mid-ocean ridges |
		Europe	Asia	
Depth (shallow-focus, intermediate-focus, or deep-focus)	shallow-, intermediate- and deep-focus	mainly shallow-focus, a few intermediate	mainly shallow-focus, a few intermediate	shallow-focus
Largest magnitude (up to magnitude 7.9, or over magnitude 8.0)	over 8.0	up to 7.9	over 8.0	up to 7.9

Activity 3.3

(a) They seem to be clustered, particularly over western Scotland, parts of Wales, the western Midlands and the middle of the North Sea. Higher-magnitude earthquakes occur in all these main locations.

(b) The answer will, of course, depend on when you access this data. At the time of writing, three earthquakes are listed in the last 30 days, with magnitudes from 1.5 to 2.2.

Activity 4.1

Task 1

The Weekly Reports do not always include information about volcanoes that have been monotonously erupting for many years. Unobserved volcanism on the sea floor cannot be reported, for obvious reasons.

Task 2

Table 4.1 summarises activity in the Weekly Report for 31 January to 6 February 2007. Blank cells in the table indicate that no information was given.

Table 4.1 Weekly Report of volcanic activity for 31 January to 6 February 2007.

Volcano name	Location	Fumaroles	Lava flows	Ash plumes and/or ash fall	Pyroclastic flows	Mud flows	Earthquakes
Karymsky	Kamchatka, Russia			plumes to 3 km			✓
Kilauea	Hawaii		✓				✓
Rabaul	New Britain Island, PNG			explosions sending plumes to 2.2 km			
Sangay	Ecuador			plumes to 9.1 km			
Santa Maria	Guatemala	✓		plumes to 4.1 km	✓		
Shiveluch	Kamchatka, Russia			plumes to 3.5–4.5 km			✓ shallow earthquakes
Soufriere Hills	Montserrat, West Indies		lava dome	plumes to 1.5 km			
St Helens	Washington, USA		lava dome				✓
Suwanose-Jima	Ryukyu Islands, Japan			explosion and plume			
Urbinas	Peru			plumes to 5.5 km			

Task 3

10 volcanoes are listed for 31 January to 6 February 2007. The most common activity was explosions leading to ash plumes (8 of the 10 volcanoes).

Activity 5.1

There are no comments on Tasks 1–5.

Task 6

Your notes on Specimen 4 should contain some or all of the following points:

Overall grey colour (but may be rusty-brown on some faces) – both dark and light-coloured minerals– individual crystals 0.5–5 mm in size – contains many small shiny flakes of a silvery-coloured mineral (sometimes rusty-brown) – some round grains of a reddish, glassy mineral about 2–3 mm across – mineral crystals arranged in alternating thin bands of darker and lighter materials – bands are wavy or contorted.

(*Note*: the specimens vary slightly; the colour banding is more pronounced in some than others.)

Task 7

Your notes on Specimen 5 should contain the following points:

Dark-coloured – crystalline texture – mainly dark material in which individual grains are barely visible with hand lens – numerous white crystals, up to about 4 mm in size – also some black blocky crystals, up to 8 mm – brown or orange staining on some surfaces – some small round holes present.

(*Note*: the specimens vary slightly; most specimens will have some brown or orange staining.)

Task 8

Crystal type 1: White crystals – up to 1 cm long, 0.5 cm wide.

Crystal type 2: Grey, glassy crystals – up to 1 cm across.

Crystal type 3: Dark crystals – typically 1–5 mm across.

Summary

Table 5.3 is a completed version of Table 5.1 and summarises the information on the five rock specimens. Note that the largest grains in a particular rock type vary from sample to sample, particularly if the rock contains rare large crystals.

Table 5.3 Completed version of Table 5.1. Observations and interpretations of rock specimens.

Specimen number	Texture	Colour(s)	Typical grain size(s)	Rock type (metamorphic, sedimentary or igneous)	Process of formation	Rock name	Additional comments
2	fragmental	creamy white or pale brown	1–4 mm	sedimentary	accumulation of sand grains	sandstone	grains are mostly quartz
3	fragmental	dark grey with pale fragments	fossils up to 1 cm long	sedimentary	accumulation of crinoid fragments and mud on sea bed	limestone	contains fossils; dissolves in acid
4	crystalline	dark grey with silvery-brown crystals	0.5–5 mm	metamorphic	recrystallisation of rock in solid state at great depth under high temperature and pressure	schist	crystals arranged in wavy bands
5	crystalline	black	very fine-grained with some larger crystals; white crystals up to 4 mm long; black crystals up to 8 mm	igneous (extrusive)	rapid cooling and crystallisation of magma at Earth's surface	basalt	contains gas bubbles
6	crystalline	pale, but with some black crystals	occasionally up to 2 cm long in some samples, but mostly under 1 cm	igneous (intrusive)	slow cooling and crystallisation of magma underground	granite	

Activity 5.2

See Table 5.4.

(Although the text in Section 5 did not explicitly state that fossils are not found in metamorphic and igneous rocks, you may have worked out that fossils are unlikely to be formed or preserved by the processes that yield metamorphic and igneous rocks.)

Table 5.4 Completed version of Table 5.2. Summary of features that distinguish sedimentary, metamorphic and igneous rocks.

	Sedimentary	Metamorphic	Extrusive igneous	Intrusive igneous
Texture (fragmental or crystalline)	fragmental	crystalline	crystalline	crystalline
For rocks with crystalline texture, do the crystals have random orientations or are they arranged in bands?	–	layers (unless platy minerals are absent, as in marble)	random	random
Can fossils be present?	yes	no	no	no
For igneous rocks, describe the grain size and how it relates to cooling rate.	–	–	small crystal size, indicates rapid cooling	large crystal size, indicates slow cooling

Activity 6.1

Summary of the computer-based activity 'Seismic waves'

There are two types of body wave, P waves and S waves. P waves are compressional waves, and S waves are transverse waves. P waves travel faster than S waves. S waves cannot travel through a liquid. There are two types of surface wave, Love waves and Rayleigh waves. Love waves move the ground surface horizontally, and Rayleigh waves move the ground both horizontally and vertically. Surface waves travel more slowly than body waves; Rayleigh waves are the slower of the two types of surface wave.

Activity 6.2

Summary of the computer-based activity 'Travel time graphs'

Beyond distances of a few hundred kilometres, the travel time graph shows an additional P wave, corresponding to waves that have travelled at a higher speed in a lower layer of the Earth, called the mantle. The upper layer, where speeds are lower, is called the crust. Seismic waves change direction as they travel from the crust into the mantle; this change in direction is called refraction. The boundary between the crust and mantle is called the Mohorovičić discontinuity, usually abbreviated to the Moho.

P-wave speeds vary between different crustal rock types. An increase in the P-wave speed will result in a decrease in the gradient of a travel time graph, and vice versa. Crustal and mantle P-wave speeds, and the depth of the Moho, can be calculated from a travel time graph.

Activity 6.3

Summary of the computer-based activities 'Modelling the mantle' and 'Down to the centre'

The seismic wave speed in the mantle suggests that the mantle is formed of peridotite. Travel time graphs for greater distances are curved due to changes in the speed and direction of seismic waves with depth, and to the Earth's curvature. Travel time curves for greater distances show shadow zones. The P-wave shadow zone is caused by refraction at the seismic discontinuity that marks the boundary between the mantle and the central part of the Earth, called the core, about 2900 km below the surface. The S-wave shadow zone occurs because the core blocks the passage of S waves. For this to happen, the outer part of the core (at least) must be in a liquid state.

Activity 7.1

Task I

(a) Figure 7.13 shows the best-fit line and an example of points where the line crosses easily read grid lines on the graph paper that reduces the degree to which the coordinates have to be estimated by reading the scale.

(b) The gradient gives a speed of 57 km Ma^{-1}, which is equal to 57 mm y^{-1}. Two significant figures are appropriate as this is the precision with which the coordinates of points on the graph can be read. Depending on exactly how you drew your line, and which points you chose, you may have got an answer that was slightly higher or lower than this.

(c) A speed of 57 mm y^{-1} is much faster than the 19 mm y^{-1} for the Mid-Atlantic ridge southwest of Iceland discussed in the text.

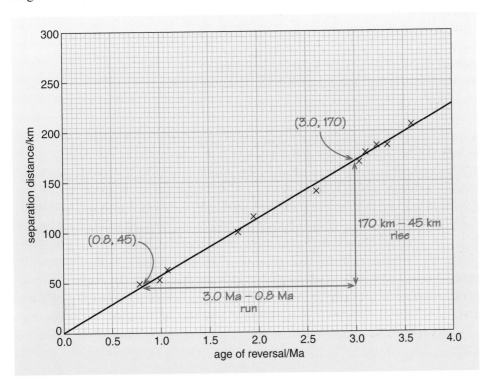

Figure 7.13 Completed version of Figure 7.11, with best-fit line and an example of how the 'rise' and 'run' could be chosen.

Task 2

(a) Figure 7.14 shows the completed plot.

(b) At any given time, the separation distance at 118.7° E is greater than that at 70.2° E (Table 7.3), so the 180.7° E site must have a faster sea-floor spreading rate. Equally, the slope of the best-fit line at 180.7° E is steeper than that at 70.2° E, indicating a faster spreading rate.

(c) The gradient of the best-fit line is 76 km Ma^{-1}, or 76 mm y^{-1}.

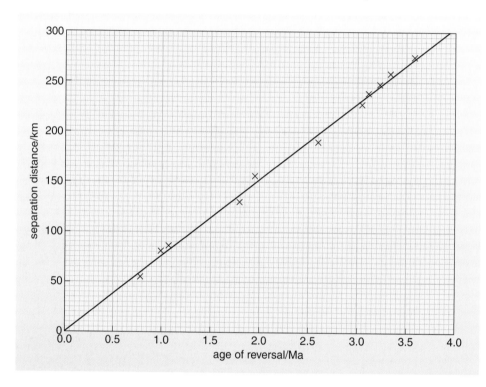

Figure 7.14   Plot of separation distance against age of magnetic reversals on the Southeast Indian Ridge at 180.7° E. Data from Table 7.3.

Task 3

Your finding that the sea-floor spreading rate is different at different points along a mid-ocean ridge is a result of the fact that the Earth has the shape of a sphere and has a fixed size (the Earth is neither expanding nor contracting). Figure 7.15 shows more data for the Southeast Indian Ridge, and you can compare how your results fit with the general pattern in Figure 7.15. The general pattern is that the sea-floor spreading rate of this mid-ocean ridge is low at the ends and increases to a maximum rate of about 77 mm y^{-1} at about longitude 118 °E. This effect comes about because the sea floor on either side of the ridge is moving over a spherical surface. Figure 7.16 shows how this happens, using the analogy of another pair of surfaces that move over a spherical surface – your eyelids when you blink or open your eyes. When your eyes are shut, your upper and lower eyelids meet along a straight line. Open your eyes and the lids separate farthest in the middle (you can check this with a friend or when you next look at yourself in a mirror). The ocean floor on either side of a mid-ocean ridge is analogous to your eyelids (Figure 7.16c).

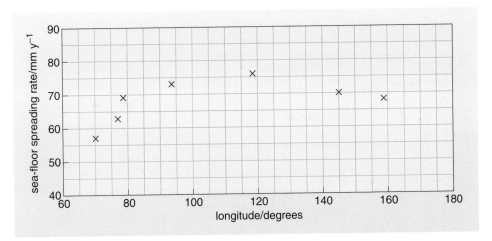

Figure 7.15 The sea-floor spreading rate varies with longitude along the length of the Southeast Indian Ridge.

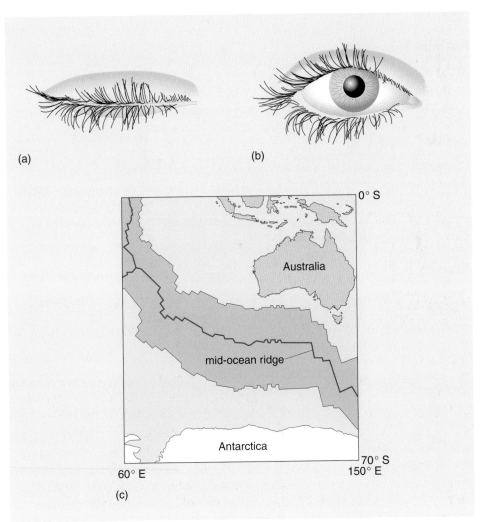

(a)

(b)

(c)

Figure 7.16 Sea-floor spreading on a spherical Earth causes different amounts of space to open up (more spreading) along the length of the ridge. (a) and (b) show that when eyelids on a spherical eyeball are opened, the gap between the lids is greatest in the middle of the eye. (c) shows that the amount of opening (sea-floor spreading) after 35 Ma is greatest part-way along the Southeast Indian Ridge (dark-blue line) as a consequence of the Earth's curvature, similar to the situation when eyelids are open in (b).

Activity 8.1

Table 8.2 Completed version of Table 8.1. The characteristics of each type of plate boundary.

Characteristic	Divergent	Convergent	Transform fault
Direction of motion of plates with respect to plate boundary	away from boundary[a]	towards boundary[a]	parallel to boundary[a]
Depth of earthquake foci (shallow, intermediate, or deep)	shallow[b]	shallow, intermediate and deep[b]	shallow[b]
Destruction or creation of lithosphere, or neither	creation[a]	destruction or thickening[a]	neither[a]
Physical features associated with boundary	mid-ocean ridge[c]	ocean trench, island arc/ mountain belt, volcanoes[c]	fault[a]

Notes on sources of information: [a]from Section 8.2; [b]from Figure 3.6 and Activity 3.2; [c]from Sections 2.2.2, 2.2.3 and 8.2 and Activity 3.2.

Activity 8.2

At the eastern plate boundary, a gap opens, indicating sea-floor spreading at a divergent plate boundary. At the western boundary, paper plate A will go under or over paper plate B; this is a convergent boundary. At the north and south boundaries the paper plates just slide past each other, and these correspond to transform faults.

You may want to use this paper-cutting technique to help you visualise what happens in some of the other example of plate motion that you will meet in this book. This was the method that Earth scientists in the 1960s originally used to consider the implications of plate motion; scientific discoveries do not always involve elaborate equipment!

Activity 8.3

Here is an example of an answer that would gain good marks if it was being assessed. Note that this account starts by clearly stating what the three types of boundary are, and then goes on to discuss three features of plate boundaries (topography, earthquakes and volcanic activity) in turn and in separate paragraphs.

Convergent plate boundaries are of three types: oceanic lithosphere converging with oceanic lithosphere, continental lithosphere converging with oceanic lithosphere, and continental lithosphere converging with continental lithosphere.

In the two cases where oceanic lithosphere is involved, subduction occurs and this produces a deep oceanic trench along the plate boundary. Subduction also produces a row of volcanoes about 200 km away from the plate boundary, on top of the plate that is not subducted. In contrast, where two pieces of continental lithosphere converge, subduction does not take place. Instead, a mountain belt is produced by the collision of the continents. The mountain belt lies along the plate boundary.

Earthquakes occur at all types of convergent plate boundary, but the distribution of earthquake foci depends on the types of lithosphere involved. Where subduction occurs, shallow-, intermediate- and deep-focus earthquakes are generated. In these cases, earthquakes occur at increasing depth away from the plate boundary, defining a Wadati–Benioff zone, which indicates the position of subducted oceanic lithosphere. However, at continental collision zones, earthquakes are confined to shallow depths and are distributed broadly across the zone of collision.

Volcanoes are associated with convergent plate boundaries only where at least one plate is oceanic. They are not found where both plates have continental lithosphere at the boundary. (*213 words*)

Your account is likely to have differed in detail, but should contain the same main points.

Activity 10.1

(a) Following weathering and erosion of the exposed sedimentary rock, mineral grains are transported by water, air or ice to a site of deposition. Once deposited, they can become compacted and cemented together to form a new sedimentary rock. Deep burial and recrystallisation of the sedimentary rock will then yield a metamorphic rock.

(b) The intrusive rock may become deeply buried and recrystallised to form a metamorphic rock. Alternatively, the intrusive rock may become exposed at the Earth's surface if erosion removes the overlying rocks. It may then be weathered and eroded to form sediments which are then turned into a metamorphic rock by following the same path as in (a).

(c) The only way for an atom to escape from the mantle is if it gets incorporated into a magma which then rises towards the surface. Thereafter, the magma could form a volcanic rock on the surface. If this undergoes weathering and erosion, then it can become a sedimentary rock. Alternatively, if the magma solidifies underground, as an intrusive igneous rock, then it will have to be uplifted and exposed by erosion before the process of forming a sedimentary rock can proceed. Other alternatives are that the intrusive rock could be metamorphosed before being exposed at the surface and eroded, or the metamorphic rock could be melted to produce another magma which could then embark on any of the previous paths before ending up as a sedimentary rock. A further possibility is if the atom in question was erupted as part of a volcanic gas. In this case, the atom could end up in a chemical precipitate or in biological material that becomes incorporated into sediment.

(d) The atmosphere can influence the rock cycle. For example, winds, rain and ice cause weathering and/or transport sedimentary material; desert sediments are mostly transported in and deposited from air.

Conversely, the rock cycle can influence the atmosphere. For example, gases are added to the atmosphere from volcanoes; rock-forming organisms such as corals (forming certain limestones) and plants (forming coal and chalk) influence the atmosphere's composition through photosynthesis and respiration.

Activity 11.1

The radius of Pluto is given as 1140 km (3 significant figures), or $r = 1.14 \times 10^6$ m. The radius cubed is $r^3 = 1.482 \times 10^{18}$ m^3. Multiplying by 4 gives 5.928×10^{18} m^3. Multiplying by π gives $4\pi r^3 = 1.862 \times 10^{19}$ m^3. Finally, dividing by three gives the volume of Pluto:

$$V = \frac{4}{3}\pi r^3 = 6.207 \times 10^{18} \text{ m}^3.$$

Written out in full, this is:

$$V = \frac{4}{3}\pi r^3$$

$$= \frac{4}{3}\pi \times (1.14 \times 10^6 \text{ m})^3$$

$$= \frac{4}{3}\pi \times 1.482 \times 10^{18} \text{ m}^3$$

$$= 6.207 \times 10^{18} \text{ m}^3$$

Equation 11.1 can now be used to calculate the density:

$$\rho = \frac{m}{V} = \frac{130 \times 10^{20} \text{ kg}}{6.207 \times 10^{18} \text{ m}^3} = 2094 \text{ kg m}^{-3}$$

$$= 2100 \text{ kg m}^{-3} \text{ to 2 significant figures.}$$

Note the initial radius of Pluto was given to 3 significant figures, but throughout the intermediate calculations, an extra figure was quoted to maintain maximum precision. The final answer, however, was given to 2 significant figures as the mass value was only given to 2 significant figures.

Table 11.2 Properties of the eight major planets and three dwarf planets (completed).

Planetary body	Radius/km	Mass/10^{20} kg	Density/kg m^{-3}
Mercury	2 440	3 302	5 430
Venus	6 052	48 690	5 240
Earth	6 371	59 740	5 515
Mars	3 389	6 419	3 910
Jupiter	69 910	18 990 000	1 240
Saturn	58 230	5 685 000	620
Uranus	25 360	866 200	1 240
Neptune	24 620	1 028 000	1 610
Ceres	470	9.5	2 200
Eris	1 200	150	2 100
Pluto	1 140	130	2 100

Doing a calculation for Earth in a similar way, gives a value of density of 5515 kg m^{-3}.

Activity 13.1

(a)(i) To determine the scale factor, the same procedure is used as in the example of the architectural model. 1.00×10^{-4} m in the model corresponds to 6.37×10^6 m in the real Galaxy, so:

$$\frac{1.00 \times 10^{-4} \text{ m}}{1.00 \times 10^{-4}} = 1 \text{ m} \text{ in the model corresponds to:}$$

$$\frac{6.37 \times 10^6 \text{ m}}{1.00 \times 10^{-4}} = 6.37 \times 10^{10} \text{ m} \text{ in the real Galaxy.}$$

So the scale of the model is $1 : 6.37 \times 10^{10}$.

(a)(ii) To find the values for the other model distances, the actual distance is simply divided by the scale factor. So for the radius of the Sun, the scale model value is:

$$\frac{6.96 \times 10^8 \text{ m}}{6.37 \times 10^{10}} = 1.09 \times 10^{-2} \text{ m} = 10.9 \text{ mm}.$$

The answer is given to 3 significant figures, the same as in the data. In the scale model, the Sun would thus have a radius of 10.9 mm. The other two values required to complete Table 13.3 were calculated in the same way, and are shown in Table 13.5.

Table 13.5 A scale model of the Galaxy, in which the Earth's radius is 0.100 mm (completed). sf denotes significant figures.

Size or distance	Actual value/m	Scale model value/m	Scale model value/mm
Radius of the Earth	6.37×10^6	1.00×10^{-4}	0.100
Radius of the Sun	6.96×10^8	1.09×10^{-2}	10.9
Average distance of the Earth from the Sun	1.50×10^{11}	2.35	2 350 (3 sf)
Distance from the Sun to the nearest star	3.99×10^{16}	6.26×10^5	626 000 000 (3 sf)

Note that the scale model values have been expressed to an appropriate number of significant figures.

The scale model values might give you a better impression of how far off the nearest star is compared with the Sun. In the model, the Sun is a couple of metres away from the Earth, but the nearest star is 626 000 000 mm (626 km) away, which is roughly the distance between London and Aberdeen, in the UK.

(b) In the second scale model the scale is $1 : \left(\dfrac{3.99 \times 10^{16}}{1.00 \times 10^{-4}} \right)$ or $1 : 3.99 \times 10^{20}$.

Therefore, each of the values in the second column must be divided by 3.99×10^{20} to obtain the values shown in the third column of Table 13.6.

Table 13.6 A scale model of the Galaxy, in which the distance from the Sun to the nearest star is 0.100 mm (completed).

Size or distance	Actual value/m	Scale model value/m	Scale model value/mm
Distance from the Sun to the nearest star	3.99×10^{16}	1.00×10^{-4}	0.100
Diameter of the globular cluster M13	1×10^{18}	3×10^{-3}	3
Thickness of the disc of the Galaxy	2×10^{19}	5×10^{-2}	50 (1 sf)
Diameter of the disc of the Galaxy	1.2×10^{21}	3.0	3000 (2 sf)

References

Powell, J.L. (2001) *Mysteries of Terra Firma: The Age and Evolution of the Earth*, Free Press/Simon and Schuster, New York, quoted by Bryson, B. (2004) *A Short History of Nearly Everything*, Black Swan.

Wegener, A. (1966 [1928]) *The Origin of Continents and Oceans* (trans. J. Biram), New York, Dover Publications Inc.

Acknowledgements

The S104 Course Team gratefully acknowledges the contributions of the S103 *Discovering science* course team and of its predecessors.

Grateful acknowledgement is made to the following sources for permission to reproduce material in this book.

Figures

Cover: Eric Heller/Science Photo Library;

Figure 1.1: NASA Langley Research Center (NASA-LaRC);

Figure 2.3: National Geophysical Data Center; Figure 2.6: Adapted from Fowler, C. M. R. (1990) *The Solid Earth: An Introduction to Global Geophysics*, Cambridge, Cambridge University Press;

Figure 3.1: Lefteris Pitarakis/AP/PA Photos; Figure 3.3: US Geological Survey/ Science Photo Library; Figure 3.5: Plafker, G. and Galloway, J. P. (1989) 'Lessons learned from the Loma Prieta, California, earthquake of October 17th, 1989', *USGS Circular 1045*, United States Geological Survey; Figure 3.6: Adapted from The British Geological Survey, World Seismicity Database, Global Seismology and Geomagnetism Group, Edinburgh; Figure 3.9: United States Geological Survey;

Figure 4.1: © Photo SCALA, Florence, British Museum 2003; Figures 4.2a and b, and 4.5: USGS/Cascades Volcano Observatory; Figure 4.2c: Original source unknown; Figure 4.2d: Newhall, C. G. and Punongbayan, R. S. (1996) *Fire and Mud*, Philippine Institute of Volcanology and Seismology and University of Washington Press; Figure 4.4a: Peter Mouganis-Mark; Figure 4.4b: Scott Rowland; Figure 4.6: Adapted from Johnson, R. W. (1993) AGSO Issues Paper No. 1, Volcanic Eruptions and Atmospheric Change, Australian Geological Survey Organisation, © Commonwealth of Australia 1993; Figure 4.7b: Copyright © Louis Maher;

Figures 5.1, 5.2 and 5.10 Andy Tindle; Figure 5.9: Neil McBride;

Figure 6.1: Andy Tindle; Figures 6.2 and 6.3: United States Geological Survey; Figure 6.9: Adapted from Plummer, C. C. and McGeary, D. (1996) *Physical Geology with Interactive Plate Tectonics CD-ROM*, 7th ed., William C. Brown Publishers. Copyright © 1996 by Times Mirror Higher Education Group Inc; Figure 6.14: Adapted from Bolt, B. A. (1982) *Inside The Earth: Evidence from Earthquakes*, New York, W. H. Freeman and Company; Figure 6.15: Francois Gohier/Science Photo Library;

Figure 7.3: Based on Smith, A. (1996) *CD-ROM of Plate Reconstructions*, Cambridge, Cambridge Palaeomap Services Ltd; Figure 7.4a: Dr Ken MacDonald/Science Photo Library; Figure 7.4b: B. Murton/Southampton Oceanography Centre/Science Photo Library; Figure 7.7: Heirtzler, J. R. et al. (1966) 'Magnetic anomalies over the Reykjanes Ridge', *Deep Sea Research*, vol. 13, pp. 427–443. Cambridge, Elsevier Science;

Index

Entries and page numbers in **bold type** refer to key words that are printed in **bold** in the text and that are defined in the glossary. Where the page number is given in *italics*, the index information is carried mainly or wholly in an illustration or table.